Real-Financial Linkages among Open Economies

Real-Financial Linkages among Open Economies

edited by
Sven W. Arndt
J. David Richardson

The MIT Press
Cambridge, Massachusetts
London, England

This book was set in Palatino by Asco Trade Typsetting Ltd., Hong Kong, and printed and bound by Halliday Lithograph in the United States of America.

Library of Congress Cataloging-in-Publication Data

Real-financial linkages among open economies.

Includes index.
1. International economic relations. 2. International finance. I. Arndt, Sven W.
II. Richardson, J. David.
HF1411.R4135 1987   337   87-15153
ISBN 0-262-01096-8

Contents

List of Contributors

Sven W. Arndt

University of California-Santa Cruz, and the Commons Institute

Bernard de Bellefroid

University of Louvain

Paul De Grauwe

University of Louvain

Koichi Hamada

University of Tokyo, Yale University, and NBER

Akiyoshi Horiuchi

University of Tokyo

Michael M. Hutchison

University of California, Santa Cruz, and Federal Reserve Bank of San Francisco

Irving B. Kravis

University of Pennsylvania and NBER

Paul Krugman

Massachusetts Institute of Technology and NBER

Robert E. Lipsey

Queens College and Graduate Center, CUNY, and NBER

Richard C. Marston

University of Pennsylvania and NBER

Charles A. Pigott

Federal Reserve Bank of New York

J. David Richardson

University of Wisconsin-Madison and NBER

Alan C. Stockman

University of Rochester and NBER

List of Tables

List of Figures

Preface

With this volume we hope to contribute toward filling an analytical and empirical gap in international economics. "Real-financial linkage among open economies" is our shorthand to describe the way exchange rates, international competitiveness, and capital movements interact with growth, industrial structure, comparative advantage, and sectoral wage patterns. The fashion in international economics is to treat financial markets independently while "holding the 'real' sector constant," and to treat "real" industrial structure and trade patterns as if exchange rates and financial markets made no long-run difference. We focus in this volume on the feedback that each tradition neglects.

We resolved to aim for a book that is significantly better in novelty, quality, and cohesion than the usual conference volume—more akin to a special issue of a refereed journal, with similar expectations of contributors, referees, and editors. To that end, we publicly solicited proposals to participate, using an Announcement and Call for Papers; appointed an advisory committee to help us judge among them competitively; appointed and paid referees (not merely discussants), one for each selected paper, to criticize the paper all through its drafting; held a "preconference" over first drafts (June 1985) with authors and referees, using it to suggest revisions for a final conference (January 1986), which had a larger audience; thoroughly edited the papers to improve them and to integrate them better with each other; tried to incorporate the suggestions of seven reviewers of the finished manuscript.

We have appreciated in these endeavors the special patience of the authors of each chapter. And we would like to thank the various referees, critics, and advisors who have played so important a role in this project: Jacques R. Artus, William H. Branson, Michael R. Darby, Michael Dooley, Barry J. Eichengreen, Robert C. Feenstra, Peter Hooper, John H. Makin,

Nancy Marion, Donald J. Mathieson, Rachel McCulloch, Stephen J. Turn-ovsky, and seven anonymous referees.

Portions of the research in this volume have been supported by National Science Foundation Grant PRA-8116459 to the National Bureau of Economic Research for its program in International Studies. Other portions of the research have been supported by the American Enterprise Institute's project on Competing in a Changing World Economy. Opinions expressed are, however, those of the authors, and not of the National Science Foundation, National Bureau of Economic Research, or the American Enterprise Institute.

I

Introduction, Perspective, and Overview

Introduction to Part I

This volume analyzes and measures linkages between the real and financial sectors of open economies. The two chapters in part I synthesize and supplement those that follow.

Chapter 1 by the editors summarizes the major real-financial linkages that concern the other contributors, attempting to integrate them among themselves and with standard international economic paradigms. Beyond summary, it adds a theoretical framework from which to view the entire volume and points out several real-financial linkages that are not well represented, for example, the way financial markets can ensure uncertain real transactions. Chapter 2 by Stockman discusses this particular linkage in more detail. The editors believe that it is becoming increasingly important for international exchange, and is a likely emphasis for any sequel to this volume.

There are two principal sources of real-financial linkage among open economies that are discussed in the subsequent chapters. One is structural, occupying chapters 3 through 5. It focuses on linkages due to imperfect competition and intersectoral differences in growth, productivity, and cross-national price parallelism. The second source is temporal, occupying chapters 6 through 8. It focuses on real-financial linkages due to fiscal policy and financing of budget deficits, international financial liberalization, and the choice of exchange rate regime.

1 Real-Financial Linkages among Open Economies: An Overview

Sven W. Arndt
J. David Richardson

1.1 International Economics, Real and Financial

A familiar separation persists in international economic analysis. There are two camps. "Real" international economics, also called "international trade," examines cross-border transactions in current goods and services. "International finance" examines cross-border transactions in "capital"— claims on the future. Typical real and financial international economists converse only superficially and develop little appreciation for each other's problems. Real-side scholars find closest kinship with colleagues in applied microeconomics, industrial organization, and public economics. Financial-side scholars find closest kinship with colleagues in macroeconomics, money and banking, and portfolio analysis. There are of course notable outliers such as W. M. Corden and Robert Mundell, and the giants of earlier generations have comfortably inhabited both camps (Gottfried Haberler, Harry Johnson, Fritz Machlup, and others). Yet today there is a chasm between international trade and international finance that is quite broad and quite deep.

The aim of this volume is to begin filling in the chasm, in the hope of stimulating research that will some day span it. To do that, the chapters focus on linkages between the real and financial variables that themselves link open economies. Thus the word "linkage" has a double meaning throughout.

The aim of this introduction is to draw the volume together, identifying overlapping and unique contributions of each chapter to the common theme. Sections 1.2, 1.3, and 1.4 describe in more detail the typical separation between real and financial analysis. Typical analysis notwithstanding, real-financial linkages among open economies spring from two fundamental sources: structural (or intersectoral) differences among economies and temporal (or intertemporal) differences among them. Some of the more important structural differences are described in sections 1.5 and 1.6. Temporal differences, which can also be conceived as circumstantial differences in a world of uncertainty, are discussed in section 1.7. Structural and temporal differences are examined together in section 1.8.

1.2   How the Typical Twain Do Not Meet

The separation described earlier can also be called a dichotomy of interest. Real-side international economics is concerned with the way cross-border transactions affect an economy's trade patterns, production structure, and factor markets. Financial-side international economics is concerned with the way cross-border transactions affect an economy's exchange rates, interest rates, and financial markets. Typical treatments of these concerns are almost completely independent of each other.

The typical pure analytic approaches to "real" international trade make exchange rates, interest rates, and capital movements irrelevant. Such financial variables are ignored or taken for granted in the most familiar general equilibrium models. Exchange rates are ignored because they are assumed to be the relative price of two moneys, both of which are "veils" that have no real effects. Money does not matter, and neither do exchange rates. They are all neutral. Interest rates do not matter because they are essentially intertemporal prices, with only second-order-of-small effects on intersectoral prices and relative factor prices. Financial capital movements may matter in a "long run" long enough for them to influence an economy's endowment of productive capital. But its endowment (stock) is often taken to be so large relative to its annual, even decennial, increments that changes in the increments can be ignored as infinitesimal. International trade in productive capital (or labor) may also be ignored if commodity trade eliminates the wage-rental incentives for factors to become mobile across borders (Mundell 1957). And since international transfers of financial purchasing power must be reversed sometime if national budget balance is to be maintained, familiar general equilibrium models insist that long-run equilibria feature no capital account (or current account) imbalance.

The typical pure analytic approaches to international finance make the sectoral structure of production and comparative advantage irrelevant. Sectoral structure is ignored in familiar macroeconomic approaches because demands for (and supplies of) financial assets are assumed to depend on aggregate real income and wealth, not on their sectoral source, and on intertemporal prices reflected in earnings and interest rates, not on intersectoral prices. Asset stocks in turn determine capital movements, exchange rates, and, in pegged exchange rate regimes, official intervention. Devaluation and revaluation in such regimes may have temporary differential impacts on sectoral outputs, prices, and employment. But sectoral structure is usually irrelevant for calculating the long-run effects of these parity changes. Even nontradables prices move to match the equilibrium shift in tradables prices from the parity change, given price flexibility and intersectoral factor mobility.

1.3   Difference in Focus on Different Relative Prices

All international economics is concerned with "foreign relative prices relative to domestic relative prices"—a double relative in every sense, and a mouthful, too. But the relative prices being compared across borders differ between international trade and international finance. The dichotomy of interest between the subareas can be clarified by describing the different relative prices that occupy each, and by discussing when one set of relative prices can be assumed independent of another. The description will also be useful in summarizing several of the chapters that follow.

We can conceive P and P^* to be indexes of prices denominated in the currencies of a domestic and foreign economy, respectively. Each index is a function of two vectors, one of tradables prices (p_t), and the other of nontradables prices (p_n). Each vector contains many elements, each representing the price of a given sector's homogeneous product.

$$P \equiv f(\mathbf{p_t}, \mathbf{p_n}); \quad \begin{bmatrix} \mathbf{p_t} \\ \mathbf{p_n} \end{bmatrix} \equiv \begin{bmatrix} \vdots \\ p_{ti} \\ \vdots \\ p_{nk} \\ \vdots \end{bmatrix}.$$

$$P^* \equiv f^*(\mathbf{p_t^*}, \mathbf{p_n^*}); \quad \begin{bmatrix} \mathbf{p_t^*} \\ \mathbf{p_n^*} \end{bmatrix} \equiv \begin{bmatrix} \vdots \\ p_{ti}^* \\ \vdots \\ p_{nk}^* \\ \vdots \end{bmatrix}. \tag{1}$$

Typical pure analytic approaches to "real" international trade are concerned with relative intersectoral prices—that is, relative prices *within* the vector p relative to those within the vector p^*. The ratios of the ratios

$$\frac{p_{ti}/p_{tj}}{p_{ti}^*/p_{tj}^*}, \quad \text{for all } i \neq j,$$

determine each economy's comparative advantage, production structure, exports, imports, and implicit factor demands. Although p's are expressed in domestic currency and p^*'s in foreign currency, exchange rates do not directly influence these relative price comparisons and are ignored in "real" analysis. Also ignored are expected and actual inflation and interest rates, which have to do with the rate of change of prices between periods 0 and 1. It is not these rates of change that concern typical "real" analysis. Its concern is the international comparison of the relative prices for period 0 and then the same comparison independently for period 1. Comparative advantage may indeed change between the periods—but if so, the reason will have been *differential* rates of change among sectoral prices, not their common rate of change (i.e., not general inflation).

Typical pure analytic approaches to international finance are concerned with relative intertemporal prices, for example P_1/P_0 relative to P_1^*/P_0^* using subscripts 0 and 1 to denote time. The ratios of the ratios

$$\frac{P_1/P_0}{P_1^*/P_0^*}, \quad \text{for all lengths of interval between 0 and 1,}$$

influence the economies' relative interest rates, and in turn the exchange rate and capital movements between them. Ratios formed from the sectoral prices that are components of each price index, such as p_{ti}/p_{tj}, have no particular implication for the value of P or P^* and are ignored in international finance. Also ignored are international differences in the sectoral composition of production, themselves the consequences of relative inter-sectoral prices. Financial assets that are issued by various sectors of the economy, as well as those issued by the government, are typically assumed to lose much of their sectoral identity as integrated capital markets "size up" their market value. The mechanism by which they are homogenized is competitive financial arbitrage, motivated by the desire of lenders to maximize their future returns and of borrowers to minimize their future debt burdens. When asset markets are well integrated within each economy in this way, the sectoral composition of production and balance sheets is irrelevant to the concerns of international finance.

1.4   "Laws of One Price" and Purchasing Power Parity

All this notwithstanding, the dichotomization of international trade and finance has never been absolute. Some real-financial linkages have always been implicit, and a few have received significant attention, especially those relating to the "law of one price" and "purchasing power parity." These venerable linkages play important roles in several of the later chapters and need elaboration.

The first step in the elaboration is to describe equilibrium price structures in open economies. One of the chief conclusions of "real" analysis is that unencumbered, perfectly competitive trade in goods and services will make the relative price of tradable i to tradable j the same in every trading economy. In special circumstances the relative prices of some *non*tradables k and l may be equated across economies—not, obviously, because they are traded but because their producers employ the same primary factors as do tradables producers and must pay competitive rates for those factors.[1] Relative factor prices themselves may become equated across economies, as perhaps the most important example of how global tradables markets may implicitly "globalize" even nontradables markets.

Typical "real" analysis has implications for price levels as well as relative prices. The same unencumbered, perfectly competitive forces of trade will bring about price level equalization for any tradable good:

$$p_{ti} = ep_{ti}^*, \quad \text{for all } i,$$

where the exchange rate e is the domestic currency price of foreign currency. This equation is called the "law of one price," and this would come close to holding for indexes of tradables prices: $P_t \approx eP_t^*$ (where P_t, P_t^* represent indexes of tradable goods alone). The "law of one price" might hold even for some nontradable goods too, for the reasons described earlier. That is why economists presume that general price indexes ought to vary similarly across economies:

P_t should vary quite closely with eP_t^*.

P should vary somewhat closely with eP^*.

These covariations are called "purchasing power parity" (PPP) relationships. The accuracy of each is enhanced by the accuracy of the component laws of one price and by similarity between the domestic and foreign weights implicit in the price index functions f and f^*. The accuracy of the second (general) PPP relationship will be further enhanced by any tendency of nontradables prices to track tradables prices due to internal competition over primary factors.

Laws of one price describe prices of homogeneous goods taken one by one. PPP relationships describe aggregations of those prices. Although laws of one price generally contribute to the accuracy of PPP relationships, they are neither sufficient nor necessary. One could see perfect validity of laws of one price and failure of PPP because of international differences in the weights that sensible aggregation suggests. One could imagine conversely that PPP relationships were reasonably accurate but that laws of one price did not describe cross-boundary prices well for certain subsets of sectors.

PPP relationships are used often to specify a norm for exchange rates: e "should" vary closely with P_t/P_t^*, or even P/P^*. Such use illustrates one of the simplest, oldest, and most important types of real-financial linkage: the relative price of both nations' moneys, a financial asset, should bear some predictable relationship to relative aggregates of their prices for current goods and services.

Of course trade barriers, international transport costs, and other encumbrances interfere with "laws" of one price, and with PPP as a consequence. Yet such barriers are often roughly proportional to prices (e.g., an ad valorem tariff). In that case these price relationships will be observable in rates of change over time, albeit not in levels. These are usually called "relative" as opposed to "absolute" versions of the price relationships. The relative version of the law of one price is

$$\%\Delta p_{ti} = \%\Delta(e p_{ti}^*) \approx \%\Delta e + \%\Delta p_{ti}^*$$

(recognizing that the percentage change in the product of two variables is approximately equal to the sum of their percentage changes). And the "relative" versions of PPP are

$$\%\Delta P_t \approx \%\Delta(e P_t^*) \approx \%\Delta e + \%\Delta P_t^*,$$

$$\%\Delta P \approx \%\Delta(e P^*) \approx \%\Delta e + \%\Delta P^*.$$

From these relations comes one of the most popular norms on which to forecast exchange rate trends: they ought to be related fairly closely to international differences in inflation rates ($\%\Delta P - \%\Delta P^*$).

These price relationships and their implicit real-financial linkages can be depicted in figure 1.1. Quadrants 1 and 3 summarize PPP tendencies that arise within each period from competitive cross-border trade in goods, as studied by "real" international trade analysts. Quadrants 2 and 4 imply the intertemporal transition relationships between exchange rates and inflation rates (and also, implicitly, rates of interest) that are studied by international financial analysts. For example, when the foreign rate of inflation is zero and the domestic rate positive, then the P_1/P_0 locus in quadrant 2 is displaced below the $45°$ line, unlike the P_1^*/P_0^* locus in quadrant 4 that

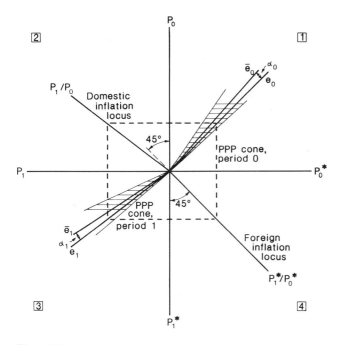

Figure 1.1
Prices across borders and time

coincides with the 45° line. This displacement brings forth a mirror-image clockwise rotation of the "PPP cone" in quadrant 3 such that the future exchange rate is consistent with differential inflation rates (and possibly with corresponding nominal interest-rate differentials between economies). The PPP relationships are drawn as cones of approximation to reflect the fact that P and P^* include nontradables and other products for which the law of one price should not be expected to hold tightly. Thus the actual exchange rates e_0 and e_1 may not be exactly equal to PPP norms $\bar{e}_0$ and $\bar{e}_1$. But if the relative version of PPP holds, then any future divergence measured by the angle α_1 ought to be equal to the current divergence, measured by α_0 ($\alpha_1 = \alpha_0$).

From these price relationships also come various measures of a nation's "international competitiveness." Sectoral competitiveness is often measured by the change in p_{ti}/ep_{ti}^* since some "normal" base period, that is, by ($\%\Delta p_{ti} - \%\Delta p_{ti}^* - \%\Delta e$). National competitiveness is often measured by the change in P_t/eP_t^* or P/eP^* since some "normal" base period, and even sometimes by the change in a ratio of nontradables prices—where wages and occasionally other factor costs are taken to be the principal components of nontradables indexes.

National competitiveness measures are frequently called "real exchange rates"; negative changes are described as "real depreciation," signifying improved competitiveness; and positive changes as "real appreciation," signifying reduced competitiveness.

International competitiveness is currently an important and controversial topic in analysis, policy, and interpretation. Recent movements in real exchange rates have been larger, more enduring, and more divergent among economies than either history or analysis had suggested. Older views and experience were that an economy's international competitiveness might rise and fall over medium-term periods but would on average, over a decade or so, approximate the norm dictated by PPP. Ebbs and flows of competitive "advantage" would appear random over time and across economies.

Events of the past ten years have undermined this confidence, especially the appearance of persistent, marked competitive advantage for Japan and competitive disadvantage for the United States.[2] Trade policy conflict has escalated as these divergences have been reflected in persistent, marked trade balance surpluses for Japan and deficits for the United States.

One of the most important questions for international economics today is what explains the persistence and size of divergences from laws of one price and purchasing power parity norms. A number of the contributions to this volume provide the beginnings of an answer.

1.5   Explaining International Competitiveness: Predictable Divergences from Laws of One Price and PPP

Three of the chapters devote explicit attention to international competitiveness, and others, implicit attention. All measure competitiveness as a sustained divergence from the law of one price or from PPP. All contribute something new to the established literature along these lines on real-financial linkage. Yet each asks a unique question, and methodologies and aggregation differ among them. Even their terminology is distinct.

Krugman (chapter 3) asks how imperfectly competitive market structure conditions the way exchange rates change international competitiveness at the industry level. Algebraically, he explores how the comparative equilibrium derivative

$$\frac{d(p_{ti}/ep_{ti}^*)}{de}$$

is altered by the presence of monopolistic price discrimination and oligopoly (among other things). The derivative itself reflects a classic issue in real-financial linkage: how an exchange rate change that is exogenous from the viewpoint of firms in an industry "passes through" into its prices at home and abroad. The exchange rate change in the denominator of the derivative is obviously "financial"; the relative price measure of industry competitiveness in the numerator is obviously "real."

Under perfect competition and the law of one price, the derivative and the real-financial linkage are zero. Krugman shows how imperfect competition, however, makes the derivative nonzero and establishes potential for indefinite divergences from the law of one price. He calls such divergences "pricing to market," because of the incentives for imperfectly competitive firms to maintain historical pricing in each distinct market despite an exchange rate shock. Exchange rates in these cases *do* influence relative prices, international competitiveness and, by implication, comparative advantage too. Imperfectly competitive market structure is a mechanism for real-financial linkage.

Marston (chapter 4) asks how differential productivity growth among sectors (among other things) affects different measures of U.S. competitiveness relative to Japan. He is particularly interested in comparative equilibrium derivatives such as

$$\frac{d\,[(P/eP^*)/(P_t/eP_t^*)]}{d\,[G/G_t)]},$$

where G_t and G stand, respectively, for productivity growth in the tradables sector and the overall economy (both tradables and nontradables). Marston calls the bracketed term in the numerator a *relative* real exchange rate, because it is a ratio of two alternative measures of international competitiveness. One of his major contributions is to show how large such derivatives are—which is also to show how divergent are alternative measures of international competitiveness when an economy's sectoral growth patterns differ radically from each other. This is very important because ratios such as P/P^* and P_t/P_t^* are used to set exchange rate (e) norms. Alternative exchange rate norms obviously diverge greatly from each other when sectoral trends do. It would be very hard then to write sensible rules for internationally coordinated monetary policy or exchange market intervention aimed at damping e fluctuations, as recommended by some plans for international monetary reform.[3] Disparate e norms would stand like multiple targets at an archery contest, some commending themselves to one country and others to others.

Like Marston, Kravis and Lipsey (chapter 5) illustrate an international linkage from real economic structure to a "financial" variable. They ask how an economy's international competitiveness is affected by its (1) per capita income, (2) sectoral structure (between t and n goods), and (3) openness to trade. Using regressions run cross-sectionally over 25 countries for various time periods, they calculate

$$\frac{d(P/eP^*)}{dZ_j} \quad \text{and} \quad \frac{d(P_t/eP_t^*)}{dZ_j}, \frac{d(P_n/eP_n^*)}{dZ_j}$$

where P_n, P_n^* denote indexes of nontradables prices, and Z_j ($j = 1, 2, 3$) stands for their three structural determinants of measured competitiveness. They use the United States as a standard against which to compare other countries, normalizing U.S. prices (P^*) to be 1.00 and then calling the 25 calculated P/e's each nation's "price level" (implicitly relative to the United States). If purchasing power parity held, every nation's price level would clearly be 1.00 too. Kravis and Lipsey show instead that divergences from 1.00 are very large, very persistent over time, and reasonably well explained (across economies) by international structural differences.

In chapter 6 Hutchison and Pigott and in chapter 7 Hamada and Horiuchi describe implicitly how fiscal policy and capital controls have impacts on a nation's international competitiveness and its distance from any PPP norms.

1.6 The Influence of Tradables/Nontradables Structure on Exchange Rates and Price Levels

Differences across economies in intersectoral trends are one of the fundamental sources of real-financial linkage. They are emphasized in both the Marston chapter and that by Kravis and Lipsey, and have a modest analytical and empirical history (Balassa 1964, and others). Among the most important implications of this work is that exchange rates, although a "financial" variable, are influenced significantly by relative product prices.

These linkages can be detailed usefully in figure 1.2, a familiar diagram that depicts production possibilities and preference contours for a small open economy. The assumption of smallness, made here for convenience only, implies that trends in the world prices of the economy's exportables and importables are exogenous. If the trends are also identical, then exportables and importables can be properly aggregated into tradables, and units of either can be measured along the vertical axis. Other assumptions

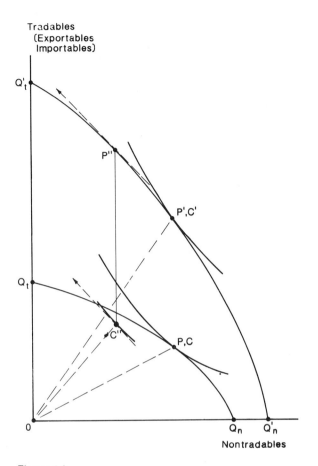

Figure 1.2
Relative tradables/nontradables structure

made for convenience are that preferences are homothetic and that the point P, C lies directly below the point P', C'.

This sort of real-financial linkage can be illustrated first across economies, in the fashion of Kravis and Lipsey, and then over time, in the fashion of Marston. Suppose that two economies differ in their real structure in the following way. One has an across-the-board technological advantage that by world standards is especially large in tradable goods. The other has a less marked absolute and differential advantage. Or to make the point more graphic, suppose that the second economy is a laggard across-the-board in productivity, and especially backward in tradables. The first economy will, of course, tend to have above-average per capita income, and the second, below average. The production possibilities curve of the rich economy can be taken to be $Q_t'Q_n'$ and that of the poor economy $Q_t Q_n$.[4] "Equilibrium" production and consumption for the rich economy in typical analyses can be identified with point P', C', and for the poor economy with point P, C. These are equilibrium points in the sense that each economy's single-period aggregate budget is balanced—aggregate spending during the period is exactly equal to aggregate income during the period. The value of national production (P) is equal to the value of national consumption (C). Each economy's trade must thus be balanced, with commodity exports equal in value to commodity imports.

When we consider intertemporal trade, we will abandon this definition of equilibrium as overly rigid and unrealistic. But it is quite typical. And it leads directly to the conclusion that the relative price of tradables to nontradables is lower in the rich economy than the poor one. That is,

$$\frac{P_t'}{P_n'} < \frac{P_t}{P_n}. \tag{2}$$

This much is familiar. It is all "real" analysis. Less familiar is its implication for financial variables, such as the national "price levels" that Kravis and Lipsey emphasize. These are defined as P'/e' and P/e, where $P' = f'(P_t', P_n')$ and $P = f(P_t, P_n)$ as in (1). Since these index functions ought sensibly to be homogeneous of degree one in all prices, they can be rewritten as

$$\frac{P'}{e'} = f'\left(\frac{P_t'}{e'}, \frac{P_n'}{e'}\right) \quad \text{and} \quad \frac{P}{e} = f\left(\frac{P_t}{e}, \frac{P_n}{e}\right) \tag{3}$$

Because each of these two economies faces the same exogenous world prices of tradables, laws of one price suggest that P_t^* will be equal to both P_t'/e' and P_t/e. Using these equalities, (3) can be rewritten as (4)

$$\frac{P'}{e'} = f'\left(\frac{P_t^*, P_n'}{e'}\right) \quad \text{and} \quad \frac{P}{e} = f\left(\frac{P_t^*, P_n}{e}\right). \tag{4}$$

and (2) can be rewritten as (5)

$$\frac{e'}{P_n'} < \frac{e}{P_n}. \tag{5}$$

Then substituting (5) into (4), it is clear that the national price level will be higher in the first (rich) economy than in the second (i.e., $P'/e' > P/e$)—as long as the price indexes f' and f are sufficiently similar.

To summarize, the cross-country real-financial linkage illustrated here is that economies with strong productivity advantage by world standards in tradables relative to nontradables will have higher price levels than naive purchasing power parity norms suggest. Economies with relatively weak productivity advantage in tradables relative to nontradables will have lower price levels than naive PPP norms suggest. These latter economies are often presumed to be poor and the former rich, a presumption based on productivity in nontradables sectors being similar worldwide.

A similar real-financial link over time is illustrated by Marston. His analysis can be summarized in figure 1.2 by assuming that $Q_t Q_n$ and $Q_t' Q_n'$ both represent Japanese production possibilities curves, the first in the 1970s and the second in the 1980s. Their difference illustrates Japanese productivity growth that was especially rapid in tradables over this period compared to the (undiagrammed) rest of the world (specifically the United States in Marston's analysis). Each of the preceding equations has its analog in Marston's analysis over time. The analog to (2) implies that prices of tradables relative to nontradables had to fall faster over this period in Japan than in the United States to maintain balanced trade (national spending equal to national income). The analog to (5) shows two financial mechanisms by which this real change might have taken place: Japanese e might have fallen, that is, the yen might have appreciated, or Japanese nontradables prices (P_n) might have risen. The analog to (4) shows that if either had happened sufficiently, Japanese prices overall would have risen relative to the U.S. price level. Or, using Marston's terminology, real exchange rates based on general price indexes would have shown yen appreciation from 1973 to 1983.

Marston shows in fact that general measures of the yen's real value hardly changed at all over this period. As a result "equilibrium" real-financial linkage could not be attained. Linkage still existed, but took on a character typically thought to imply disequilibrium. The sense in which it does can be illustrated in figure 1.2. Because neither e nor P_n moved sufficiently from 1973 to 1983, Japan's price of tradables relative to non-tradables remained unduly high. This had consequences. Consumption of tradables relative to nontradables was discouraged, including consumption of imports. Production of tradables relative to nontradables was encouraged, including production for export. Japanese consumption in the 1980s was better depicted by the point C'' than C', Japanese production by P'' instead of P'. The implied gap between national income and national spending is precisely the distance $C''P''$ measured in units of tradables, and is identically the Japanese trade surplus (more exactly its growth over the period). Instead of generating a rise in the Japanese price level relative to the world, the unusually strong Japanese productivity growth in tradables generated a Japanese trade surplus. It may furthermore last a long time. Some of Kravis and Lipsey's regressions toward the end of their chapter suggest trade balance effects of price level misalignments that stretch over the ensuing decade!

It is next appropriate to address the issue of whether Marston's illustration is necessarily a disequilibrium real-financial linkage. The next section shows that it is not necessarily so if economies are allowed to trade intertemporally, that is, to finance or "save" single-period differences between national spending and national income. In allowing for such intertemporal trade, additional mechanisms for real-financial linkage appear.

1.7   The Influence of Intertemporal Considerations on Real-Financial Linkage

Differences across economies in intertemporal preferences and in capabilities for intertemporal transformation are a second fundamental source of real-financial linkage. They are emphasized by Hutchison-Pigott and Hamada-Horiuchi in chapters 6 and 7, and are behind the scenes of the Marston paper.

They are also emphasized by Stockman in chapter 2, yet with added generality. What economists often mean by intertemporal trade is contingent trade—trade across uncertain circumstances, not necessarily across time. For example, if persons are currently employed, they may decide to consume less than they earn, trading away current consumption in order to increase consumption if they become unemployed. There is no need to analyze their contingent decision making intertemporally. The circumstantial problem and the intertemporal problem have exactly the same structure. Financial markets facilitate not only intertemporal transactions but transactions under uncertainty too.

. Thus what we describe here as intertemporal linkages could also be conceived as circumstantial linkages, those caused by uncertainty. It is from this perspective that De Grauwe and de Bellefroid (chapter 8) analyze the effect of exchange rate variability on a very long-run, decade-spanning measure of international trade volume. They are not surprised to find a significant negative correlation between variability and volume because they recognize the inadequacies (even nonexistence) of financial markets for hedging risk over decade-long horizons. They thus illustrate one of Stockman's key conclusions: a spectrum of financial markets is often necessary to support any particular "real" transaction; in the absence of the right financial markets, the real transaction may not take place.

Real-financial linkages from intertemporal differences across economies can be detailed usefully in figure 1.3. $Q_f Q_c$ represents an economy's production-possibilities curve between "current" goods and "future" goods, both assumed homogeneous and tradable. If the economy is closed to international transactions, then the vertical axis is typically considered also to measure capital goods output—produced increments to the economy's endowment (stock) of productive capital—which is the way a closed economy's claims on future goods can be increased (or maintained, when there is depreciation). For convenience it is assumed that national preferences are homothetic (less defensible than sometimes because of the presence of a preexisting background stock of claims on the future, implied by the interrupted vertical axis below the origin labeled 100).

Intertemporal linkages identified by both Hamada-Horiuchi and Hutchison-Pigott can be described in this diagram. Hamada and Horiuchi focus on preferences, in particular, on financial liberalization given differences between economies in intertemporal preferences. Hutchison and Pigott focus on availability of unique financial instruments, in particular, on differences between economies in "production" rates of government securities through fiscal policies that create budget deficits.

Financial Liberalization and Differences in Preferences

Japan's national saving rate is high by world standards, and for purposes of reference, we might suppose that the Japanese economy is closed not only by capital controls but to trade as well. Then Japan's equilibrium could be described by point P_J, C_J on the preference contour through that point. Real interest rates, reflected in the slope of the tangent line, would be low. If the rest of the world has a lower saving rate but is otherwise identical to Japan (for convenience, and let us call it the United States), then its equilibrium

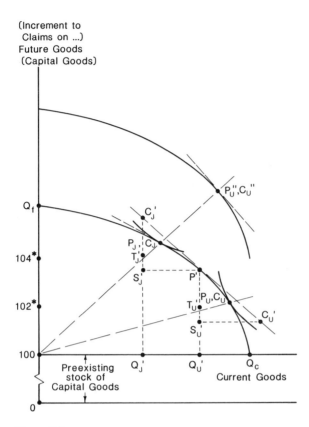

Figure 1.3
Intertemporal trade (the asterisk indicates growth rates of the capital stock of 2 and 4
percent, respectively)

could be described by point P_U, C_U. Real interest rates would be higher than in Japan.

Liberalization of commodity trade alone between the two economies would add a very simple real-financial linkage. But most economists would consider this strictly a "real" experiment. Each economy would produce at P'. Japan would consume at C'_J, importing S'_J C'_J of capital goods and exporting $S'_J P'$ of consumer goods. The United States would consume at C'_U, with the mirror-image trade pattern. Trade would be balanced; there would be no trade surpluses or deficits or international capital movements as usually defined. Real interest rates would be higher in Japan and lower in the United States than they were before trade. As a result Japan's current consumption would decline and her purchases of investment goods would increase, with an increased growth rate of her capital stock and gross national product (GNP) being the result. U.S. effects would be opposite: current consumption would rise, and investment and growth would decline (though U.S. welfare would rise). With these effects the two economies could not remain identical in periods subsequent to the one depicted. The production possibilities curve for Japan would shift outward faster than that for the United States.

Removing capital controls and liberalizing international financial trade could change the picture still further. This is what Japan did in the late 1970s and early 1980s, as Hamada and Horiuchi discuss. The principal change is that the allocations among nations of the world's capital stock and its wealth can be independent of each other.[5] A simple way to describe the change is to assume that what additionally could be traded freely was ownership certificates to the productive capital stock—pieces of paper that entitle the owner to the income of a machine whether it is in his/her backyard or far away. Now, if newly produced machines do not differ from existing machines, then some of Japan's excess demand for claims on future goods might be satisfied by Japanese purchases of ownership certificates, not by physical shipment of the capital goods themselves. U.S. exports of capital goods may in fact decline. It is cheaper, among other things, to transport pieces of paper than machines! A U.S. deficit on commodity trade could develop, offset of course by a U.S. surplus in exchanges of financial assets. In fact a stable, recurrent Japanese demand each period for U.S. financial assets would cause the U.S. dollar to appreciate to a stable higher level in real terms, thus generating the sustained trade deficit and making the United States appear "uncompetitive." The requisite exchanges of goods for paper could continue indefinitely at stationary levels each period among growing economies like those pictured.

Debt service and investment income are other important aspects of intertemporal real-financial linkage that can be introduced in this simple scenario. To do this, it is helpful to discuss one of an infinity of equilibria (an infinity due to the assumption that financial ownership certificates and physical machines are perfect substitutes in trade). In the equilibrium that we examine each economy would produce at P'. Japan would consume at C'_J, importing $S'_J C'_J$ of *ownership claims* to U.S. capital (not the machines themselves) and exporting $S'_J P'$ of consumer goods. The United States would consume at C'_U, with the mirror-image trade pattern. Commodity trade would no longer be balanced as it was before financial liberalization. Japan would have a current account *surplus* equal to $S'_J P'$ (or $S'_J C'_J$ in value) and a capital account deficit of the same size. The United States would have mirror-image imbalances of the same size—a current account deficit and capital account surplus. If Japan plowed back the periodic earnings on its U.S.-domiciled capital into future purchases of such capital, then there would be no repatriated international investment income or debt service. Current account imbalances would be identical in size to trade imbalances.

In this case, the Japanese-owned capital stock would be growing at $Q'_J C'_J$ per period, just as it was before financial liberalization. But the Japanese-domiciled share of this increment would be growing at only $Q'_J S'_J$; $S'_J C'_J$ would represent "net foreign investment" in the United States by Japan. The growth rate of the capital stock in *geographical* Japan would be lower than previously, as would the growth rate of Japanese GNP. In fact Japanese growth rates would be identical to those of the geographical United States in this equilibrium (because $Q'_J S'_J$ is equal to $Q'_U P'$). The geographical economies would remain identical in periods subsequent to the one depicted. But Japanese residents would own a larger and larger share of the growing U.S. capital stock as time went on, with corresponding claims over a larger and larger share of U.S. GNP. (Note that although U.S. residents' ownership *shares* would fall, their claims over future goods would still be rising at $Q'_U S'_U$ per period.)

Debt service and investment income then become a natural aspect of intertemporal linkage as Japan reaches the point of wanting to repatriate earnings on its U.S.-domiciled capital rather than reinvesting them. A simple way to represent that development in the diagram is to assume that $S'_J T'_J$ of repatriation is carried out in machinery, Japan's importable. This repatriation causes a decline in the Japanese trade surplus (U.S. trade deficit) and other adjustments in international balances and real exchange rates that are summarized in table 1.1. It also causes the two geographical economies

Table 1.1
Differing intertemporal preferences: financial liberalization, debt service, international balances, and real exchange rates[a]

	No financial liberalization	Financial liberalization	
		Without repatriation	With repatriation
Trade balances[b]	Zero	J: $S_J'C_J'$, surplus U: $S_U'P'$, deficit	J: $T_J'C_J'$, surplus U: $T_U'P'$, deficit
Investment income/debt service[b]	Zero	Zero	J: $S_J'T_J'$, income U: $S_U'T_U'$, service
Current-account balances[b]	Zero	← J: $S_J'C_J'$, surplus → ← U: $S_U'P'$, deficit →	
Capital-account balances[b]	Zero	← J: $S_J'C_J'$, deficit → ← U: $S_U'P'$, surplus →	
Real exchange rates	"Normal"	Highest (lowest) real value of dollar (yen)	High (low) real value of dollar (yen)

a. Japan (J) is assumed in the table to have a higher national saving rate than the rest of the world, represented by the United States (U).
b. Measured in units of capital goods.

to begin growing apart again, losing their identical character, with Japan's investment and GNP growth exceeding that of the geographical United States.

Budget Deficits and Differences in "Production" Rates of Government Securities

Suppose that we introduce a further difference across the economies by allowing the U.S. government to run (and increase) a budget deficit financed by issues of new Treasury securities every period, precisely the situation analyzed by Hutchison and Pigott in chapter 6. If the United States were a completely closed economy, nothing might change from introducing this feature. The Treasury securities might be considered "inside," not "outside" assets; some U.S. residents and generations would "owe" them to other U.S. residents and generations. In this extreme case (Ricardian equivalence) there would be no real change in the U.S. production possibilities curve in figure 1.3, nor therefore in capabilities for transforming present goods into claims on future goods. Nor of course would there be any burden of the public debt.

But in the open economy setting, matters are quite different, whatever one believes about the burden of the debt and Ricardian equivalence. From Japan's point of view, U.S. Treasury securities are clearly "outside" assets, purchases of which *would* represent increased Japanese capability to consume future goods. Japan may even see them as perfect substitutes for ownership certificates to the U.S. capital stock, taking account of risk, liquidity, and all aspects of financial assets. From the point of view of Japanese decision making, the increased U.S. government budget deficits and the increased issue of new Treasury securities every period shift the U.S. production possibilities curve *vertically* by exactly the increased deficit/issue. The United States produces wonderful Treasury securities every year and equally wonderful capital goods! There is of course not necessarily any real shift from the U.S. point of view, but that is irrelevant for what concerns us.

One of Hutchison-Pigott's important points is a difference in intertemporal transformation opportunities. Even a perceived shift in Japan's ability to use external trade to transform present goods into claims on future goods establishes a real-financial linkage. To show the motive for such trade in its starkest simplicity, assume that U.S. and Japanese intertemporal preferences were identical after all, and depicted by the preference contours through point P_J, C_J. Then because from a Japanese perspective U.S. Treasury securities are outside assets, and because the perceived U.S. production possibilities curve has been shifted vertically, Japan will also perceive higher potential real rates at P_U'', C_U'' than at P_J, C_J, as reflected in the steeper tangent price line. Japanese residents (unlike U.S. residents) will be prepared to bid for assets at prices between those implied by the two tangents. Trade will be thereby encouraged in which Japan exports consumer goods to the U.S. in return for Treasury securities (as well as assets and capital goods that may be perfect substitutes for the Treasury securities). The United States will incur a trade account deficit and probably debt service obligations, offset by a capital account surplus, plus other consequences discussed by Hutchison-Pigott.

A purist might object to this real-financial linkage by observing that the *world* production possibilities curve that could be constructed from figure 1.3's true U.S. and Japanese curves would be unaffected by any issue of government securities. That observation is correct but focuses only on production of real goods. It neglects "production" of financial assets, which is an equally important element of generalized supply in this perspective, and especially important when the asset is "inside" to some agents and "outside" to others. Real-financial linkage follows directly. It arises in an open economy for precisely the same reason that it would arise in a closed economy with "distribution effects" caused by two groups of agents, one that considers government securities to be net wealth and one that does not.

1.8   Structural and Intertemporal Linkages Jointly Considered

Combining the intertemporal and structural perspectives on real-financial linkage is valuable for its suggestive richness. It also allows fuller reference to the Hutchison and Pigott chapter and to familiar macroeconomic linkages that have been deemphasized in this volume.

Every economy in reality has an array of differentiated current goods and assets (claims on future goods). It has proved helpful above to recognize this very simply in the distinction between tradable and nontradable current goods. Now it is helpful to conceive symmetrically of tradable and nontradable assets, identifying the first with government securities and ownership claims to capital goods and the second with money. It is also helpful to conceive of wealth owners holding a portfolio of tradable assets and "their own" (but not the other) nontradable money, just as current goods consumers buy tradables and "their own" nontradable (but not the other).

General equilibrium in this conception includes stock equilibrium in all asset markets, characterized in ways that are captured in monetary, portfolio balance, and stock adjustment models of international finance. Figure 1.4 summarizes what is familiar from these models and draws out their implications for real-financial linkages along with figure 1.5.

In figure 1.4 asset market equilibrium is described in quadrant 1, where schedules HH and FF describe pairs of (nominal) interest rates (r) and exchange rates (e) that make portfolio managers content to hold the existing stock supplies of (nontradable) money and (tradable) foreign securities. At the interest and exchange rate common to both schedules, the stock supply of domestic securities must be willingly held too, because existing wealth is constrained to be held in either money, domestic securities, or perfectly substitutable foreign securities. Conditions for equilibrium can be written

$$\frac{H}{P} = L(y, v, r)$$

$$\frac{eF}{P} = F(y, v, r),$$

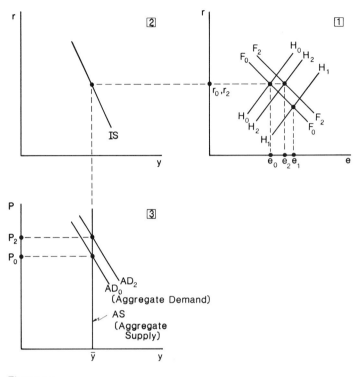

Figure 1.4
A familiar real-financial model

where H and F stand for existing nominal stocks of money and foreign securities in an economy's portfolio, and P is an index of prices of current tradables and nontradables as in equations (1).

The real demand for money varies directly with real income (y) and real wealth (v), and inversely with the domestic rate of interest on tradable securities (r).[6] The real demand for foreign securities varies inversely with real income and the domestic rate of interest and directly with real wealth. The foreign rate of interest can be treated exogenously and ignored if for convenience we focus on a small economy.

The FF curve in figure 1.4 is negatively sloped because a rise in e (appreciation of foreign currency) creates an excess supply of foreign securities, requiring a fall in the domestic rate of interest to correct it.[7] The HH curve is positively sloped because a rise in e creates an excess demand for domestic money which must be offset by a rise in the domestic rate of interest.

The real sector is typically linked to this financial sector by an equilib-

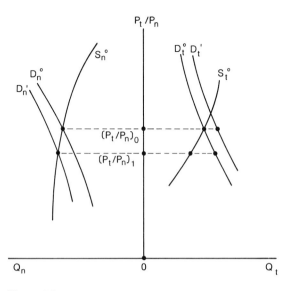

Figure 1.5
Structural disaggregation underlying the familiar real-financial model

rium condition equating supplies of and demands for domestically produced current goods in the open economy:

$$T\left(\frac{P_t}{eP_t^*}, y, y^*\right) + D = S(y, r) - I(r),$$

where any excess of private real saving (S) over investment (I) is either
invested abroad, creating a real trade surplus (positive T) to match the
negative balance on capital account, or absorbed by government budget
deficits (D). The trade balance is usually assumed to be directly related to
foreign real income, and inversely do domestic real income and the real
exchange rate. Private saving is usually assumed to be directly related to
income and the interest rate, and private investment inversely to the
interest rate. This equilibrium condition yields an "IS curve" depicted in
quadrant 2 of figure 1.4, and an aggregate demand curve in quadrant 3.
When factor markets are free of distortions (factor price rigidities, money
illusion, etc.) so that the economy operates on its production possibilities
curve in figure 1.3, then the aggregate supply curve in figure 1.4 can be
taken to be vertical.[8] The point $\bar{y}$ in figure 1.4 in fact corresponds to points
like P' in figure 1.3. Furthermore the "IS curve" in figure 1.4 is precisely the
demand curve generated by the preference map of figure 1.3, and distances
corresponding to T, D, S, and I can be found in figure 1.3.

With this framework we can see more clearly the contributions of Hamada-Horiuchi and Hutchison-Pigott. Hamada and Horiuchi discuss the linkage effects of Japanese regulation and deregulation of the use of yen assets as transactions media (H behavior) and as stores of value (F behavior). Hutchison and Pigott discuss the linkage effects of government budget deficits (D), controlling implicitly for whether they are financed by money creation (H behavior) or securities issue (F-equivalent behavior). Given a value of D, of course this choice of whether to finance it by money creation or securities issue is equivalent to the choice of some open market exchange (operation) of money for securities. This kind of open market exchange is easy to analyze in our framework in order to introduce the importance of tradables/nontradables structure in questions of real-financial linkage.

To that end, consider monetary expansion by way of an open market purchase of domestic securities. This increases H and shifts the HH curve down in quadrant 1 of figure 1.4, initially bringing down the rate of interest and depreciating the domestic currency. These developments stimulate domestic demand and shift expenditure from foreign to home goods, as indicated by the shift in aggregate demand. Because the aggregate supply curve is vertical, though, the monetary expansion leaves real income unaffected. In the new equilibrium, the nominal exchange rate and the price level rise in proportion to the change in money supply.

The rise in domestic prices restores the original values of H/P and e/P, and shifts the HH and FF curves up, returning the interest rate to its original level. The new equilibrium is characterized by neutrality, with real variables remaining unaffected while prices and the nominal exchange rate rise in proportion to the rise in the money stock. Linkage is absent.

Structural differentiation of the real economy does not alter this. Linkage will still be absent. Distinguishing between tradables and nontradables makes no difference to the neutrality conclusion. We can demonstrate this in figure 1.5, where the price of tradables relative to non-tradables (P_t/P_n) is measured vertically. In the right-hand panel, the demand for tradables is a negative function of the relative price and a positive function of overall expenditure, while supply is a positive function of relative price. In the left panel, the demand curve for nontradables slopes up from right to left and the supply curve slopes down from right to left to reflect the fact that the relative price of nontradables falls as we move up along the price axis. (These supply and demand curves could in fact be derived directly from figure 1.2 by rotating a price line respectively around the production possibilities curve and the indifference curve that is tangent to it.)

The initial equilibrium in figure 1.5 shows both markets to be cleared at relative price $(P_t/P_n)_0$ and thus reflects the familiar constraint in pure trade theory that the market for nontradables must clear and that trade must be balanced. Monetary expansion causes the initial depreciation of domestic currency from e_0 to e_1 in figure 1.4 to raise P_t (incipiently) in figure 1.5 if the law of one price holds. But a rise in the price ratio creates excess demand in nontradables as well as a trade surplus. For small economies it is clear that in the absence of shifts in demand or supply, the original price ratio is the only equilibrium relative price. Hence the excess demand in the non-tradables sector serves to raise the price of nontradables, ensuring that its movement keeps pace with the nominal depreciation. In this situation we will observe the law of one price not only for tradables but for nontrad-ables as well. The rise in P_n in turn feeds back to the financial sector by raising the price level, shifting HH and FF up. In the new equilibrium, P_t, P_n, E, and P will have all risen proportionately while real variables remain the same.

During the adjustment process any decline in the rate of interest that increases aggregate expenditure has the effect of shifting out the D_t and D_n curves, thereby adding to the disequilibrium in the nontradables sector, while reducing the trade surplus. That same transitional decline in the interest rate can, however, also cause both the exchange rate and tradables prices to "overshoot" their ultimate equilibrium values (Dornbusch 1976; Kouri 1976).

The importance of e, P_t overshooting for our purposes is that their variance over time might be greater than the variance of P_n, nontradables prices. This difference in variance might be expected especially in an economy with floating exchange rates and monetary "shocks" that domi-nate real "shocks." This in turn might explain the withdrawal of risk-averse resource owners from tradables sectors and the reduction in trade volumes under floating exchange rates that De Grauwe and de Bellefroid seem to detect. Thus real-financial linkages that are absent in comparisons of equilibria that feature neutrality may nevertheless be present during adjust-ment periods or under uncertainty. Stockman's chapter describes why we should not be surprised by this conclusion.

Hutchison and Pigott's securities-financed fiscal expansion gives struc-tural differentiation an even stronger role. Consider first an increase in government expenditure (and D) in which the entirety goes to purchase nontradables. The demand for nontradables shifts to D_n^1 in figure 1.5, creating an excess demand at the initial relative price and requiring a fall in the relative price of tradables if equilibrium in nontradables is to be restored.

The needed decline in the price ratio can be achieved by currency appreciation and/or a nominal price rise in nontradables. The fall in the relative price of tradables is needed to liberate resources for use in nontradables production and to crowd out private demand for nontradables. As price falls in tradables, increased private consumption of tradables is met by imports. Hence the budget deficit and the rise in public demand for nontradables leads directly to a trade deficit, matched of course by a capital account surplus that represents the sale abroad of a portion of each period's additional issue of government securities. What happens to internal relative prices, and relative production and consumption of the two types of goods, is in fact completely analogous to the discussion of Kravis and Lipsey's and Marston's work in section 1.6. There, however, the impetus comes from supply-side shocks, whereas in Hutchison and Pigott the impetus is from the demand side.

In the financial sector the fiscal expansion raises the stock of domestic securities, whose effect depends to some extent on whether domestic money and securities are considered part of domestic wealth or whether foreign ("outside") securities are the only financial asset representing wealth. There exists considerable disagreement on this issue, as implied in section 1.7, but we will assume that wealth is increased at least somewhat. The rise in wealth shifts the HH and FF curves upward, hence raising the rate of interest. The IS curve in quadrant 2 of figure 1.4 would also shift up in response to the fiscal expansion.

Given fixed aggregate supply (albeit changed in its composition) and a fixed money stock, the overall price level P will tend to move directly with velocity, which rises due to the higher interest rate. Although it seems possible that prices of both tradables and nontradables rise due to the fiscal expansion, P_n must rise more than P_t in order to bring about the required decline in equilibrium P_t/P_n. And the nominal exchange rate e must fall in this case enough to bring about the real appreciation (higher P_t/eP_t^*) that is required to generate the trade-balance deficit required. (We assume the economy is too small to affect P_t^*.)

The preceding illustrates a set of linkages between the real and financial sides of the economy due to fiscal policy. It also provides a useful insight into the efficacy of exchange market intervention.

Suppose that the authorities were dissatisfied with the required appreciation (lower e) and they attempted through exchange market intervention to reverse it. Suppose further that this was accomplished by official purchases of foreign securities added to reserves which shift the FF curve up in the first panel of figure 1.4, bringing about the nominal rise in e, at least as far as the financial side of the economy is concerned. The depreciation would push up the price ratio in figure 1.5 and create excess demand in the nontradables sector while reducing the trade deficit. This outcome cannot be sustained, however, for the relative price must fall again to restore equilibrium in nontradables. The ensuing rise in the price of nontradables would have secondary effects in the financial sector, pushing the two curves up. The upshot of the intervention policy would be a depreciation of the dollar in nominal terms but no change in the price ratio, nor in the real exchange rate, and hence no improvement in the trade balance.

Exchange market intervention of the type discussed is a nominal or financial policy, while the trade balance deficit is a real phenomenon. Intervention fails to budge the trade balance because it has no effect on the domestic relative price.

The preceding discussion assumes that the fiscal policy increases purchases of nontradables. If by contrast, the increased government expenditure were to fall entirely on traded goods, represented by a shift in the D_t curve to D_t^1, the initial real side effect is a trade balance deficit at the original relative price $(P_t/P_n)_0$. Meanwhile the financial sector repercussions are as before. The price relative cannot change, however, since that would break equilibrium in the nontradables sector. Thus the nominal exchange rate and the price of nontradables must rise (or fall) together, preserving the price relative, while the trade balance moves into deficit by an amount equal to the increase in government spending. The real exchange rate remains unaffected.

The clear lesson is that the real-financial linkages from fiscal policy are ambiguous! They depend not only on the type of differentiated asset that the government uses to finance its budget deficit but also on the type of differentiated goods that it buys. Nominal and real exchange rates, relative prices, and several other variables ought to respond differently to fiscal policy in different economies, depending on these considerations. Therefore it is no surprise, and is in fact an important contribution, that Hutchison and Pigott find different configurations of quantitative effects for different countries in their sample.

Notes

We have benefited greatly from the comments of Michael Hutchison, Richard C. Marston, Robert E. Lipsey, Charles Pigott, and several other anonymous referees.

1. This prediction depends on a conception of nontradables as comparable goods from economy to economy, only perhaps facing prohibitive transport costs, for

example, personal services such as hair styling, shoeshines, and dry cleaning. To apply the prediction to unique national nontradables, for example, judicial services, would be nonsense because factor requirements will obviously be themselves unique to each economy.

2. "Competitive advantage," measured say by $\%\Delta(P_{ti}/eP_{ti}^{*})$, is obviously a quite different concept than "comparative advantage, measured by $(p_{ti}/p_{tj})/ (p_{ti}^{*}/p_{tj}^{*})$. The two concepts are often confused.

3. For discussion and references, see, for example, Goldstein (1984).

4. In interpreting the two production possibilities curves as belonging to two economies, we are adopting the conception that one economy's nontradables are comparable to the other's, and measuring both along the same horizontal axis; see note 1.

5. This particular wording is Charles Pigott's.

6. Real wealth can be visualized in figure 1.3 as the vertical distance between the points C and the horizontal axis beginning at O.

7. The presence of at least one asset with a nominally fixed face value, of which money is the best example, is necessary for this conclusion.

8. Real-financial linkages in open economies with factor market distortions are the meat of many open economy macroeconomic models, and receive little attention in this volume because of their familiarity. One might think of open economy macroeconomics and this volume as describing real-financial linkages, respectively, on and below the production possibilities curve of figures 1.2 and 1.3 or on and to the left of the vertical aggregate supply curve of figure 1.4.

References

Balassa, Bela, 1964. The Purchasing Power Parity Doctrine: A Reappraisal. *Journal of Political Economy* 72 (December): 584–596.

Dornbusch, Rudiger. 1976. Expectations and Exchange-Rate Dynamics. *Journal of Political Economy* 84 (December): 1161–1176.

Goldstein, Morris. 1984. The Exchange Rate System: Lessons of the Past and Options for the Future. Occasional paper, no. 30. Washington: International Monetary Fund.

Kouri, Pentti J. K. 1976. The Exchange Rate and the Balance of Payments in the Short Run and in the Long Run. *Scandinavian Journal of Economics* 78 (May): 280–304.

Mundell, Robert A. 1957. International Trade and Factor Mobility. *American Economic Review* 47 (June): 321–335.

2   Some Interactions between Goods Markets and Asset Markets in Open Economies

Alan C. Stockman

This chapter provides a brief overview of some links between real and financial markets in open economies. There are two main sources of the links discussed here. First, the opportunity sets of individuals and the economy's set of feasible resource allocations depend in part on the availability of financial markets. Second, portfolio allocations, financial transactions, and prices of financial assets depend on characteristics of goods markets such as production opportunities, consumers' preferences for goods, and opportunities for trade in goods markets. The links between real and financial markets operate in both directions.

My discussion is restricted to interactions that exist irrespective of the nature of the monetary regime or the effects of monetary policies. Connections between monetary policy and the real economy, which are subject to considerable controversy, may create additional interactions between real and financial markets that are not discussed here.

Financial markets permit individuals to transfer resources over time and across alternative states of nature. Consequently opportunities to trade on financial markets affect real resource allocations, incomes, and relative prices. The division of output between consumption and investment, the allocation of time to labor or leisure, the allocation of factors of production to alternative industries and sectors of the economy, the balance of trade, and the international pattern of comparative advantage and trade are all affected by the availability of financial markets. Relative prices of various goods at a point in time, intertemporal relative prices of goods, the size and distribution of income and welfare are also affected by the available set of financial markets. The structure of financial markets and the set of financial assets available is in turn affected by characteristics of goods markets.

These interactions are not peculiar to "international" financial markets; the links also operate within each country. But there are some uniquely international aspects to the some of the links I discuss here. In addition these links between financial markets and goods markets are particularly important in many international applications.

Considerable theoretical work in international economics has been devoted to studying the effects *on* goods markets of changes *in* goods markets, such as changes in production opportunities, preferences, and trading opportunities. Many simple models of international trade abstract from financial markets in order to concentrate on these issues. Although this is a useful way to investigate many issues, it poses dangers in other applications because it can give misleading results in certain cases, as I will explain.

The relative neglect of financial markets in international economics may have been justified at times in the past when national governments imposed severe restrictions on international financial markets and when those markets were at earlier stages of development. But international financial markets have developed over the past decade in both scope and sophistication, and the prospects for continuation of this trend are great. These developments have progressed well beyond the establishment of the Eurocurrency market in the 1960s and 1970s. Stock markets and credit markets, for both short- and long-term debt, have become increasingly integrated internationally. Future contracts and currency options are traded on organized markets. The development of swaps, some of which have become so standardized that they are traded as commodities, has created opportunities for trade in almost any contingent asset that market participants can invent. Such trades are increasingly commonplace among firms engaged in international trade. Trade in equities of firms permits indirect access to these markets for smaller investors.

2.1   Real-Financial Links in a World without Uncertainty

Consider a world without uncertainty about the future. The single role of financial markets in such a world is to permit intertemporal trade. The types of trading opportunities available on financial markets affect demands and supplies for goods. In the presence of a full set of intertemporal trading opportunities (i.e., assets for every maturity), and in the absence of other distortions in the economy, all contemporaneous and intertemporal marginal rates of substitution will be equalized across consumers. Similar statements could be made regarding marginal rates of transformation in production, and other conditions for an efficient allocation. At the other extreme, without any intertemporal trading opportunities, marginal rates of substitution between consumption at different dates may differ across consumers. The same is true in the intermediate case in which financial markets exist but offer only limited opportunities for trading intertemporally (or across states of the world if there is uncertainty).

The inability to engage directly in financial transactions when those markets are incomplete leads consumers to substitute into alternative, imperfect ways of reallocating consumption over time. Suppose two countries have deterministic seasonal variations in production opportunities and are identical except for the seasons during which production opportunities are particularly good (e.g., one has better opportunities in winter, the other in summer). To make the example concrete, suppose that marginal physical products of factors are independent of the season, so that seasonal variation occurs in average but not marginal product. With a complete set of financial markets, consumption can be completely smoothed over time in each country, with alternating trade surpluses and deficits. Without financial markets, consumption in each country must vary seasonally. (This is similar to Mundell's 1973 example in which there are no international financial markets but trade in international reserves under a fixed exchange rate system can substitute for those missing financial markets). But these seasonal fluctuations can be mitigated somewhat by changes in behavior in goods markets and factor markets. Labor supply, for example, will be varied seasonally to increase production in bad seasons and reduce it in better seasons. This allows the economy to smooth consumption over time at the expense of greater variability in leisure. In equilibrium the motivation for this seasonal variation in labor supply is variation in domestic real interest rates—which differ across countries—and so in the value of the marginal product of labor. If inventories of goods can be held at some cost, then they will also be used to reduce seasonal variation in consumption. If some products have greater seasonal variation in production than do others, then factors will move seasonally between the most variable industries and other industries in response to seasonal variation in relative prices. These factor movements help smooth seasonal movements in domestic production of the most variable products at the cost of additional seasonal variation in production of other goods. These reallocations in goods markets and factor markets occur because financial markets are incomplete and so do not permit seasonal variations to be pooled across countries.

The same type of argument obviously applies in other contexts. The general point is that reallocations in product and factor markets can partially substitute for the ability to trade on asset markets. When asset markets are limited, therefore, goods markets are organized differently in order to smooth consumption, take advantage of unique investment opportunities that cannot be financed by borrowing from abroad, or accomplish others goals that would involve financial trades if such trades were possible. The level and composition of production, international trade, incomes, and relative prices are all affected by limitations on international financial markets and would all be changed by expanded opportunities to trade on those financial markets. Clearly any limitations on financial markets can have these kinds of effects on allocations and prices in goods markets, whether they result from government restrictions (e.g., capital controls, exchange controls, regulation of financial markets, and taxation of income from financial assets) or from problems of private information related to hidden actions (moral hazard) or hidden information (adverse selection).

The availability of financial markets not only affects resource allocation and prices on goods markets but also the way that goods markets respond to exogenous disturbances. Consider the previous example in which two countries are identical except for the season in which production opportunities are particularly good. Assume that agents in these economies are infinitely lived (an overlapping generations model would give slightly more complicated results, but the main point would be similar). Call the home country the one with good opportunities in summer, and the foreign country the one with good opportunities in winter. Suppose that, in year T, the home country gets (temporarily) slightly better production opportunities in winter than usual but that they are still inferior to those in the summer.[1] This exogenous, temporary increase in production is assumed to have been perfectly anticipated in advance, because assuming otherwise would violate the perfect foresight assumption. (Unanticipated disturbances are discussed in the next section.) In a world with complete international financial markets, the home country will have capitalized this increase in production into its wealth and consumed more than otherwise prior to the date T winter. Because of this greater domestic demand for goods prior to date T winter, the foreign country will have consumed less than otherwise.

During the date T winter, both home and foreign consumption rise in equilibrium.[2] Variations in labor supply, inventories, etc., will occur in both countries as they attempt to smooth consumption over time. In the absence of any international financial markets, foreign consumption is unaffected by the increase in home production opportunities at date T winter.[3] Adjustments in labor supply, inventories, etc., are greater in the home country and may not occur at all in the foreign country.[4] Clearly the ability to trade on international financial markets alters the responses in goods and factor markets to exogenous changes in supplies or demands. Note that financial markets affect the results of changes in government policies just as they affect the results of other exogenous changes. Further discussion of these points is postponed until the next section in which uncertainty is introduced.

Another link between financial markets and goods markets is due to the role of financial markets in permitting governments to precommit themselves credibly to future policies. Lucas and Stokey (1983) examined the time consistency of optimal government policy in a closed economy, and concentrated on the optimal time path of distorting taxes for a given time path of government expenditure. They found that the optimal government policy when the government can precommit itself (credibly and costlessly) to future policies is identical to the optimal policy when the government *cannot* credibly precommit itself as long as the economy has complete financial markets. They also found that if financial markets are incomplete in the sense that there are not assets traded for *every* maturity (and, in their stochastic model, for every state of the world), then the optimal government policy differs from the full precommitment policy, and the resulting equilibrium is Pareto inferior. These results imply the existence of a link between financial markets and goods markets that differs from the links discussed earlier. The full range of financial markets permits the government at each date to alter the incentives of future governments, by restructuring the term structure of the government debt, so as to duplicate a situation of full (and credible) precommitment.

Persson and Svensson (1986) extended the Lucas-Stokey model to an open economy setting. They found that the government of an open economy can duplicate the full precommitment policy if an only if international financial markets are complete and the domestic country is sufficiently large to be able to affect world interest rates at each maturity. Under these conditions, of course, it is feasible to improve welfare in the domestic country with the imposition of capital controls to take advantage of the economy's market power in world capital markets. An economy that is unable to affect all (state-contingent) prices on world financial markets cannot use the Lucas-Stokey method to duplicate the precommitment equilibrium, even if international financial markets are complete and even if the government imposes capital controls so that it can affect domestic interest rates. Governments can duplicate the optimal precommitment policies only be affecting world interest rates (for each maturity and, when there is uncertainty, for each state). If governments of different countries have different objectives or opportunity sets (e.g., time profiles of tax bases), then it is infeasible for more than one government to duplicate the optimal precommitment equilibrium (even if all have market power on complete international financial markets). This has interesting implications for issues of international cooperation and policy coordination that have yet to be examined.

The set of financial markets required for Pareto efficiency depends on tastes and production opportunities. In an economy without uncertainty and without endogenous government policies subject to problems of time consistency, the required financial assets are minimal. Assets need only permit wealth to be transferred across time periods, so a set of one-period loans, for all periods, is generally sufficient. However, the problem of time consistency of optimal government tax policies creates an additional link between goods markets and financial markets. As a consequence, if pre-commitment is a problem, then a complete set of assets for all possible maturities may be required to support the Pareto-optimal equilibrium.

Another link between financial markets and goods markets operates in open economy, monetary economies where money is held for transactions purposes (e.g., the general equilibrium versions of Baumol-Tobin models such as Jovanovic 1982) or cash-in-advance models (Lucas 1980; Stockman 1980; Svensson 1985a, b). The requirements on asset markets for a Pareto-optimal equilibrium in these monetary models are greater than in real models. The source of the additional requirements lies in the use of moneys to buy goods. In contrast to barter models, in these monetary models individuals must obtain "liquidity," represented by money, in order to purchase goods; a large enough level of wealth is not sufficient. In international applications moreover individuals must obtain enough liquidity in each currency, in each period, to finance purchases in that period requiring that currency. These additional constraints on purchases in goods markets imply that the set of financial assets required to support a Pareto-optimal equilibrium is larger than it would be in a barter economy.

2.2 Uncertainty and Real-Financial Links in Open Economies

When the economy is subject to uncertainty, international financial markets permit trade across states of nature as well as trade over time. Trade across states of nature allows individuals to allocate risk optimally. Availability of financial markets to trade across alternative states affects allocations and prices in goods markets for the same reasons as does availability of financial markets to trade over time. Pareto efficiency of allocations in goods markets now generally requires that financial assets exist to trade across every possible state as well as every period of time. Limitations on asset markets induce the same kinds of substitution and reallocations in goods markets that were discussed in the previous section, though they now can take new forms (e.g., altering the composition of goods produced in a country to reduce aggregate risk from productivity shocks when international financial markets cannot be used to diversify risks of production shocks in various industries). Because the arguments are the same as in the previous section, with "states of the world" replacing "time periods," no more need be said about these real-financial links.

Just as the effects of exogenous changes differ depending on the availability of financial markets in a world without uncertainty, so they do with uncertainty. Consider the example in the previous section with two economies that are almost identical. Rather than assuming deterministic seasonal variations in production opportunities, suppose those variations are stochastic. An exogenous disturbance to the economy consists of a high (or low) realization of a random variable. Suppose that during the date T winter, output in the home economy is high relative to its mean. This is an unexpected increase in home output at T in the sense that actual output exceeds expected output. An assumption of rational expectations guarantees that individuals knew in advance that this might occur, because output is subject to stochastic shocks. With complete international financial markets (and countries that are identical except for realizations of random variables and the season in which output is high on average), the two countries will pool risks of productivity shocks in such a way that they both share in an unexpected increase in output at T in the home country. Both countries might share the increase equally, as in Lucas (1982). Alternatively, it is easy to construct examples in which the sharing is unequal; for example, if the shock raises the marginal product of labor in the home country, labor will rise in the home country but fall in the foreign country (through a wealth effect on leisure). If the marginal utility of consumption is a function of leisure, then the equilibrium with complete financial markets will allocate the increased output differently to the home and foreign countries. Note that it is possible (e.g., if utility is separable in leisure and consumption) that utility in the home country falls at date T because of the fall in leisure at home (while the increase in output is shared by the two countries). This would not happen if there were no international financial markets; nevertheless, expected utility is higher with than without those markets.

In Lucas's model this sharing of the increased output in the home country is accomplished through international trade in equities of firms. On the other hand, if international financial markets are limited (by either governments or nature through private information problems), then this risk sharing may be infeasible. In that case the initial equilibrium is different because (as noted previously) each country will substitute into alternative forms of self-insurance. Note that this link between financial markets and goods markets occurs because of the *possibility* of future disturbances and the desire to mitigate the associated risk. In addition the effects of an *actual* disturbance, such as an increase in home production opportunities at date T, has different effects if financial markets are limited. Because of the absence of ex ante risk sharing in financial markets, the increase in home opportunities at T would raise home consumption by more, raise home output by less (through adjustments to factor supplies), and would generally have a smaller effect on goods markets in the foreign country than if international financial markets had been complete. Some related issues are analyzed by Cole (1986), who examines a more general model in which limitations on financial markets raise the variability of consumption across countries, reduce the covariation between domestic and foreign consumption, affect employment, and reduce the variability of output in each country.

The effects of changes in government policies are also altered by the set of international financial markets. In a perfect foresight model, by definition, the effects of unexpected changes in government policies (or in other exogenous variables) cannot be examined. Comparative statics can be used to contrast two different economies whose policies (or technologies, etc.) differ but cannot generally be used to show the effects of an unexpected change within a single economy. The reason is that if risk-averse individuals do not *expect* a change in policy but know that there is some *possibility* that a change will occur, then (in this environment of uncertainty) they have an incentive to insure against the risk involved. The existence of international financial markets permits individuals to purchase insurance by altering their portfolios of assets. Because national government policies frequently have different effects on domestic residents than on foreign residents, the possibility of a change in policy creates risk that differs across countries. This difference creates gains from trade on financial markets even if tastes for risk are the same across countries, and imparts a particularly "international" flavor to this real-financial interaction. The trades that occur on financial markets feed back on goods markets: they alter the effects of a change in policy if and when it actually occurs. Because individuals have used financial markets to insure (at least partially) against the risk of a change in policy, the response of consumption, investment, and other allocative decisions differs from what it would have been in the absence of those financial markets. This link between asset markets and goods markets means that changes in the availability of financial assets can have substantial effects on the results of government policies, sometimes even reversing the results (Stockman and Dellas 1986; Stockman 1987).

The set of assets that are required to support the Pareto-optimal equilibrium depends, as in the case of certainty, on the economy's production and trading opportunities and on individuals' preferences. Also as in the certainty case these characteristics of goods markets affect portfolio allocations and asset prices. Links between goods markets and asset markets continue to operate in both directions. Cole (1986), for example, examines the conditions under which international trade in equities, which are claims only to the *residual* income of firms after payment for labor and other costs, supports an equilibrium in goods markets that duplicates the (Pareto-optimal) equilibrium with complete international financial markets. Not surprisingly, those conditions can be rather strict; for example, if claims to income from human capital cannot be directly traded (which is a standard assumption because of the moral hazard problems involved), then the equilibrium allocation will be Pareto inferior unless those claims are unneccesary because the income from human capital is perfectly correlated with the income from an asset that is traded. That condition would require special assumptions about the form of production technology (and the opportunities for trade in other assets). The inability to trade claims to income from human capital leads to partly offsetting reallocations on goods markets as individuals attempt to reduce risk in alternative ways. It also leads to alternative forms of the organization of firms and contracts to reduce the magnitude of the moral hazard problem.

These effects on goods markets of limitations in financial markets are mirrored in the effects of the structure of goods markets on portfolio allocations and asset prices. For example, the greater the importance of human capital as a factor of production and the greater the moral hazard problems (e.g., the greater the incentive to shirk rather than work), the lower the degree of optimal portfolio diversification for the agent who has the incentive to shirk. By reducing his diversification and adding a component of wealth that is tied to his output, the agent's cost of shirking can be raised. Portfolio choice and asset prices are also affected by limits on international trade in goods. The existence of nontraded goods, for example, induces domestic and foreign residents to choose different portfolios of assets because they want to hedge against price changes of different bundles of goods (Stulz 1981; Stockman and Dellas 1984). Similar effects of the structure of goods markets on portfolio allocations and asset prices involve costs of transportation, information, or transacting, which can create potential deviations from the law of one price in response to various disturbances. These potential price changes affect optimal portfolio choices and, in equilibrium, asset prices.

2.3   Conclusions

There are many subtle links between markets for financial assets and markets for goods and services in open economies. Some of these links have a distinct "international" aspect to them because of differences across countries in governments and their policies, differences in supply (or demand) conditions in goods markets, or differences in the consumption bundle across countries. The links that involve attempts by individuals to insure against the risk of future changes in government policies, and those that involve the time consistency of optimal government policies, have particularly "international" characters and important applications to open economies. Much theoretical work remains to be done on all of these links.

I have ignored links that involve nonneutralities of money, largely because of the controversies and uncertainties that those issues involve. But, because almost all theories about monetary nonneutralities postulate mechanisms in which the availability of financial markets plays an important role, additional real-financial links will appear. For example, financial markets can provide valuable information about underlying disturbances that play an obvious role in business cycle models based on confusion of nominal and relative price changes. Models based on contracts in labor or product markets generally postulate the absence of certain financial opportunities for some people (e.g., workers), so the availability of financial markets plays a key role in the results.

Whatever the additional real-financial links in open economies created by conditions that result in nonneutralities of money, the links I discuss in this chapter will continue to operate. Further work on these links is required to understand the causes and effects of the recent (and current) rapid development of international financial markets. These new financial markets may profoundly influence the organization of markets for goods and factors and the pattern of international trade.

Notes

I would like to thank Sven Arndt, David Richardson, and Michael Dooley for helpful comments.

1. The two countries are no longer identical (except for seasonality in production) because production in the foreign country is not subject to a change in year T.

2. If utility functions are intertemporably separable, then the world short-term interest rate falls at T until world consumption rises sufficiently for equilibrium.

3. If the two countries differed in that home and foriegn products were different, then the foreign country would be affected at date T even in the absence of international financial markets, because the increase in home production would reduce the home country's terms of trade. But this terms of trade effect operates whether or not there are international financial markets. So the main point of the example, that the effects of exogenous changes differ depending on the availability of international financial markets, would still go through.

4. It is possible that some readjustments will occur in the foreign country, depending on the detailed assumptions of the model. For example, if each country produces many products, reallocations of factors across industries in the home country (in response to the exogenous change at T) may alter relative prices of goods that can be traded internationally, and these relative price changes would then induce adjustments in factor and goods markets in the foreign country.

References

Cole, Harold. 1986. Financial Structure and International Trade: A General Equilibrium Analysis. Working paper. Department of Economics, University of Pennsylvania.

Jovanovic, Boyan. 1982. Inflation and Welfare in the Steady State. *Journal of Political Economy* 90 (June):561–577.

Lucas, Robert E. Jr. 1980. Equilibrium in a Pure Currency Economy. *Economic Inquiry* 18:203–220.

Lucas, Robert E. Jr. 1982. Interest Rates and Currency Prices in a Two-Country World. *Journal of Monetary Economics* 10:335–360.

Lucas, Robert E., Jr., and Nancy Stokey. 1983. Optimal Fiscal and Monetary Policy in an Economy without Capital. *Journal of Monetary Economics* 12:55–83.

Mundell, Robert. 1973. Uncommon Arguments for Common Currencies. In H. G. Johnson and A. K. Swoboda (eds.), *The Economics of Common Currencies* . London: George Allen and Unwin.

Persson, Torsten, and Lars E. O. Svensson. 1986. International Borrowing and Time-Consistent Fiscal Policy. *Scandinavian Journal of Economics* 88, no. 1:273–295.

Stockman, Alan C. 1980. A Theory of Exchange Rate Determination. *Journal of Political Economy* 88:673–698.

Stockman, Alan C. 1986. Fiscal Policies and International Financial Markets. Rochester Center for Economic Research working paper no. 36. Forthcoming in Proceedings of NBER Conference on Fiscal Policy in Open Economies, edited by Jacob Frenkel, 1987.

Stockman, Alan C., and Harris Dellas. 1986. Asset Markets, Tariffs, and Political Risk. *Journal of International Economics* 21 (November): 199–213.

Stockman, Alan C., and Harris Dellas. 1984. The Roles of the Terms of Trade and Nontraded Good Prices in Exchange Rate Variations. NBER working paper no. 1342.

Rene Stulz. 1981. A Model of International Asset Pricing. *Journal of Financial Economics* (December): 383–406.

Svensson, Lars E. O. 1985a. Currency Prices, Terms of Trade, and Interest Rates: A General Equilibrium Asset-Pricing, Cash-in-Advance Approach. *Journal of International Economics* 15 (February): 17–41.

Svensson, Lars E. O. 1985b. Money and Asset Prices in a Cash-in-Advance Economy. *Journal of Political Economy* (October): 919–944.

II Structural Sources of Real-Financial Linkages

Introduction to Part II

Real exchange rates have fluctuated significantly since the onset of floating and departures from purchasing power parity have been frequent and persistent. The three chapters that comprise part II are intent on exploring some possible reasons.

In chapter 3 Krugman examines the proposition that import prices do not adjust to exchange rate changes to the extent suggested by purchasing power parity theory because foreign exporters "price to market." A review of the empirical evidence involving U.S.–EC trade, and German exports in particular, supports the conclusion that pricing to market did indeed take place during the dollar appreciation of the early 1980s, but that it was specific to the machinery and transport equipment sector. Krugman estimates that 35 to 40 percent of the real appreciation of the dollar was absorbed by foreign exporters in a rise in their supply prices to the United States relative to other markets.

Krugman examines several potential theoretical models to explain this phenomenon and finds that pricing to market is best explained in a dynamic model of imperfect competition, where supply (cost) and demand (reputation, product differentiation) considerations both play a role.

Marston, in chapter 4, focuses on competition among the tradables producers of countries and on the use of general price levels in the calculation of real exchange rates. He notes that if productivity growth is substantially faster in Japan than in the United States, then the dollar must depreciate against the yen in order to prevent U.S. goods from becoming relatively expensive. If the rapid growth in productivity is concentrated in traded goods, then the real value of the dollar based on the general price level must fall by even more in order to prevent an erosion of competitiveness for U.S. tradables producers. Discrepancies among countries in productivity growth in traded goods production can thus bring significant departures from purchasing power parity.

Marston tests this proposition by constructing several measures of the real exchange rate using general price levels such as the CPI and WPI and then comparing movements in real exchange rates. He concludes that the real exchange value of the dollar would have had to fall by very large amounts since 1973 in order to keep U.S. tradables producers from slipping in relation to Japan. In the absence of such needed adjustments, U.S. competitiveness did in fact suffer significantly.

Also focusing on comparisons of national price levels, Kravis and Lipsey, in chapter 5, maintain that purchasing power parity does not provide an adequate norm for the evaluation of equilibrium exchange rates. Theirs is a search for methods that would provide better, more meaningful, and more consistent estimates of medium- and long-term equilibrium price structures among countries. They conclude that structural variables such as real per capita income and trade openness provide superior explanations for differences in national price level movements and offer more reliable and meaningful guidelines for evaluating changes in the equilibrium values of relative price levels than purchasing power parity.

3

Pricing to Market When the Exchange Rate Changes

Paul Krugman

It has been widely remarked that the prices of many imports into the United States did not fall to the degree that one might expect given the strong dollar of the early 1980s. The most conspicuous example was that of European luxury automobiles, whose prices actually rose in U.S. dollar terms despite huge declines in European currencies against the dollar. Since prices in Europe, in European currencies, did not rise dramatically, the effect was to create large differences between prices of the same automobiles in the United States and Europe. The price differential gave rise to "gray markets" in which individuals and firms bypassed normal distribution channels to import automobiles directly from Europe.

The phenomenon of foreign firms maintaining or even increasing their export prices to the United States when the dollar rises may be described as "pricing to market" (PTM). Pricing to market is an interesting subject for both practical and intellectual reasons. The immediate practical concern is with the effects of a declining dollar on inflation. Although many economists expect a declining dollar to contribute to a resurgence of inflation, some observers from the business community have disputed this. They argue that foreign firms did not cut their prices as the dollar rose, and that they will maintain their pricing to market as the dollar falls. Thus these observers argue that the effects of a decline in the U.S. dollar on import prices will in fact be small.

The intellectual interest of pricing to market is that it offers evidence on the role of market structure in international trade. For the past decade theorists have been proposing new models of international trade that stress imperfect competition and dynamic aspects. These models have unfortunately often proved difficult to test. The phenomenon of pricing to market, however, offers a possible new piece of evidence. As I will argue, pricing to market properly understood almost certainly involves both imperfect competition and dynamics, so that its apparent importance is a confirmation of the practical importance of "new wave" models of trade. Furthermore, as we will see, the importance of pricing to market appears to vary widely across industries. This raises the prospect that by correlating the importance of pricing to market with industry characteristics we will be able to distinguish between alternative unconventional trade models.

In this chapter I do not pretend to offer either a full empirical examination or a definitive analytical treatment of the phenomenon of pricing to market. I instead offer a preliminary overview of the subject. I begin with some rough evidence on the extent to which pricing to market has actually occurred, and on the relative extent of PTM in different industries. I then turn to some possible theoretical models of PTM. The intention of this theoretical discussion is to be provocative rather than definitive; that is, I offer a large batch of suggestive models (six in all) without attempting to settle on any one as the right one.

3.1   Some Empirical Evidence

Conceptual Issues

Before examining some admittedly rough empirical evidence, it is important to be more precise about what we mean by pricing to market. In general, we mean that import prices fall "too little" when a currency appreciates. This should not be taken to mean, however, that PTM is present whenever import prices fail to fall in proportion to the exchange rate appreciation. For a large country like the United States, a less-than-proportional response of import prices to the exchange rate is not surprising, and need not lead us to look for exotic explanations.

The best way to define when PTM is and is not occurring is to consider an example. Suppose that we measure the real exchange rate using unit labor costs and that the U.S. experiences a real appreciation in this sense against both France and Germany. For simplicity, let us in fact take nominal unit labor costs as fixed in each country. Suppose also that France exports wine to the United States and Germany exports BMWs. Wine is traded on an arms'-length basis by agents who are prepared to arbitrage any international price differences; BMW shipments are arranged by the manufacturer, who therefore sets CIF prices in each market rather than simply setting a single FOB price in Germany.

Now even though the law of one price will apply to wine, we would not be too surprised if the dollar price of wine fails to fall as much as the U.S. real appreciation. As French wine becomes cheaper in the United States, we will buy more; if the U.S. market is a significant share of French demand, this will drive up the price of wine in francs. The price of wine will not fall as much as the real dollar rises, but the price of French exports to the United States will not rise relative to the prices on domestic sales or exports to Germany. This is an example of a case in which the import price appears to fall "too little," yet we would *not* want to call this a case of pricing to market.

By contrast, suppose that BMW decides for some reason to keep both its dollar prices in the United States and its mark prices in Germany constant. In this case the price of BMWs will certainly not fall as much as the dollar rises, but that is not the distinctive point. What would be striking would be that prices of autos in Germany and prices of German exports to France would fall relative to export prices to the United States. Indeed, if the prices diverged far enough, there would be an incentive for individuals to bypass BMW's distribution channels and create a gray market. This is the situation that I have in mind when discussing pricing to market.

Notice that when we look at aggregate price indexes, it does not matter whether the import price effects of an exchange rate change are dampened by garden variety supply and demand considerations, as in the case of wine, or by noncompetitive pricing practices, as in the case of BMWs. The reason for distinguishing PTM is analytical and microeconomic. We understand the competitive model of traded goods prices pretty well (although empirically the behavior of commodity prices in response to exchange rate changes is rather puzzling; see Dornbusch 1985). Thus I focus instead on what seems harder to explain, pricing to market that involves divergent movements in different markets.

The implication of our distinction is that the usual way in which price effects of exchange rate changes are assessed, by comparing some price change directly with an exchange rate movement, will not do in this case. We always need to compare the price change with some measure that takes into account any effect of the exchange rate on *world* prices of the imported good, so that we can exclude these effects from our measure of PTM.

I have attempted to measure the extent of pricing to market using three kinds of comparison. (Unfortunately, in all cases the price data are unit value indexes rather than true price indexes. The problems with these measures are well known, but there do not seem to be better numbers.) The first is a comparison of aggregate U.S. manufactures import prices with a "predicted" import price index using export prices of major U.S. trading partners. The second is a comparison of Germany's prices on exports to other European Community countries with her prices on extra-European exports. The third is a comparison of prices of German exports to the United States and to the rest of the world.

Aggregate U.S. Manufactures Import Prices

The first comparison is shown in figure 3.1. Three series are shown. First, we show how the actual unit value of U.S. manufactures imports changed from 1980 to 1984. This measure of the import price rose imperceptibly, by 0.5 percent, over the period. Second, we show a "predicted" U.S. import price. This is an average of the manufactures export unit values in dollars of Canada, Japan, the European Community, and developing countries, weighted by their shares in U.S. imports in 1980. This index fell by 9.2 percent from 1980 to 1984. Finally, for reference we include the U.S. manufactures export unit value, which rose 21 percent in four years.

To interpret these series, suppose that each country exported only a single manufactured good and that this good were sold at a single world price—that is, that there were no pricing to market. Then we would expect the aggregate U.S. import price index to fall in proportion to our "predicted" price index. The extent to which this fails to happen can then be interpreted as our measure of PTM.

Clearly U.S. manufactures import prices fell "too little," by 9.7 percent. If we use the divergence between U.S. and trading partner export prices—30.5 percent—as a measure of the real exchange rate change, then PTM was 9.7/30.5 = 0.32 of the real exchange rate movement.

Aggregate German Exports

Figure 3.2 shows our second comparison. It makes use of the convenient fact that Germany reports separate unit value series for trade with other European Community (EC) countries and trade with the rest of the world. This is useful because during the first half of the 1980s Germany had fairly stable exchange rates against most of the EC, while the European Currency Unit (ecu) depreciated sharply against the dollar and to a lesser extent against the yen.

Two series are shown, both for finished manufactures. First, we show the ratio of German import unit values from EC countries to those from outside the community. This series can serve as an indicator of the extent to which the mark depreciated more in real terms relative to the world at large than it did relative to the EC. By 1984 this measure had declined by 9.4 percent. This is not as large a change as in the case of the United States, so that

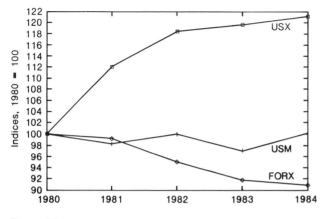

Figure 3.1
Actual vs. predicted U.S. import prices: USX = unit value of U.S. manufacture exports;
USM = unit value of U.S. manufactures imports; FORX = unit value of manufactures
export by U.S. trading partners. Sources: U.S. data from Department of Commerce, *United
States Trade: Performance in 1984 and Outlook*; foreign data from UN, *Monthly Bulletin of
Statistics*.

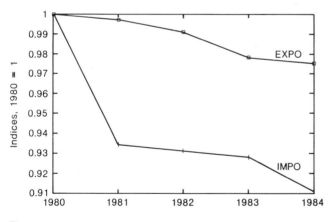

Figure 3.2
German trade prices, EC vs. non-EC: EXPO = ratio of prices of finished manufactures
exports from Germany, EC/non-EC destinations; IMPO = ratio of prices of finished
manufactures imports into Germany, EC/non-EC sources. Source: *Statistisches Jahrbach*.

problems of measurement error become even more acute. Nevertheless, there is some evidence of PTM.

The evidence is contained in the second series, which compares German export unit values to the EC with those on exports to the rest of the world. This series shows a decline of 2.5 percent. If Germany did not engage in any pricing to market (and if the price indexes for EC and rest of world exports were truly comparable), this number should be zero. Clearly we do not want to lay too much stress on this number, which is within the bounds of measurement error. For what it is worth, however, the implied extent of PTM is 2.5/9.4 = 0.26, which is not too inconsistent with our results for U.S. import prices.

German-U.S. trade

Our last evidence is shown in figure 3.3. Here an attempt is made to compare the movement of German export prices to the United States with prices to other countries from 1980 to 1983. Again if Germany did not engage in any pricing to market (and if the price indexes were comparable), these movements would be identical.

To construct these numbers, the following procedure was used. First, unit values were constructed for German three-digit SITC exports to the United States and to all other trading partners for both 1980 and 1983.

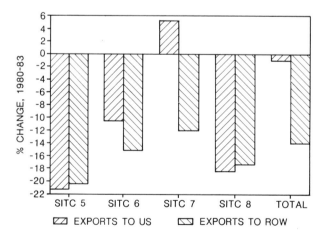

Figure 3.3
Changes in German export prices: SITC 5 = chemicals and related products; STIC 6 = basic manufactures; SITC 7 = machines and transport equipment; SITC 8 = miscellaneous manufactured goods. Source: UN, *Commodity Trade Statistics*.

Then "price indexes" were constructed by applying these unit values to the bundle of three-digit export quanta that Germany exported to the United States in 1980. That is, the measures are supposed to measure what the 1980 bundle of U.S. imports from Germany would have cost if the United States had been able to buy these imports at the prices other countries were paying. These indexes were calculated both for one-digit categories and for German manufactured exports as a whole. The weaknesses of this method are severe enough to make us treat the results with great caution. Nevertheless, it is interesting to have a look, however crude, at the disaggregated pattern of pricing to market.

Let us consider first, however, the aggregate change. The German price index for manufactured exports to the United States, in dollars, appears on our calculation to have fallen by only 1 percent from 1980 to 1983. (The mark fell by 29 percent in nominal terms). Meanwhile the price of the same bundle of exports to other countries fell in terms of dollars by 14 percent. This gives us a PTM divergence of 13 percent. Over the same period U.S. export unit values, as reported in *International Financial Statistics*, rose 33 percent relative to Germany's, so that the extent of PTM may be estimated at $13/33 = 0.39$—a number again reasonably consistent with our estimate for U.S. aggregate imports.

When we look at the data by single-digit SITC, the basic result seems so dramatic that it is hard to discount, the limitations of the data notwithstanding. This is that PTM, instead of being comparable across sectors, in fact occurs in only one sector, machinery and transport equipment. In this sector the export price to the United States actually rises by 5 percent, while the price to other countries falls by 12 percent. Admittedly this is a large sector, but PTM is absent in other large German export sectors such as chemicals and basic manufactures. This selectivity of the occurrence of pricing to market is one of the things that we would like our theoretical analysis to explain.

Summarizing the Evidence

Our examination of the data may be summarized as saying two things. First, pricing to market when the exchange rate changes is a real phenomenon: both our examination of aggregate U.S. import prices and our data on U.S.-German trade suggest that more than 30 percent of the real appreciation of the dollar was reflected in a divergence between prices of U.S. imports and prices of the same goods in other markets. Second, however, PTM is not universal. Our disaggregated U.S.-German evidence seems to say that pricing to market is limited to the transportation equipment and machinery industries.

We should note that the evidence does not support the extreme claims some have made about the failure of exchange rate changes to be reflected in import prices. A good deal less than half of the rise in the dollar was reflected in a divergence between U.S. and foreign prices of U.S. imports. This is because pricing to market seems to be selective across sectors, and perhaps also because even when it occurs it is not complete.

On the other hand, the extent of PTM is clearly enough to be significant for macro analyses. That will not, however, be the concern of this chapter. Instead, I will now turn to the microeconomic question: How can we explain pricing to market?

3.2   Theoretical Analysis: Static Models

In our theoretical discussion of the pricing to market phenomenon, we will consider a series of models. These models fall into two classes. First are *static* models. What I mean by a static model in this context is a model in which the belief on the part of firms that the dollar's rise is temporary does not play any role in their pricing behavior. That is, in these static models the pricing to market would last even if the real appreciation of the currency were expected to remain unchanged indefinitely. It seems a priori unlikely that a static approach would be adequate here, but it makes sense to consider the simplest option first.

Then we will turn to dynamic models. In these models it is assumed to be crucial that the dollar's rise is taken to be temporary. That is, in these models foreign firms are for some reason pricing based on their expected long-run costs rather than on their temporarily low costs during a period of a strong dollar. The point is of course to explain why the firms should adopt such a long-run pricing rule.

Let us begin, however, with the static models. Three such models will be considered. First is simple supply and demand. It will become clear that this model cannot account for the key phenomenon of divergent prices, but it is still illuminating to consider what it can explain. Second, we consider monopolistic price discrimination. This model turns out to be somewhat ambiguous in its implications. Finally, we turn to a simple oligopoly model. This has some nice features but is ultimately implausible as an explanation of what we observe.

Supply and Demand

The supply and demand model of the price implications of exchange rates goes back at least to Haberler (1949) and has recently been restated by Dornbusch (1985). Thus it needs only brief restatement here. We imagine a world of two countries, the United States and EC, and two currencies, the dollar and ecu. Let P be the dollar price of some U.S. importable, P^* the ecu price, and e the number of ecus per dollar. Also let $S(P)$, $S^*(P^*)$ be the supply from each region, while $D(P)$ and $D^*(P^*)$ are the demands. Then equilibrium may be described by two equations. First, we have world market clearing:

$$S(P) + S^*(P^*) - D(P) - D^*(P^*) = 0. \tag{1}$$

Second, we have the law of one price:

$$P^* = eP. \tag{2}$$

Equilibrium and the effects of a dollar appreciation may be illustrated as in figure 3.4, which follows Dornbusch. Clearly a dollar appreciation, though it lowers the dollar price, raises the ecu price. Thus the dollar price does not fall in full proportion to the appreciation. Obviously this depends on the United States being a large country: specifically, the elasticity of the ecu price with respect to the exchange rate is

$$\frac{d(S - D)/dP}{d(S - D + S^* - D^*)/dP}.$$

Thus the extent to which import prices will fall "too little" will be equal to the U.S. share in the response of world excess demand to price. Since the United States *is* a large country, if the failure of import prices to fall as much as the dollar has appreciated was the only puzzle, the simple supply and demand model might be sufficient.

What this model cannot explain, however, is the pricing to market phenomenon of divergence between prices of goods sold to the United States and to other markets. Indeed, equation (2), by asserting the law of one price, rules this out by assumption. That is, this analysis can explain why the dollar prices of Volvos and BMWs fail to fall in proportion to the dollar's rise, but it cannot explain why these prices have fallen in Europe relative to the United States (i.e., literally, a fall in P^* relative to eP).

To explain such price divergence, we would have to add another element: we would have to have some kind of specificity of supply to the U.S. market. Suppose, for example, that there were an upward-sloping supply

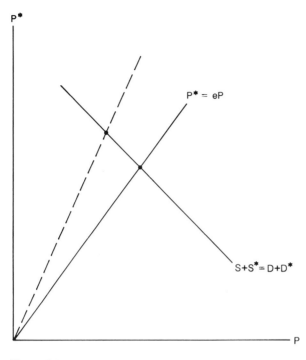

Figure 3.4
Supply and demand model of the price effect

curve for transportation of importables to the U.S. market. Then the law of one price would be replaced with a new relation of the form

$$P^* = eP - t,$$ (2')

where t is marginal transport cost, and is increasing in the volume of U.S. imports:

$$t = t(D - S).$$ (3)

Without working this out in full detail, we can immediately see how this would work. A rise in the dollar would be accompanied by a fall in the U.S. price, and thus a rise in U.S. imports. The rise in imports would however be associated with a rise in marginal transportation costs, and thus with a widened wedge between United States and EC prices.

There are, however, several problems with a formulation like this. First, how plausible is it to suppose that marginal transportation costs are strongly upward sloping? Surely we would imagine that, given time, the supply of transportation is highly elastic. There could be short-run bottlenecks—but this then brings us into the issue of dynamic response, which we will deal with in the next section. Also this formulation does not account for the specificity of the pricing to market: Why should marginal costs of transport of machinery and transport equipment be much more steeply upward sloping than those for other manufactures?

A possible answer is that what matters are not transport costs per se so much as other costs such as marketing and distribution. These could be highly specific to a particular set of products and arguably might be more important for autos than for other goods. The marketing and distribution issue is, however, inevitably a dynamic one; thus we reserve fuller discussion until the next section.

Monopolistic Price Discrimination

We turn next to the possibility that pricing to market can be explained by monopolistic price discrimination. To make the point most clearly, let us assume that a monopolistic firm can sell either in the United States or the EC and that it has a constant marginal cost in ecus. Transport costs will be ignored—although we assume that consumers are not able to arbitrage goods across markets. Then the monopolist's optimal pricing rule is

$$P^* = \frac{c^* E^*}{(E^* - 1)},$$ (4)

$$eP = \frac{c^* E}{(E - 1)},$$ (5)

where c^* is marginal cost in ecus, and E and E^* are the elasticity of market demand in the United States and EC, respectively. E and E^* may of course depend on P and P^*.

If P^* does not change, neither will E^*, the elasticity of demand in the EC market. Thus P^* is invariant to e. The question is whether a rise in e will produce a more or less than proportional change in P.

This question corresponds exactly to a more familiar question in the recent theoretical literature on protection under imperfect competition; namely, will a tariff be partly absorbed by foreign firms? As Brander and Spencer (1984), among others, have shown, the result depends on the shape of the demand curve. Clearly, if the demand curve has constant elasticity, the U.S. price will fall in full proportion to the exchange rate change. In order to get pricing to market, we must have a fall in the elasticity of demand; that is, the elasticity of demand must be increasing in the price (so that it falls as the price falls).

Unfortunately this means that the predicted behavior of a monopolist depends crucially on the shape of the demand curve—or more accurately, on the monopolist's perception of the shape of the demand curve. We might hope to put some bounds on what can happen by looking at the two most popular assumed demand curves, constant elasticity and linear. The problem is that these bounds are very wide indeed. In the constant elasticity case we have already seen that there will be no pricing to market. In the linear case, on the other hand, the percentage fall in the U.S. price will *always* be less than half of the percentage exchange rate change. Let E be the initial elasticity of demand, with the monopolist facing linear demand schedules; then we can show that the elasticity of P with respect to e is $(E - 1)/2E$, which is always less than 0.5.

In principle, then, price-discriminating monopoly can explain pricing to market if demand curves have the right shape. It is disturbing to rely so heavily on the shape of demand curves, however. Surely we would prefer to have shifts in the perceived elasticity of demand result from some more fundamental cause. One possibility is that such shifts arise from shifting market share in an oligopolistic market, which we consider next.

Oligopoly

Suppose now that the European firm, which still has constant marginal ecu cost of c^*, faces a U.S. competitor with constant dollar marginal cost c. How will this affect pricing?

Let us assume in this case that the firms compete in Cournot fashion, each firm taking the other's deliveries to the market as given. Also, to isolate the new element added by imperfect competition, let us assume constant elasticity of market demand, so that there would be no pricing to market by the European firm if it did not have to face a domestic competitor (for an analysis in the linear case, see Dornbusch 1985).

The basic rule of Cournot competition in the constant elasticity case is that a firm will face a perceived elasticity of demand equal to E/s, where E is the market elasticity and s is the firm's market share. Let s be the market share (in the U.S. market) of the U.S. firm, and $s^* = 1 - s$ be the market share of the EC firm. Then the pricing rules of the two firms will be

$$P = \frac{cE}{(E - s)} \tag{6}$$

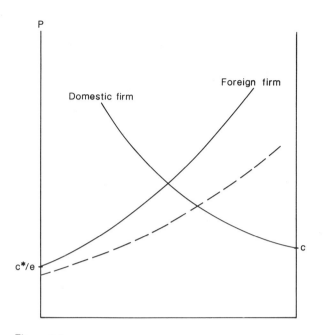

Figure 3.5
Pricing under oligopoly

for the U.S. firm and

$$P = \frac{c^* E}{e(E - s^*)} \qquad (7)$$

for the EC firm. In equilibrium, market shares must be such that these two pricing rules coincide.

To see the implications of (6) and (7), consider figure 3.5. The higher is the import market share, the lower the elasticity of demand perceived by the foreign firm and thus the higher its price for any given marginal cost. Similarly the higher the import share, the higher the elasticity of demand perceived by the domestic firm and thus the lower the domestic firm's price.

Now suppose that e rises. The foreign firm's pricing schedule will shift down proportionately to this change. Its actual price will not fall by as much, however, because its market share will rise, and thus its perceived elasticity of demand will fall.

The exchange-rate change then will not be fully passed on to domestic prices. This need not represent pricing to market, however, if the foreign firm also raises its price abroad. It is straightforward to show that if transport costs and other barriers to trade are absent, market shares of U.S. and foreign firms will actually be the same in both markets. In this case pricing behavior in the two markets will be identical, and there will be no pricing to market. To get divergent movement in the U.S. price, we need to invoke some obstacle that prevents U.S. firms from competing on equal terms in foreign markets.

We should note further that our pricing result depends crucially on two unrealistic assumptions. First, we are assuming that the domestic and foreign firm produce perfect substitutes. This is empirically unreasonable for the industries in which we actually seem to see PTM; those manufacturing sectors in which German and U.S. goods would seem likely to be near-perfect substitutes, such as chemicals and basic materials, show no evidence of PTM in practice. Second, competition is assumed to be Cournot in form. Obviously Bertrand competition will lead to a collapse of either imports or domestic production in the perfect substitutes case.

A more realistic model, then, would be one in which the firms produce differentiated products and probably engage in Bertrand competition. The general point here is that there is no general point: whether the perceived elasticity of demand of the EC firm rises or falls depends on the particular functional form, bringing us back to the problems of the discriminating monopolist.

3.3   Dynamic Models

The models described in the last section were static in the sense that neither the actual nor the expected duration of the exchange rate change affect the extent of pricing to market. That is, the extent to which import prices fall is independent of whether the dollar has just risen or has been high for a number of years and is also insensitive to whether the current strength of the dollar is regarded as permanent or soon to be reversed. Intuitively this seems implausible. The extent of pricing to market in the United States is often regarded as being due at least partly to the belief of foreign firms that the dollar will fall again in the not too distant future. In this section I present three models that offer possible rationalizations for the idea that import prices will fall less than proportionately to the exchange rate change when that change is either unanticipated or expected to reverse. The first of these models stresses dynamics that arise from the supply side. The second asks whether slow adjustment of demand to the market price will give rise to a slow adjustment of the price itself. Finally, the third attempts to justify price stickiness by a concern of firms for reputation.

Supply-Side Dynamics

In our discussion of the supply and demand approach to import prices it was pointed out that increasing marginal transportation costs could explain a failure of import prices to fall as much as one might expect following an appreciation. I suggested, however, that marketing and distribution costs were more likely candidates than transport costs per se, especially given the apparent disparity in the extent of pricing to market across sectors. It was also suggested that upward-sloping marginal cost in this case was more likely to be a short-run phenomenon than a permanent feature. What we would like to do, then, is to formalize the idea that pricing to market can result from temporary bottlenecks to changing import volume.

To do this, let us return to the model of a price-discriminating monopolist introduced in the last section, but make one change: we will now suppose that the monopolist has costs to changing deliveries to the market. We might imagine, for example, that foreign auto manufacturers cannot expand their sales without also providing an expanded sales, distribution, and service "infrastructure." To expand this infrastructure is costly, and presumably more costly the more rapid the attempted expansion. Suppose that the dollar rises suddenly. Then there will be no point in cutting prices immediately if there is no capacity to meet the expanded demand. Instead, we would expect prices to fall gradually as the infrastructure is put in place. Furthermore, if the dollar's rise is seen as temporary, foreign firms will not see it as worth their while to expand the infrastructure much to begin with. So this apporach says that the degree of pricing to market should depend on both how recently the exchange rate has changed and how long the change is expected to last.

We can model this formally as follows. There is an EC firm that sells a good in the U.S. market. It faces a demand curve which we write in inverse form:

$$P = P(x), \tag{8}$$

where x is the rate of deliveries to the U.S. market. If we want to make a clean separation of the dynamic reasons for pricing to market from the static ones we considered earlier, we can assume that the demand curve has constant elasticity.

The EC firm's costs will be assumed to consist of two parts. First, there is production cost; marginal production cost will be taken to be constant in ecus. Second, we will attempt to capture the dynamic aspects of marketing and distribution by assuming that there are costs to adjusting the level of U.S. sales (i.e., an adjustment cost which is increasing in the deviation of dx/dt from zero). Let us write this adjustment cost as $h(dx/dt)$; then the firm's instantaneous profits will be

$$V = \frac{Px}{e} - c^*x - h\left(\frac{dx}{dt}\right). \tag{9}$$

What the firm will want to do is to maximize the present discounted value of V. Problems of this sort are by now familiar in many parts of economics (e.g., see Sargent 1979), so it should not be necessary to rework the solution. Instead, let us simply review the basic characteristics of the outcome. The most useful way to think about the problem is to regard the firm as placing a shadow price on output. If this shadow price is positive, it will expand output; if it is negative, it will contract. The evolution of this shadow price itself depends on the marginal profitability of an increase in x. The optimal solution takes the form of a saddle path.

Suppose that we now shock this system by changing the exchange rate e. The result depends on how permanent the shock is assumed to be. Figure 3.6 illustrates how the price of imports would behave following a permanent and a temporary exchange rate change. In the case of a permanent appreciation the price would fall only gradually as x rose, in the long run finally falling by the full amount of the appreciation. In the case of a temporary appreciation the price would not only begin rising again after the exchange rate returned to its initial level, it would fall more slowly from the start and might actually begin to rise before the exchange-rate reversal.

Allowing for costs of adjustment, then, can rationalize pricing to market. The extent of PTM in this case turns out to depend on both how long the appreciation has lasted and how persistent it is expected to be. These are reasonable things to include in our model, and probably there is a good deal of truth to this explanation. I would doubt, however, whether it is sufficient. In particular, if the divergence of prices between the U.S. and EC markets is wholly due to marginal costs of distribution, etc., how do we explain the emergence of gray markets, that is, of individuals bypassing the normal distribution channels? To explain this would seem to require that this model be supplemented with some additional considerations affecting the pricing decision.

P

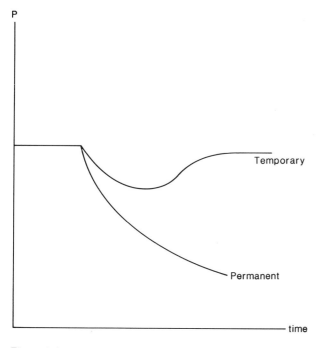

Temporary

Permanent

time

Figure 3.6
Supply dynamics following exchange rate appreciation

Dynamics of Demand

Another possible route to a dynamic account of pricing to market might be to appeal to slow adjustment of demand. Suppose that there are lags in the effect of price on demand. Then a firm's pricing decision will in effect have an investmentlike component, trading off lower profits now for higher sales later. It seems intuitively reasonable that when the lags are long pricing will be dictated by long-run cost rather than short-run fluctuations.

Somewhat surprisingly, this intuition is by no means easy to confirm. Analyzing optimal pricing under lags in demand is in general fairly difficult, but the main points can be conveyed with a two-period example. This example gives some presumption that transitory exchange-rate shocks will have less effect on prices than permanent ones, but it is no more than a presumption.

Consider a foreign firm that plans to sell a good in the United States over two periods. In the first period it faces a demand $D_1(P_1)$, in the second a demand $D_2(P_1, P_2)$, where subscripts refer to periods. Marginal costs are c^*/e_1, c^*/e_2, respectively. The firm will seek to maximize

$$(e_1 P_1 - c^*) D_1(P_1) + R(e_2 P_2 - c^*) D_2(P_1, P_2),$$

where R is a discount factor.

The question we need to answer is whether the price in the first period will fall more if the exchange rate rises in both periods than if it rises only in the first period. That is, will an exchange rate appreciation that is regarded as temporary have less effect on the price than one that is regarded as permanent? What writing out the model in this way shows is that this question is equivalent to asking whether an increase in e_2 will lead to a fall in P_1.

The answer to this question hinges on how the second-period appreciation affects the incentive of the firm to keep its first-period price down. We note that the derivative of second-period profits with respect to P_1 is

$$\left(\frac{dX_2}{dP_1}\right)(e_2 P_2 - c^*) < 0,$$

where X_2 is second-period sales.

This may be rewritten as

$$\frac{[(dX_2/dP_1)(P_1/X_2)][(e_2 P_2 - c^*) X_2]}{P_1}.$$

The first term in square brackets here is the cross elasticity of demand; the second term is second-period profits. The direction of the effect of e_2 on the price in the first period can be determined by asking how the size of this expression is affected holding P_1 constant; if it increases in absolute value, there will be an increased incentive to hold down the first-period price.

What we can say definitely is that the second term will increase: a rise in e_2 will definitely increase second-period profits. If we could assume that the cross elasticity of demand would remain unchanged, then we would be sure that a rise in second-period e would lead to a fall in first period P. Unfortunately we cannot be sure of this. Here as elsewhere in our analysis, the answer seems to be contingent on functional form.

Reputation and Pricing

We have now seen that an ad hoc model of dynamic demand, in which lagged as well as current prices are simply assumed to affect the quantity sold, provides only a presumption that pricing to market will be profitable. On wonders, however, whether some less ad hoc formulation of demand dynamics might give a clearer reason for a failure to pass cost reductions on in price reductions. As our final theoretical model, I will suggest a particular version of dynamics that could justify the stickiness of prices without appeal to particular functional forms or arbitrary lags in price effects.

The basic idea is that purchase of imported goods is a two-stage process. First, potential buyers must decide whether to put themselves in the market for a product—for example, whether to visit the showroom and test-drive a particular firm's automobiles. We must presume that putting oneself into a market is costly, and will be done only if the price is expected to be sufficiently attractive. Second, those in the market must then decide whether in fact to purchase, and how much to buy.

The effect of this two-stage process will be that demand depends not only on the actual price but on the price that customers expect to pay when they decide whether or not to put themselves in the market. The question then is how the expected price gets determined. In practice, the way this seems to happen is that firms cultivate a reputation over time for being in a certain price range. For example, I know that in looking for a car, it is sensible to look at the major Japanese imports but not worthwhile to look at Volvos or Mercedes given my resources. We can formalize this process in a simplified way by imagining that a firm announces a price and that customers arrive on its doorstep, provided that they expect it to honor its announcement. If the firm fails to honor its announcement, in future periods it will not be believed.

Let P^e be the price expected by potential customers to prevail, and let N be the number of customers that actually enter a firm's market. Then what we will say is that

$$N = N(P^e). \tag{10}$$

Letting X be the quantity sold, we will then have a demand function

$$X = X(N, P). \tag{11}$$

To see the implications of this formulation, consider figure 3.7. Two demand curves are illustrated. The first, labeled DD, is what we might call the "ex ante" curve: it represents the eventual quantity sold if the expected price P^e is validated by the actual price P. Corresponding to DD is a marginal revenue curve, MR. Given marginal cost c^*/e^*, we show the profit-maximizing price given this demand curve.

Once customers have committed themselves to entering the market,

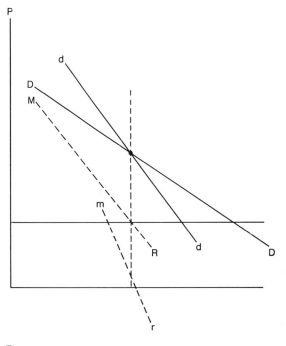

Figure 3.7
Pricing with reputation

however, the firm will face a less elastic demand curve, illustrated by the "ex post" curve *dd*. Short-run profit maximization would then lead the firm to charge a higher price than P^e, as shown by the fact that the corresponding marginal revenue curve, *mr*, lies below marginal cost when the price equals P^e. If the firm takes advantage of its full short-run market power in this way, however, the result will be that customers will no longer believe its future announcements and will expect that the firm will always exploit its ex post monopoly power. Provided that the discount rate is not too high, the cost of this loss of reputation will exceed the benefits of exploiting short-run market power, and the firm will thus choose to keep $P = P^e$.

How does this explain price stickiness? The answer seems clear for *increases* in marginal cost. An unexpected rise in marginal cost, provided that it is not too large, will be not be passed on in higher prices so as not to lose reputation. Less obvious, perhaps, is that decreases in marginal cost will also not be passed on if they are not too large. The reason is that short-run marginal revenue lies below marginal cost, with price increases prevented by the need to retain reputation. A fall in marginal cost that does not bring it below short-run marginal revenue will therefore not provide an incentive to cut the price; in effect, a firm will treat it as a windfall that allows it to exploit short-run monopoly power without breaking its implicit promise not to charge a price in excess of P^e.

In context, this implies a story something like the following: at 1981 exchange rates (say) a European auto manufacturer calculates that its long-run profit-maximizing price is $20,000. Its short-run profit-maximizing price would, however, be higher, because ex post demand is less elastic than ex ante, so that if reputation were not an issue the price would be $30,000. Now suppose that there is a rise in the dollar that lowers marginal cost, so that the short-run profit: maximizing price is $24,000. If this rise is not expected to persist, the firm will not find it worthwhile cultivating a reputation as a lower priced seller; and the short-run incentives will not lead it to cut its price.

An interesting feature of this story is that it suggests that pricing to market will be more likely to happen where there are substantial firm-specific costs to entering a market, so that ex ante and ex post demand elasticities are very different. One might guess that this will happen where buyers make occasional discrete purchases rather than continuous small ones, and where the products are complex and differentiated enough that the information costs of evaluating quality and thus interpreting prices are high. This combination of features might explain why pricing to market is apparently confined to the machinery and transport equipment sector.

3.4 Conclusions

Pricing to market appears to be more than just a curiosus related to luxury European automobiles. The aggregate estimates reported in the first part of this paper suggest that 35 to 40 percent of the real appreciation of the dollar since 1980 has been absorbed by foreign exporters in a rise in their prices to the United States compared with prices in other markets. If the German case is representative, however, and if the crude data are to be believed, the phenomenon of pricing to market is not general but is specific to the machinery and transport equipment sector.

Explaining pricing to market is not as simple as one might hope. It seems clear that a perfectly competitive model will not do the trick. Static models of imperfect competition could explain it in principle, but there are serious objections to both a simple explanation in terms of price-discriminating monopoly and a slightly more complex explanation in terms of non-cooperative oligopoly.

The best hope of understanding pricing to market therefore seems to come from dynamic models of imperfect competition. At this point my preferred explanation would stress the roles of both supply dynamics, resulting from the costs of rapidly adjusting the marketing and distribution infrastructure needed to sell some imports, and demand dynamics, resulting from the need of firms to invest in reputation.

What is needed at this point is not so much more theory as more data. Clearly the next step will have to be to focus on particular industries, where it is possible both to construct better series on pricing and to use institutional knowledge about the particulars of industries to inform the assumptions of our models.

References

Brander, J., and Spencer, B. 1984. Tariff Protection and Imperfect Competition. In H. Kierzkowski (ed.), *Monopolistic Competition and International Trade*. Oxford: Oxford University Press.

Dornbusch, R. 1985. Exchange Rates and Prices. NBER working paper no. 1769.

Haberler, G. 1949. The Market for Foreign Exchange and the Stability of the Balance of Payments: A Theoretical Analysis. *Kyklos* 3 : 193–218.

Sargent, T. J. 1979. *Macroeconomic Theory*. New York: Academic Press.

4

Real Exchange Rates and Productivity Growth in the United States and Japan

Richard C. Marston

The recent misalignment of the dollar relative to the yen has obscured the effects of a longer-term influence on the relative competitiveness of the two economies, productivity growth in Japan. For the past few decades productivity growth has been much more rapid in Japan than in the United States. Such a gap in productivity performance would not ordinarily affect real exchange rates except that productivity growth is concentrated in the traded sectors of both economies. Thus through time, the prices of traded relative to nontraded goods must adjust to reflect productivity gains, but this adjustment is much more extensive in Japan. As a result the U.S. general price level must continually fall relative to the Japanese price level, when both are measured in a common currency, just to keep U.S. traded goods competitive.

In the extensive literature on the purchasing power parity (PPP) theory of exchange rates, a number of studies have cited productivity differentials between the nontraded and traded sectors of economies as a prime cause of deviations between any exchange rate and its PPP value. Several of these studies, including Balassa (1964, 1973), De Vries (1968), Clague and Tanzi (1972), and Officer (1976b), have reported empirical tests of this phenomenon but have differed widely in their conclusions about whether productivity differentials explain deviations from PPP.[1] Hsieh's (1982) recent study using time series rather than cross-sectional data, however, has provided strong evidence supporting the role of productivity differentials.[2]

The real exchange rates used in the present study, defined as the nominal exchange rate (yen/dollar) adjusted for the relative prices of U.S. and Japanese goods, measure departures from PPP defined in terms of several alternative price indexes. This study, however, is less concerned with whether PPP holds or does not hold than with assessing the quantitative effects of productivity growth differentials between the United States and Japan on the alternative real exchange rates between the yen and dollar.

The rapid productivity growth in the traded sector of the Japanese economy requires a continuing adjustment of real exchange rates between the yen and dollar measured in terms of general price indexes to keep U.S. goods competitive with Japanese goods. Similarly, the sharp changes in the prices of raw materials since 1973, which have affected the U.S. and Japanese economies in different ways, also require adjustments in real exchange rates.

Movements in real exchange rates over time are influenced by numerous short-term demand factors in addition to the supply factors emphasized in this chapter. The *differential movement* between two real exchange rates, however, should be primarily influenced by supply factors such as productivity growth differentials rather than short-term demand factors. For that reason the expressions we develop below measure the real exchange rate based on one price series *relative* to that based on an alternative price series.[3] In the case of the United States and Japan, supply factors lead to a widening gap between real exchange rates based on the consumer price index or wholesale price index and those based on traded goods alone. Estimating the magnitude of this gap is important since the relative competitiveness of these two economies is often determined by examining movements in real exchange rates based on the broader price indexes. The analysis will show that any appreciation of the yen large enough to restore real exchange rates based on such indexes to their levels prior to the recent misalignment would fall far short of restoring U.S. traded goods to their previous levels of competitiveness. For the same reasons both nominal and real wages in the United States would have to decline relative to those in Japan just to restore previous levels of competitiveness.

The chapter is also concerned with productivity performance within the manufacturing sector alone and its effects on relative prices within that sector. The analysis shows that the differentials in productivity growth between the United States and Japan at the industry level are highly correlated with the rates at which relative prices change within these same industries. Because these productivity changes have been so different across industries within manufacturing, with Japanese productivity growth exceeding U.S. growth by widely differing margins depending on the industry, the relative competitiveness of individual industries has changed radically. This would continue to be true even if the real exchange rate for manufactured goods as a whole were restored to historical levels.

Section 4.1 develops equations for real exchange rates defined in terms of value-added deflators, relative unit labor costs, and general price indexes. These equations relate real exchange rates to productivity differentials in the nontraded and traded sectors of each economy and, in the case of general price indexes, to the real prices of raw materials. Section 4.2, the empirical section, begins with an analysis of how much real exchange rates based on the GDP deflator and consumer price index must diverge from those based on the prices of traded goods in order for the two economies to remain competitive. Section 4.3 examines the implications of these movements in real exchange rates for relative wages in the two countries. In the final section disaggregated data for manufacturing are used to examine the productivity and relative price behavior of individual industries.

4.1 Sectoral Production Patterns and Real Exchange Rates

Real exchange rates based on alternative price indexes can diverge sharply when there are changes in productivity and relative prices within national economies. This section develops expressions for several real exchange rates to show how they are affected by such supply factors. The real exchange rates range from one based on the value-added deflator for traded goods to a broader series based on the consumer price index.

Output and Prices

We begin by outlining a simple production structure that distinguishes between gross output and value added and that divides output into traded and nontraded sectors. The production and gross output in one sector is assumed to be separable into value added and two types of inputs, raw materials and the output of the other sector. For simplicity, all production functions are assumed to be of the Cobb-Douglas form, although the expressions developed below could be interpreted as linearizations of a CES production function.[4] Equation (1a), or (1b), expresses value added in the traded (nontraded) sector, V_T, as a function of employment in that sector, L_T, and capital, K_T, as well as a productivity factor represented by a time trend.

$$V_T = (1 - c_T) L_T + c_T K_T + h_T t, \tag{1a}$$

$$V_N = (1 - c_N) L_N + c_N K_N + h_N t. \tag{1b}$$

All variables are expressed in logs with their differences interpreted as percentage changes in the underlying variables. Equation (1c) expresses gross output in the traded sector, Z_T, as a function of value added in that sector as well as output in the nontraded sector used in the traded sector, Z_{NT}, and the input of raw materials, I_T. Equation (1d) expresses gross output in the nontraded sector, Z_N, in analogous fashion.

$$Z_T = c_{T1} V_T + c_{T2} Z_{NT} + c_{T3} I_T, \quad c_{T1} + c_{T2} + c_{T3} = 1, \tag{1c}$$

$$Z_N = c_{N1} V_N + c_{N2} Z_{TN} + c_{N3} I_N, \quad c_{N1} + c_{N2} + c_{N3} = 1. \tag{1d}$$

This specification, which allows the output of one sector to serve as an input in the other sector, is especially necessary in the case of traded goods since (nontraded) services often constitute a significant proportion of the final value of traded goods.

Parallel to these production functions is a set of price equations that implicitly defines the value added deflators for each sector. The price of gross output in the traded (nontraded) sector, P_T, is a function of the value-added deflator for that sector, the gross output price in the other sector, and the price of raw materials.

$$P_T = c_{T1} P_{VT} + c_{T2} P_N + c_{T3} P_I, \tag{2a}$$

$$P_N = c_{N1} P_{VN} + c_{N2} P_T + c_{N3} P_I. \tag{2b}$$

Because the price equations are dual to the production functions, the same production parameters appear in the production and price equations. These equations suggest that gross output prices can diverge from their value-added counterparts either because of price developments in the other sector or changes in raw materials prices.

We are also interested in the relationship between the value-added deflator, on the one hand, and wages and productivity, on the other hand. The marginal productivity relationships derived from (1a) and (1b) give such a relationship, provided that we assume that the markups of prices over marginal costs are constant:

$$P_{VT} = W_T - H_T, \tag{3a}$$

$$P_{VN} = W_N - H_N. \tag{3b}$$

Equation (3a) relates P_{VT} to wages in the traded sector, W_T, and to productivity, H_T, which is defined as

$$H_T = V_T - L_T = c_T(K_T - L_T) + h_T t.$$

This productivity variable, H_T, reflects not only the productivity factor in the production function, $h_T t$, but also the capital deepening factor, $K_T - L_T$. It is this measure of productivity that affects value-added prices, and hence the relative competitiveness of economies. Similarly equation (3b) relates value added in the nontraded sector to wages and productivity in that sector.

The value-added deflators in the two sectors together make up the value-added deflator for the economy as a whole, P_V, which is defined as

$$P_V = gP_{VN} + (1 - g)P_{VT}. \tag{4}$$

We choose to define the value-added deflator as a weighted average (a geometric average in levels of the sectoral prices) of the sectoral deflators for simplicity, even though in practice this equation must be regarded as only an approximation to the deflator series appearing in the national income accounts.

Real Exchange Rates: GDP Deflators

The first series for the real exchange rate that is of interest is that based on the GDP deflator as a whole and the deflator for traded goods alone:

$$R_V = P_V^* + X - P_V,$$

$$R_{VT} = P_{VT}^* + X - P_{VT}.$$

We define this series for the yen-dollar exchange rate, X, where the starred variables represent those of the United States and the unstarred variables those of Japan. (Japan thus is the "home country"). Equation (5) expresses the aggregate real exchange rate *relative* to the real exchange rate for traded goods as the difference of two relative prices: the relative price of nontraded to traded goods in the United States and the corresponding relative price in Japan.

$$R_V - R_{VT} = g^*(P_{VN}^* - P_{VT}^*) - g(P_{VN} - P_{VT}). \tag{5}$$

The coefficients, g and g^*, represent the share of nontraded goods in total value added. The equation shows that a rise in nontraded relative to traded prices in Japan leads to a *real appreciation* of the yen in terms of the GDP deflator as a whole relative to the traded goods deflator. Thus the yen has to appreciate in terms of the aggregate index in order for U.S.-traded goods to remain competitive. We later provide estimates of how large that appreciation has to be.

The real exchange rate for traded goods alone can be expressed in terms of relative wages and relative productivity if we use equation (3a) and its counterpart for the foreign country (assuming as before that markups are constant):

$$R_{VT} = R_{ULCT} = [(W_T^* + X - W_T) - (H_T^* - H_T)]. \tag{6}$$

The expression in brackets on the right side of equation (6) represents relative unit labor costs (in this case, in the traded sector alone), R_{ULCT}. Substituting this expression into equation (5) along with the expressions for the sectoral prices (equations 3a, 3b), we obtain an equation for R_V in terms of the production factors.

$$R_V = R_{ULCT} + g^*[(W_N^* - W_T^*) - (H_N^* - H_T^*)]$$

$$- g[(W_N - W_T) - (H_N - H_T)]. \tag{7}$$

This equation states that the aggregate real exchange rate (that based on the GDP deflator) is influenced by two factors: relative unit labor costs in the traded sectors of the United States and Japan and unit labor costs in one sector of each national economy relative to the other sector. If unit labor costs in the traded and nontraded sectors of each country move together, then the real exchange rate will follow relative unit labor costs in the traded sectors of the two countries. But if, for example, there is a faster rate of growth of productivity in the traded sector of Japan, then the real exchange rate of the yen will have to appreciate relative to R_{ULCT} in order to keep the traded sector of the United States competitive. The relatively greater productivity in the traded sector of Japan will induce higher wages in that sector, and in the nontraded sector as well unless the labor market is segmented. As a result the relative price of nontraded goods will rise in Japan, thus pushing up the GDP deflator relative to traded prices or unit labor costs in the traded sector. If the yen depreciates in nominal terms enough to keep the real exchange rate based on the GDP deflator constant, Japanese traded goods will gain a price advantage. To keep U.S. traded goods competitive, therefore, the yen has to appreciate in real terms when measured relative to the GDP deflator (i.e., R_V has to fall relative to R_{ULCT}).[5]

Real Exchange Rates: Final Goods Prices

The real exchange rates that have received the most attention recently are not those based on GDP deflators, but on final goods prices. The two most frequently cited are the real exchange rates based on the consumer price index (CPI) and wholesale price index (WPI). In this section we develop expressions for two real exchange rates, one defined in terms of the final price of traded goods alone and another defined in terms of a general price index.

We begin by defining general price indexes for final goods, P_F and P_F^*, consisting of domestic traded and nontraded goods, traded goods originating from the other country, and traded goods originating from third countries (with a dollar price of P_W^*):

$$P_F = a_1 P_T + a_2 P_N + a_3(P_T^* + X) + a_4(P_W^* + X), \tag{8a}$$

$$P_F^* = a_1^* P_T^* + a_2^* P_N^* + a_3^*(P_T - X) + a_4^* P_W^*, \tag{8b}$$

where $a_1 + a_2 + a_3 + a_4 = 1$ and similarly for the foreign country coefficients. P_F and P_F^* may be considered idealized forms of the consumer price index (with geometric weighting). The real exchange rate defined in terms of these general price indexes, $R_F = P_F^* + X - P_F$, can be expressed in terms of several relative prices as follows:

$$R_F = (1 - a_3^* - a_3 - a_4)(P_T^* + X - P_T) + (a_4^* - a_4)(P_W^* - P_T^*)$$
$$+ a_2^*(P_N^* - P_T^*) - a_2(P_N - P_T). \tag{9}$$

According to this equation, R_F is affected by the relative prices of traded goods originating from the United States and Japan, world prices relative to U.S. prices (although only to the extent that the coefficients of third country goods differ between the two countries), and by two terms representing sectoral relative prices in the two countries.[6]

To see how R_F varies relative to real exchange rates defined for traded goods alone, we first express P_T and P_N in terms of value-added deflators and the prices of raw materials by solving equations (2a) and (2b):

$$P_T = c_{11} P_{VT} + c_{12} P_{VN} + c_{13} P_I, \tag{10a}$$

$$P_N = c_{21} P_{VT} + c_{22} P_{VN} + c_{23} P_I, \tag{10b}$$

where $c_{11} = c_{T1}/C$, $c_{12} = (c_{T2} c_{N1})/C$, $c_{13} = (c_{T3} + c_{T2} c_{N3})/C$, $C = 1 - c_{T2} c_{N2} > 0$, and $c_{11} + c_{12} + c_{13} = 1$. The coefficients $c_{2j}(j = 1, 2, 3)$ are defined analogously. Using equation (10a) and its counterpart for the foreign country, we obtain an expression explaining the movement of R_T *relative* to R_{VT}, the real exchange rate based on gross output prices for traded goods $(P_T^* + X - P_T)$ relative to that based on value-added deflators for traded goods:

$$R_T - R_{VT} = c_{12}^*(P_{VN}^* - P_{VT}^*) - c_{12}(P_{VN} - P_{VT}) + c_{13}^*(P_I^* - P_{VT}^*)$$
$$- c_{13}(P_I - P_{VT}). \tag{11}$$

According to this equation there are two sets of influences on $R_T - R_{VT}$: the relative price of nontraded to traded goods in each country, reflecting primarily the bias in productivity growth between sectors, and the real price of raw materials (in terms of traded goods) in both countries.

We can now express the real exchange rate based on the general price index in terms of that based on the value-added deflator for traded goods alone:[7]

$$R_F - R_{VT} = c_1(P_{VN}^* - P_{VT}^*) - c_2(P_{VN} - P_{VT}) + c_3(P_I^* - P_{VT}^*)$$

$$- c_4(P_I - P_{VT}) - c_5 R_T + c_6(P_W^* - P_T^*), \tag{12}$$

where

$$c_1 = (1 - a_2^*) c_{12}^* + a_2^* c_{22}^*,$$
$$c_2 = (1 - a_2) c_{12} + a_2 c_{22},$$
$$c_3 = (1 - a_2^*) c_{13}^* + a_2^* c_{23}^*,$$
$$c_4 = (1 - a_2) c_{13} + a_2 c_{23},$$
$$c_5 = (a_3^* + a_3 + a_4),$$
$$c_6 = (a_4^* - a_4).$$

According to this equation, the gap between R_F and R_{VT} is influenced by changes in the relative prices of nontraded to traded goods or in the real prices of raw materials as well as by changes in the relative prices of traded goods. The yen appreciates *more* in terms of the broader index if there is a relatively greater rise in nontraded relative to traded prices in Japan. The reasoning is the same as in the comparison between the real exchange rate based on the GDP deflator and the narrower deflator for traded goods. In order to keep the United States competitive in its traded sector, the yen must have a real appreciation in terms of the broader general price index. A rise in the real price of raw materials in Japan (for a given real price of raw materials in the United States) also causes a greater appreciation in the broader index than in that based on traded goods alone. Finally, the gap between R_F and R_{VT} widens if there is an increase in the real exchange rate for traded goods, R_T. (The effects of a rise in third country prices are indeterminate.)

In the next section, we will use these expressions for the various real exchange rates to interpret the movements of the yen relative to the dollar over the past 20 years. We begin by examining the GDP deflators derived from the national income accounts.

4.2 Real Exchange Rates in Practice

The OECD has published national accounts statistics defined on a consistent basis for the years 1964 to 1983. We have used the real and nominal GDP statistics disaggregated by type of activity to generate series for traded and nontraded goods. The corresponding employment figures disaggregated by type of activity start in 1970, so the series we generate for productivity by sector only extend back to that year.

Finding operational counterparts to the traded and nontraded aggregates in equation (1) is not an easy task. The national accounts statistics of the OECD provides a breakdown of total value added into ten subsectors ranging from manufacturing to wholesale and retail trade. We have designated two subsectors as traded:

Manufacturing

Agriculture, hunting, fishing, and forestry

A third subsector, mining and quarrying, undoubtedly has a large traded component, but this category includes energy products with prices very sensitive to OPEC price policy. Since we are interested in the relative impact of technological change on the traded and nontraded sectors, we chose to exclude any energy-intensive subsectors. The nontraded sector includes six of the remaining seven subsectors but excludes one category, electricity, gas and water, because of its energy content. The nontraded subsectors are:

Construction

Wholesale and retail trade, restaurants, and hotels

Transport, storage, and communication

Finance, insurance, real estate, and business services

Community, social, and personal services

Government services

The division chosen is inevitably somewhat arbitrary. The manufacturing subsector, for example, includes goods that never enter into international trade. But this division is, in our judgment, the best available. The value-added deflators for traded and nontraded goods are weighted averages of the subsector deflators, the weights being the relative size of value added in 1980. These same weights are used for all series subsequently defined for the traded and nontraded sectors.

Table 4.1
Real exchange rates based on GDP deflators and productivity differences between sectors
(trend movements from 1973 to 1983)

R_V	R_{VT}	$(H_N^* - H_T^*)$	$(H_N - H_T)$
−0.3%	26.7%	−13.2%	−73.2%

The Real Exchange Rate Based on the GDP Deflator

The GDP deflator is a broad based price series reflecting price movements in both traded and nontraded sectors of an economy. Real exchange rates based on this series might be expected to provide a fairly reliable guide to the relative competitiveness of national economies. In comparisons between Japan and the United States, however, the GDP deflator offers a very distorted view of relative competitiveness because the traded and nontraded sectors follow quite divergent paths in one economy compared to the other. We begin by examining broad trends in real exchange rates as well as trends in productivity by sector. In table 4.1 we report percentage changes in these series obtained by fitting each series to an exponential time trend over the 1973–83 period. The year 1973 is chosen as the starting point for the trend calculations because it is after the realignments associated with the Smithsonian agreement on exchange rates and coincides with the advent of general floating in early 1973.[8] The variables appearing in table 4.1 are defined as follows:

R_V = the real exchange rate based on the GDP deflator,

R_{VT} = the real exchange rate based on the traded goods portion of the GDP deflator,

$H_N^* - H_T^*$ = productivity in the nontraded sector relative to the traded sector in the United States,

$H_N - H_T$ = productivity in the nontraded sector relative to the traded sector of Japan.

The percentage changes in these series are quite revealing.

First, in this period, the real exchange rate based on the GDP deflator followed a much different path than the real exchange rate based on the deflator for traded goods alone. From 1973 to 1983 the yen appreciated in terms of the GDP deflator by 0.3 percent, while the real exchange rate defined in terms of the deflator for traded goods alone rose by 26.7 percent, representing a sizable real *depreciation* of the yen or real *appreciation* of the dollar over the 11-year period. (This appreciation of the dollar is exceeded even further by the rise of 35.1 percent in the real exchange rate based on the deflator for manufacturing alone.) If we were to focus exclusively on an aggregate index like the GDP deflator, we would conclude that the dollar had not appreciated much relative to the yen over the 1973–83 period.[9] Focusing on the traded sector, in contrast, leads to a very different conclusion. With a real appreciation of the dollar by 26.7 percent (or a real appreciation in manufacturing alone of 35.1 percent), it is evident that the realignment following the Smithsonian Agreement has been undone by the strength of the dollar.

Second, what accounts for this divergence between the real exchange rates based on the GDP and traded goods deflators? The relatively small real depreciation in terms of the GDP deflator is explained by relative productivity movements in the traded and nontraded sectors of the United States and Japan. As equation (5) indicates, the difference between R_V and R_{VT} is a function of relative prices or, given similar sectoral wage trends, relative productivity movements in the traded and nontraded sectors of each country.[10] Productivity in the U.S. traded sector grew by 13.2 percent faster than in the U.S. nontraded sector. But in Japan productivity growth in the traded sector was 73.2 percent greater than in the nontraded sector. We can use equation (7) to calculate the trend differential between R_V and relative unit labor costs in the traded sector, R_{ULCT}, based on these rates of productivity growth. The shares of nontraded goods in total GDP in the United States and Japan in 1980 were 0.733 and 0.657, respectively, giving a differential between R_V and R_{ULCT} as follows:[11]

$$R_V - R_{ULCT} = -0.733[H_N^* - H_T^*] + 0.657[H_N - H_T] = -38.4\%.$$

The markedly higher productivity growth differential in Japan required a substantial real appreciation of the yen in terms of the GDP deflator, by 38.4 percent according to this calculation, to keep U.S.-traded goods competitive. This relative appreciation, however, was accomplished not by R_V falling, but by R_{ULCT} rising. Because R_V was nearly constant over the period, relative unit labor costs in the traded sector, and hence the relative prices of U.S.-traded goods, rose significantly, by 38.1 percent. This sharply reduced the relative competitiveness of U.S. exports.

Movements in real exchange rates over time are influenced by numerous short-term demand factors in addition to the supply factors emphasized here. The *difference* between two real exchange rates, however, should be strongly influenced by supply factors. In the case of the value-added deflators, these factors include the relative productivity movements in the nontraded and traded sectors of each economy. Below we report a regression for equation (5), relating the difference between R_V and R_{VT} to the price differential in the nontraded and traded sectors of each country. All variables are expressed as *first difference in the logs*, so they can be interpreted as percentage changes of the corresponding variables from one year to the next. The numbers in parentheses below the coefficients are *t*-statistics.

Sample Period 1971–83:

$$(R_V - R_{VT}) = 0.543(P^*_{VN} - P^*_{VT}) - 0.679(P_{VN} - P_{VT}),$$
$$(3.72) \qquad\qquad (-10.4)$$

$$\bar{R}^2 = 0.708,$$

$$DW = 1.97$$

$$SE = 0.00891.$$

According to this equation, a rise in nontraded relative to traded prices in the United States leads to a rise in R_V relative to R_{VT}, while a rise in nontraded relative to traded prices in Japan leads to a fall in R_V relative to R_{VT}. Both coefficients are statistically significant at the 1 percent level, suggesting that annual movements in the real exchange rates relative to one another are strongly influenced by sectoral relative prices.

The annual movement of R_V relative to R_{ULCT} is also closely related to supply factors as suggested by equation (7). The second equation relates (the percentage change in) R_V to (the percentage changes in) relative unit labor costs and sectoral productivity differentials in each country:[12]

Sample Period 1971–83:

$$R_V = 0.843R_{ULCT} - 0.943(H^*_N - H^*_T) + 0.692(H_N - H_T),$$
$$(7.40) \qquad (-1.40) \qquad\qquad (2.32)$$

$$\bar{R}^2 = 0.844,$$

$$DW = 1.55,$$

$$SE = 0.044.$$

In this equation (the percentage change in) R_{ULCT} should enter with a positive coefficient close to one, depending on the markup of prices over marginal costs, while (the percentage changes in) $H^*_N - H^*_T$ and $H_N - H_T$ should have negative and positive coefficients, respectively. All of the coefficients therefore are of the correct sign, although the coefficient of $(H_N^* - H_T^*)$ is not statistically significant. Fitting this equation to the trend movements in the series reported in table 4.1, we find that the gap between R_V and R_{ULCT} grows by -44.3 percent over the 1973–83 period, a little larger than in the previous calculation based on sectoral shares.[13] But the implications are similar: the yen must appreciate significantly in real terms when measured against the GDP deflator as a whole if traded goods are to remain competitive.

Real Exchange Rates Based on the Prices of Final Goods

The prices of final goods follow patterns similar to those of GDP deflators, although in the case of the prices of final goods we have to take into account the influence of raw materials prices and the prices of final goods from third countries. We begin by examining trends in some of the key series over the post-Smithsonian period as reported in table 4.2. The variables appearing in this table are defined as follows:[14]

$$R_C = \text{real exchange rate based on the consumer price index,}$$

$$R_{WPI} = \text{real exchange rate based on the wholesale price index,}$$

$$R_{VT} = \text{real exchange rate based on the value-added deflator for traded goods,}$$

$$(P_{VN}^* - P_{VT}^*), (P_{VN} - P_{VT}) = \text{relative GDP deflators for nontraded and traded goods in the United States and Japan,}$$

$$(P_I^* - P_{VT}^*), (P_I - P_{VT}) = \text{real price of raw materials in the United States and Japan (price of raw materials deflated by the value added deflator for traded goods).}$$

Over this 11-year period the real exchange rate based on the CPI *fell* by 9 percent (thus suggesting a real *appreciation* rather than depreciation of the

Table 4.2
Real exchange rates based on the WPI and CPI indexes and relative price changes across sectors, United States and Japan (trend movements from 1973 to 1983)

R_C	R_{WPI}	R_{VT}	$(P_{VN}^* - P_{VT}^*)$	$(P_{VN} - P_{VT})$	$(P_I^* - P_{VT}^*)$	$(P_I - P_{VT})$
-9.0%	4.4%	26.7%	12.3%	56.9%	8.0%	120.1%

yen), while all other real exchange rates rose. The real exchange rate based on the WPI rose only 4.4 percent, however, a rate far below that based on the value-added deflator for traded goods. This pattern of much greater real depreciations of the yen in the case of real exchange rates based on traded goods can be attributed to the sharp changes in relative prices evident in the second part of the table. The relative price of nontraded to traded goods rose much more in Japan than in the United States. When real exchange rates for final goods are being analyzed, the real prices of raw materials are also quite important. In table 4.2 we report a much larger increase in the real price of raw materials in Japan than in the United States, the gap between the two countries being 112.1 percent. This larger increase can be attributed to two factors: the greater increase in the local currency price of raw materials in Japan than in the United States (greater by 46.7 percent), and relatively greater productivity in the traded sector of Japan which leads to a much smaller rise in the deflator for Japan, accounting for the rest of the differential in real terms.[15]

Equation (12) summarizes the different influences on the real exchange rate based on a general price index such as the CPI. To illustrate the quantitative importance of these different influences, we assign values to the parameters appearing in equation (12) and then calculate the trend change in $R_F - R_{VT}$ consistent with the trend changes in the independent variables appearing in table 4.2. We have no estimates of R_T, the real exchange rate based on the traded prices of the United States and Japan. (Japan has an export price series for the 1973–83 period, but the United States only has series for individual commodities extending back that far.) For this reason the calculations that follow are based on the assumption that *relative traded prices are constant*. Thus in effect we are asking how much would R_F have to vary relative to R_{VT} in order for traded prices to be held constant over the 1973–83 period.[16]

To simplify the analysis, we assume that the production and consumption parameters are identical for the United States and Japan. The values we assign to the parameters underlying those in (12) are as follows:[17]

$$a_2 = 0.6, \quad c_{T1} = 0.65, \quad c_{T2} = 0.2, \quad c_{T3} = 0.15,$$

$$c_{N1} = 0.8, \quad c_{N2} = 0.15, \quad c_{N3} = 0.05.$$

With these parameters and the actual trends in the relative prices appearing in equation (12), we find that $R_F - R_{VT}$ should have fallen by 37.4 percent over the 1973–83 period. This contrasts with an actual gap between the real exchange rate based on the CPI and that based on the value-added deflator for traded goods of 35.7 percent.[18] The actual gap was achieved not by a fall in R_F, but primarily by a rise in R_{VT}.

We cannot estimate equation (12) as written since we have no series for R_T, the real exchange rate based on the final prices of traded goods. Instead, we estimate a modified version of (12) with R_T omitted.[19] All variables in the equation are expressed as first differences of the logs; the GDP data are available beginning in 1964, so the sample period spans 19 years.

Sample Period 1965–83:

$$(R_C - R_{VT}) = 0.877(P^*_{VN} - P^*_{VT}) - 1.035(P_{VN} - P_{VT})$$
$$\phantom{(R_C - R_{VT}) =}\ (4.03)\phantom{0.877(P^*_{VN} - P^*_{VT})}(-10.2)$$

$$+\ 0.082(P^*_I - P^*_{VT}) + 0.015(P_I - P_{VT}),$$
$$(1.78)\phantom{0.082(P^*_I - P^*_{VT}) +}(0.52)$$

$$\bar{R}^2 = 0.753,$$

$$DW = 1.97,$$

$$SE = 0.0146.$$

The coefficients of all variables with the exception of the last one have the correct sign, although neither of the coefficients for materials prices are statistically significant at the 5 percent level. The relative sectoral prices (the ratio of nontraded to traded prices) play a major role in this equation. The coefficients of these sectoral prices, in fact, may be larger than they should be given reasonable values of the underlying behavioral parameters. (Given the parameters assumed earlier, the first two coefficients in the regression should be about 0.6 in absolute value.) The equation as a whole predicts a larger gap between R_C and R_{VT} than occurred over the 1973–83 period analyzed in tables 4.1 and 4.2. Given the trends in relative prices for the independent variables in the estimated equation and the coefficients estimated here, there should have been a real appreciation of R_C relative to R_{VT} of 45.6 percent, whereas in fact the relative appreciation was 35.7 percent (a sizable one, nevertheless). Despite the likely overestimation of the effects of Japanese sectoral prices, the equation reported explains a large proportion of the relative movement of the two real exchange rates, especially considering the fact that equation (12) on which this estimated equation is based abstracts from many short-term influences on relative prices.

Implications for Relative Wage Growth

The tremendous growth in productivity in Japan, even if largely confined to the traded goods sector, has meant rising wages and standard of living in that country. In this section we use the model developed earlier to study the growth of wages in Japan relative to that in the United States implied by productivity growth and other factors affecting the relative competitiveness of traded goods in the two economies. We pose the following question: If during the 1973–83 period exchange rates had adjusted to keep traded goods competitive, what would have been the implications for relative wages in the two countries? The answer to this question differs considerably depending on whether we examine relative nominal wages or relative real wages.

We, first, determine the percentage change in relative nominal wages required to keep traded goods competitive. We substitute equations (6), (3a), and (3b), relating value-added deflators to unit labor costs into equation (11) for R_T to obtain

$$R_T = (W^* + X - W) - (H_T^* - H_T) - c_{12}^*(H_N^* - H_T^*)$$
$$+ c_{12}(H_N - H_T) + c_{13}^*(P_I^* - P_{VT}^*) - c_{13}(P_I - P_{VT}). \qquad (11')$$

If the real exchange rate for traded goods is held constant (for convenience we set its log, R_T, equal to zero), we can express relative nominal wages as follows:

$$(W^* + X - W) = (H_T^* - H_T) + c_{12}^*(H_N^* - H_T^*) - c_{12}(H_N - H_T)$$
$$- c_{13}^*(P_I^* - P_{VT}^*) + c_{13}(P_I - P_{VT}). \qquad (13)$$

Nominal wages in the United States relative to Japan (both expressed in dollars) are proportional to the following variables:

$H_T^* - H_T =$ the gap between productivity in the traded sectors of the United States and Japan,

$H_N^* - H_T^*, H_N - H_T =$ the intersectoral productivity gap in each country,

$P_I^* - P_{VT}^*, P_I - P_{VT} =$ the real price of raw materials in each country.

In table 4.3, we list the trend changes in the five variables appearing in equation (13) over the 1973–83 period.

The most interesting figure in this table is the huge gap of 83.4 percent between productivity growth in the traded sectors of the United States and Japan.

Table 4.3
Trend changes in productivity and raw materials prices (trend movements from 1973 to 1983)

$H_T^* - H_T$	$H_N^* - H_T^*$	$H_N - H_T$	$P_I^* - P_{VT}^*$	$P_I - P_{VT}$
-83.4%	-13.2%	-73.2%	8.0%	120.1%

Using the figures for trend changes in table 4.3, we can calculate the change in relative nominal wages necessary to keep the relative prices of traded goods constant over the 1973–83 period. With the same production coefficients assumed earlier, the trend change in $(W^* + X - W)$ is -55.0 percent (expressed as a total percentage change over the 1973–83 period). This relative wage change could occur through a greater rise in Japanese wages than U.S. wages when each is expressed in its own currency, or by a depreciation of the dollar. The actual trend change in relative wages was -19.4 percent, which suggests just how far U.S. wages must fall relative to Japanese wages, or more realistically, how much the yen must appreciate relative to the dollar in order to keep the real exchange rate for traded goods constant over the 1973–83 period.

The required growth of *real wages* is not as divergent as the growth of nominal wages because the growth of real wages in Japan is held down by the slow productivity growth in the nontraded sector. To calculate the growth of real wages in one country relative to the other, we must first obtain an estimate of the rate of change of the consumer price index consistent with the real exchange rate for traded goods remaining constant. We substitute into equation (9) expressions for the gross output prices of traded and nontraded goods (equations 10a and 10b) and use equations (3a) and (3b) to express relative value added deflators in terms of productivity differentials. We then set the real exchange rate for traded goods equal to zero (as well as the relative price of third country goods) to obtain an expression for R_F (or its empirical counterpart, R_C):

$$R_F = R_C = -a_2^*(c_{22}^* - c_{12}^*)(H_N^* - H_T^*) + a_2(c_{22} - c_{12})(H_N - H_T)$$
$$+ a_2^*(c_{23}^* - c_{13}^*)(P_I^* - P_{VT}^*) - a_2(c_{23} - c_{13})(P_I - P_{VT}). \tag{14}$$

Using the coefficients assumed earlier, we find that in order for the real exchange rates for traded goods to remain constant, the real exchange rate for the CPI (R_C) must fall by 17.7 percent.

Real wages in the United States relative to that in Japan can be written as follows:

$$(W^* - P_C^*) - (W - P_C) = (W^* + X - W) - R_C. \tag{15}$$

If R_C falls by 17.7 percent over the 1973–83 period, then real wage growth in Japan must exceed that of the United States by 37.3 percent, a sizable amount but considerably smaller than the differential for nominal wages (55.0 percent). In both countries the slow rate of growth of productivity in the nontraded sector holds down the growth of real wages. But the imbalance between productivity growth in the two sectors of Japan is so great that the real exchange rate based on the CPI must fall significantly in order to keep traded goods competitive. This dampens the growth of real wages in Japan relative to the United States.

The Manufacturing Sector

Since such a large proportion of the traded sector consists of manufacturing goods, it is useful to examine manufacturing in more detail. There is considerable variation in productivity growth and competitiveness among the subsectors of manufacturing in the United States and Japan. This variation is superimposed on the trends within the manufacturing sector as a whole, so that some subsectors in the United States might fare well even in recent times when the dollar has been overvalued while other subsectors might suffer even during times of undervaluation.

The most extensive data providing a breakdown of manufacturing into subsectors are drawn from the GDP accounts of the United States and Japan. These data give a nine-sector breakdown for nominal and real GDP as well as employment, so we are able to construct real exchange rates based on value-added deflators and productivity measures on a disaggregated basis.[20] The nine subsectors are listed in table 4.4 together with the weights in the U.S. and Japanese GDP's. The third subsector, "wood and wood products, including furniture," is of negligible importance for Japan, so we have omitted this subsector from our analysis. Subsector 8, "fabricated metal products, machinery and equipment," represents 44 percent of U.S. manufacturing and 50.3 percent of Japanese manufacturing, so the relative competitiveness of that subsector is of particular importance.

We begin by examining the real exchange rates or relative price for each subsector of manufacturing. These are illustrated in figure 4.1 for eight subsectors as well as for manufacturing as a whole. In this figure a rise in the real exchange rate or relative value-added deflator for a given subsector represents a real depreciation of the yen or a gain in Japanese competitiveness in that subsector. In manufacturing as a whole the real exchange

Table 4.4
Subsectors for manufacturing

1: Food, beverages, and tobacco
2: Textile, wearing apparel, and leather industries
3: Wood and wood products, including furniture
4: Paper and paper products, printing and publishing
5: Chemicals and chemical petroleum, coal, rubber and plastic products
6: Nonmetallic mineral products except products of petroleum and coal
7: Basic metal industries
8: Fabricated metal products, machinery and equipment
9: Other manufacturing industries
M: Total for manufacturing

GDP weights for 1980

Sector	1	2	3	4	5	6	7	8	9
United States	0.113	0.065	0.043	0.087	0.140	0.029	0.069	0.440	0.015
Japan	0.081	0.037	0.000	0.023	0.096	0.029	0.104	0.503	0.126

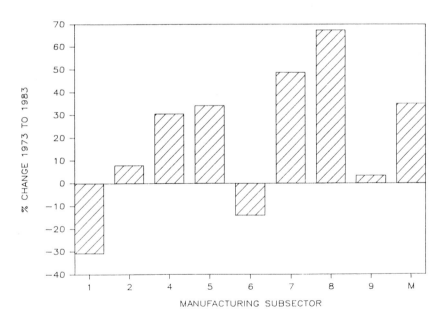

Figure 4.1
Relative value-added deflators by sectors: U.S. vs. Japanese prices

rate based on the value-added deflator rose by 35.1 percent (measured by fitting the real exchange rate series to a trend between 1973 and 1983). As figure 4.1 illustrates, this trend for manufacturing masks a wide variation across subsectors. At one extreme subsector 1, representing food, saw a real appreciation of the yen by 30.8 percent over the 1973 to 1983 period. But at the other extreme subsector 8 registered a real depreciation of 67.5 percent. This pattern across subsectors reflects shifts in comparative advantage as Japan increased its competitiveness in machinery and equipment, for example, at the expense of food, textiles, and other less technologically advanced products.

These shifts in comparative advantage are most easily seen if we imagine that the real exchange rate for manufacturing as a whole had remained constant over the period; in that case the real exchange rate for subsector 1 would have fallen by over 60 percent, while that for subsector 5, representing chemicals and petroleum products, would have remained constant and that of subsector 8 would have increased by about 35 percent. In the United States, these shifts in comparative advantage would have implied shifts of employment *within* the manufacturing sector rather than necessitating net shifts *out of* manufacturing into the nontraded sector. These shifts within manufacturing would not necessarily have involved shifts in employment out of subsector 8, since relative prices are only one determinant of employment and since the United States could have maintained a price advantage relative to other competitors.

The pattern of real exchange rates across subsectors is closely related to relative productivity growth in the two countries. Figure 4.2 shows productivity growth in the United States and Japan measured as a trend over the 1973–83 period for the eight subsectors as well as manufacturing as a whole. In all but two subsectors productivity growth in Japan exceeds that of the United States in the same subsector, in several cases by large percentages. But the magnitude of the gap varies widely. In subsector 9 that gap is only 22 percent over the 11-year period, while in subsector 8 the gap is 155 percent (productivity growth being 178 percent in Japan and 23 percent in the United States). For manufacturing as a whole, the gap is 86 percent.

The magnitude of the gap between productivity growth is important because it helps to determine how much relative unit labor costs vary between the two countries. The behavior of each sectoral real exchange rate in turn should be influenced very strongly by relative unit labor costs in that sector, and thus indirectly by relative productivity growth. This influence is confirmed by a comparison of the sectoral patterns in figures

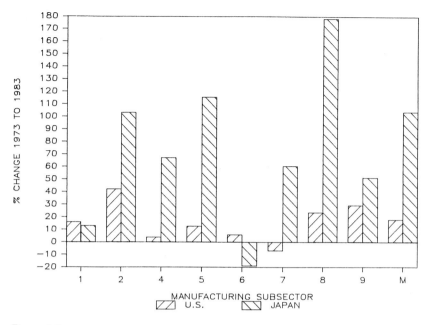

Figure 4.2
Rates of growth of productivity: trend growth by sector, 1973–83

4.1 and 4.2. The two subsectors where U.S. productivity growth exceeds that of Japan, food and nonmetallic mineral products (sectors 1 and 6), for example, are those where the relative price of U.S. goods has fallen over the same period. Similarly the subsector where the gap between Japanese and U.S. productivity growth is greatest, subsector 8, is the one experiencing the greatest rise in U.S. prices relative to those of Japan.

Over the 1973–83 period changes in real exchange rates reflected macroeconomic factors in addition to the structural influences emphasized in this chapter. But the behavior of each sectoral real exchange rate *relative* to the real exchange rate for manufacturing as a whole should be primarily determined by differences in productivity growth. To examine this relationship, we modify equation (3a) so that it explains the value-added deflator for manufacturing as a whole or, alternatively, each subsector of manufacturing. Define R_{VM}, R_{Vi} as the real exchange rates for manufacturing and for subsector i, respectively. Then the *difference* between these real exchange rates can be expressed as follows:

$$R_{Vi} - R_{VM} = [(W_i^* - W_M^*) - (W_i - W_M)]$$

$$- [(H_i^* - H_i) - (H_M^* - H_M)]. \tag{16}$$

Subsector i will experience a greater rise in its real exchange rate to the extent the U.S. wages rise relatively faster in that subsector than in manufacturing as a whole (or Japanese wages rise more slowly). Similarly the growth in R_{Vi} will exceed that of R_{VM} to the extent that Japanese productivity growth in that subsector exceeds that for manufacturing as a whole (or U.S. productivity growth falls short in that subsector).

We have no reliable data for wages by subsector. But we can compare productivity growth in subsector i with that for manufacturing as a whole as well as the corresponding real exchange rates. Using the trend changes in these variables calculated previously (and reflected in figures 4.1 and 4.2), we can determine the percentage changes in $R_{Vi} - R_{VM}$ and $-[(H_i^* - H_i) - (H_M^* - H_M)]$ over the 1973–83 period. The correlation between these two series over the 11-year period is 0.906. This suggests that the pattern of changes in relative sectoral real exchange rates is strongly influenced by the pattern of productivity growth across sectors. The relative price changes that have occurred in the manufacturing sectors of these two countries therefore are longer-term phenomena that will persist even if the current misalignment of the dollar is corrected.

4.3   Conclusion

This chapter has provided estimates of the effects of relative productivity growth on real exchange rates and relative wage growth in the United States and Japan. With Japanese productivity growing 73.2 percent faster in its traded sector than in its nontraded sector over the 1973–83 period, real exchange rates based on broad price indexes needed to adjust sharply to keep U.S.-traded goods competitive. Since the adjustment of these real exchange rates has been minimal at best, U.S.-traded goods have become much more expensive relative to Japanese goods. To maintain the competitiveness of the U.S.-traded sector, the real exchange rate based on the GDP deflator would have had to fall by almost 40 percent relative to unit labor costs in the traded sector during the 1973–83 period. Similar adjustments would have had to occur in the real exchange rate based on the CPI and in relative nominal and real wages in the two countries. The recent misalignment of the dollar has prevented such adjustments. If U.S. traded goods are to regain their earlier competitiveness relative to Japanese traded goods, then the yen must appreciate considerably (relative to 1983 levels) when measured in terms of any broad-based price indexes.

Even if such a major adjustment in relative prices occurs, we will be left with equally large changes in competitiveness within the manufactured sector due to productivity differentials between subsectors of manu-facturing. Japanese productivity growth in machinery production, for example, is nothing short of phenomenal (150 percent above the United States over the 1973–83 period). These major shifts in relative prices taking place within the manufacturing sector compound an already serious problem of relative price adjustment.

Notes

Prepared for the Conference on Real-Financial Linkages in Open Economies, American Enterprise Institute, Washington, D.C., January 30–31, 1986. I would like to thank the discussant of this paper, Rachel McCulloch, as well as William Branson, Barry Eichengreen, Koichi Hamada, Paul Krugman, Robert Lipsey, and Charles Pigott for their helpful comments on an earlier draft. I would especially like to thank J. David Richardson for providing many useful suggestions concerning both content and presentation.

1. Officer (1976b) provides a detailed description and critique of previous empirical studies. For more general studies of PPP, see the survey by Officer (1976a), Kravis et al. (1975), as well as the papers in the symposium on purchasing power parity in the May 1978 issue of the *Journal of International Economics*.

2. Unlike Hsieh's study, most previous tests used cross-sectional data and focused as much on the level of the exchange rate as on its rate of depreciation.

3. The Kravis and Lipsey study (chapter 5) also investigates the relationship between productivity and prices, although they use cross-sectional data for 25 countries to study the link between productivity levels (as reflected in per capita income) and price levels rather than the productivity growth rates and trends in real exchange rates studied here.

4. Marston and Turnovsky (1985) develop a two-level production function model in which value added has a Cobb-Douglas form and gross output a CES form (so that the elasticity of substitution between value added and raw materials can be below one). A linearization of the CES function results in an equation in the percentage changes of the variables very similar to those presented here.

5. There is an interesting parallel between the traded-nontraded model and a model of three traded goods developed by W. Arthur Lewis (1978). The three traded goods in Lewis's model are primary commodities (produced by a devel-oping country), manufactures (produced by a developed country), and an agri-cultural good such as wheat (common to both countries). In both models pro-ductivity in producing the common good determines wages in the respective economies and, indirectly, prices for the other good. I am indebted to William Branson for pointing out this parallel.

6. We might also have allowed for different price indexes for world goods im-ported into Japan and the United States, respectively.

7. To obtain equation (12), first substitute equations (9) and (11) into the expression $R_F - R_{VT} = (R_F - R_T) + (R_T - R_{VT})$. In the resulting equation, replace $P_N - P_T$ and $P_N^* - P_T^*$ by their value-added counterparts, using equations (10a) and (10b) (and the corresponding equations for the foreign country): $P_N - P_T = (c_{22} - c_{12})(P_{VN} - P_{VT}) + (c_{23} - c_{13})(P_I - P_{VT})$.

8. We do not attempt to assess whether the yen and dollar were in equilibrium in 1973, nor to measure the current equilibrium value of the yen-dollar exchange rate. Artus and Knight (1984) and Williamson (1985) discuss some of the conceptual problems involved in determining the equilibrium value of an exchange rate, including trying to assess the optimal pattern of foreign investment. In measuring trend changes in real exchange rates over the 1973–83 period, we are instead trying to assess the impact of differential productivity trends on movements in real exchange rates *relative* to one another.

9. The corresponding figure of 49.3 percent over the shorter period from 1978 to 1983 is more alarming, but that is measuring the appreciation of the dollar from a period of unusual weakness.

10. There are no reliable data on wages in the nontraded sector of the economy, so the growth in the wage differential between sectors is omitted from the equations described here. If labor is mobile between sectors, or if bargaining over wages is strongly influenced by wages in the other sector, any growth in intersectoral wage differentials should be small compared with the gap in productivity growth rates between sectors.

11. The share of nontraded goods in total GDP, represented by the coefficients g^* and g in equations (5) and (7), is likely to change through time as relative productivity differentials reduce traded prices relative to nontraded prices. Equation (7) therefore will hold only as an approximation even if the markup of prices over unit labor costs is constant over time.

12. In the measurement of relative unit labor costs, we employ U.S. Bureau of Labor Statistics (BLS) data on hourly compensation in manufacturing which are among the most reliable data available.

13. The coefficient of R_{ULCT} is not significantly different from one at the 5 percent level. If we set this coefficient equal to one, the implied change in R_V relative to R_{ULCT} is -38.3 percent, almost identical to the figures based on sectoral shares.

14. The CPI and WPI indexes as well as the spot exchange rate (period average) are taken from the IMF's *International Financial Statistics*. The prices of raw materials, which include fuel as well as other materials for processing, are taken from the disaggregated wholesale price statistics of each country.

15. The smaller increase in raw materials prices in the United States can be attributed in part to the price controls on petroleum products which were maintained through much of the period, although it is doubtful that this factor alone could account for such a large differential between the United States and Japan.

16. The relative prices of traded goods between third countries and the United States are also assumed constant.

17. The share of nontraded goods in GDP is about 0.7 in both countries, so we assign a value of 0.6 to its share in gross output. We allow nontraded goods to play a somewhat larger role in traded goods production than vice versa to reflect the relatively larger service component of traded goods. Notice also that the share of raw materials in gross output is larger in the traded than in the nontraded sector.

18. The gap between the real exchange rate based on the wholesale price index and that based on the value added deflator for traded goods is only 22.3 percent, but the WPI is heavily weighted toward manufacturing goods.

19. R_T should have a relatively small effect on the differential, $R_C - R_{VT}$, since the coefficient c_5 should be small. Its omission from the equation therefore should not make much difference. The third country price variable is even less likely to be important in an equation explaining bilateral exchange rates. (See the coefficient c_6 which is equal to the difference between the country coefficients.) When we proxied R_T with R_{VT}, the real exchange rate based on the value-added deflator for traded goods, the coefficient of R_{VT} (0.022) was statistically insignificant (with a t-statistic of 0.341) and the remainder of the equation remained almost unchanged. The adjusted R-squared fell from .753 to .737.

20. The disaggregated GDP data are undoubtedly of less uniform quality than the aggregate GDP data, but the broad trends in these data should be instructive, nevertheless.

References

Artus, Jacques R., and Malcolm D. Knight. 1984. Issues in the Assessment of the Exchange Rates of Industrial Countries. Occasional paper no. 29. Washington D.C.: International Monetary Fund.

Balassa, Bela. 1964. The Purchasing Power Parity Doctrine: A Reappraisal. *Journal of Political Economy* 72:584–596.

Balassa, Bela. 1973. Just How Misleading Are Official Exchange Rate Conversions: A Comment. *Economic Journal* 83:1258–1267.

De Vries, Margaret G. 1968. Exchange Rate Depreciation in Developing Countries. *International Monetary Fund Staff Papers* 15:560–578.

Clague, Christopher, and Vito Tanzi. 1972. Human Capital, Natural Resources, and the Purchasing Power Parity Doctrine: Some Empirical Results. *Economia Internazionale* 25:3–18.

Hsieh, David A. 1982. The Determination of the Real Exchange Rate: The Productivity Approach. *Journal of International Economics* 12:355–362.

Kravis, Irving, Zoltan Kenessey, Alan W. Heston, and Robert Summers. *A System of International Comparisons of Gross Product and Purchasing Power*. Baltimore: Johns Hopkins Press.

Lewis, W. Arthur, 1978. *The Evolution of the International Economic Order* (Eliot Janeway Lecture, 1977). Princeton: Princeton University Press.

Marston, Richard C., and Stephen J. Turnovsky, 1985. Imported Materials Prices, Wage Policy, and Macroeconomic Stabilization. *Canadian Journal of Economics* 18:273–284.

Officer, Lawrence. 1976a. The Purchasing Power Parity Theory of Exchange Rates: A Review Article. *International Monetary Fund Staff Papers* 23:1–60.

Officer, Lawrence. 1976b. Productivity Bias and Purchasing Power Parity: An Econometric Investigation. *International Monetary Fund Staff Papers* 23:545–579.

Williamson, John. 1985. *The Exchange Rate System*. Policy Analyses in International Economics 5, 2d ed. Washington, D.C.: Institute for International Economics.

5   The Assessment of National Price Levels

Irving B. Kravis
Robert E. Lipsey

It has been evident for some time that there are large country-to-country differences in national price levels. Equality of price levels—sometimes referred to as the "law of one price" or "purchasing power parity"—is not the norm.[1] International comparisons of prices and incomes from the U.N. International Comparison Project (ICP) have shown that price level disparities often involve spreads of 2 to 1 and can be as big as 3 to 1 (Kravis 1984; Kravis, Heston, and Summers 1982). Other independent investigations lead to the same conclusion.[2] Also the time-to-time variability of exchange rates in recent years, clearly unmatched by the changes in price levels called for by the theory, have tilted the weight of opinion against the validity of the relative version of the purchasing power parity theory. Offsetting changes in international price movements and in exchange rates are not the norm either.

Nevertheless, the purchasing power parity theory of exchange rates continues to be invoked as a reference point in discussions of exchange-rate behavior, such as those relating to over- or under-valuation of currencies and overshooting. The implicit assumption often is made that the exchange rates of some past period were normal and that equilibrium will be attained when the exchange rates of that period, or the exchange rates adjusted for differences in inflation (real exchange rates), are restored. In the latter case the assumption is that the "real exchange rate" would be constant in equilibrium. This means, in other words, that the relationship between the price levels of different countries would be constant. A large part of the reason for the use of the PPP theory in these contexts is that there is no other reference point.

This chapter represents an attempt to provide an alternative (see also work along these lines by Clague 1986). Our approach is based on the notion that there is a structural relationship between price levels and basic national economic characteristics, such as per capita income and propensity to trade. We investigate the hypothesis that the price level of each country tends toward a norm, changing slowly over time, which can be established on the basis of this structural relationship, rather than on the assumption of identical price levels or identical changes in price levels. Price level differences in this view may be expected to be persistent, and they are not necessarily inconsistent with trade equilibrium. Although the relationships of the price levels of different countries are determined by long-run factors, short-run influences can cause price levels to deviate from their structural norms.

Some of these issues were explored in terms of a 1975 cross section in an earlier work (Kravis and Lipsey 1983). Here we extend the investigation to the period 1960–83, focusing on explaining long- or intermediate-term movements of price levels.

The international differences in price levels provide a link between the price level, which can be regarded as a financial variable, and the key real variables in the economic system. In some versions of the monetary theory of the balance of payments, the law of one price is assumed to prevail and the price level is a financial variable with little or no lasting effects. In the view taken here, which we believe reflects reality better, the general price level for GDP as a whole has embedded in it sets of prices that can and do differ from country to country, thereby directly and indirectly influencing the nation's transactions with its trading and financial partners. Some of these prices affect the flows of goods; others the flows of capital. The literature dealing with the influence of prices on trade flows is voluminous; that dealing with the role of prices in affecting capital flows is much sparser.[4] Neither is assessed here; our focus is on the price level itself as an important link in the real-financial economic nexus. However, we do investigate whether deviations from our price level "norms" have any power in predicting changes in trade balances.

5.1 Background

The Price Level and the Real Exchange Rate

The price level (PL), on which this work focuses, is defined as the ratio of the purchasing power parity (PPP) of a currency to its exchange rate (ER), both taken relative to the U.S. dollar as the numeraire currency.[5] Purchasing power parity is defined in turn as the number of units of a currency that have the same command over GDP as a U.S. dollar. Reliable purchasing power parities require careful price comparisons for a sample of commodities and services representative of GDP (Kravis, Kenessey, Heston, and Summers 1975, chaps. 6–12). When the extrapolations on which this study is based were performed, parities for 1975 were available from the U.N. International Comparison Project (ICP) for 34 countries.[6] The basic data used in this chapter are these purchasing power parities extrapolated on an annual basis backward, for the most part to 1960, and forward to 1983, using each country's implicit GDP deflators. For some of the 34 countries, data necessary for the analysis were not available for all the years of the period, and the discussion in this chapter is therefore based on 25 or sometimes only 19 countries.[7] In some cases countries were dropped because exchange rates that reflected the large preponderance of the country's international transactions were not available. In other instances data on the division of GDP between tradables and nontradables were missing for some years, and it was not possible to construct figures on implicit deflators for tradables and nontradables.[8] Even for included countries there are sometimes uncertainties about the choice of a representative exchange rate, especially in the cases of some developing countries. Errors in the exchange rates are imparted to the PLs and if the time-to-time movement of the exchange rate series is also different from the true series, errors are introduced also into our time-to-time movements of PL.

Our focus on the price level differs from the usual formulation in terms of intertemporal indexes of "real exchange rates" found in the substantial theoretical and empirical literature on exchange rate determination. The most common definition of the real exchange rate (RER) is the intertemporal movement of the nominal rate corrected for the relative movement of prices.[9] The intertemporal index of PL (IPL) and the RER are reciprocals, provided that the same price indexes are used in constructing the two measures.

Previous Work

The starting point for the present effort was a pair of equations that were found in Kravis and Lipsey (1983) to account for over 80 percent of the cross-country variation in the national price levels of 34 countries in 1975. The price level was taken as the dependent variable, and the independent variables were real GDP per capita (r), openness (OP) defined as exports plus imports (from national accounts data) divided by GDP, and the share of nontradables in final expenditures on GDP (SN). Corresponding equations based on the 25 ICP countries used for this chapter are as follows:[10]

$$PL(75) = 24.20 + 0.897r + 16.68OP, \tag{1}$$
$$(4.48) \; (11.19) \qquad (2.31)$$

$$\bar{R}^2 = 0.852,$$

$$RMSE = 12.3,$$

No. Obs. $= 25;$

$$PL(75) = -5.29 + 0.671r + 11.57OP + 0.96SN, \tag{2}$$
$$(0.40) \quad (5.67) \qquad (1.69) \qquad (2.42)$$

$$\bar{R}^2 = 0.879,$$

$$RMSE = 11.1$$

No. Obs. $= 25.$

Equations such as these for single years are subject to a good deal of short-run variability. Because we are interested here in relatively long-term or medium-term changes, we rely on equations based on averages for three-year periods. We show the one-year equations here only for comparison with the earlier work.[11]

The rationale for the selection of the basic explanatory variables has been outlined previously (e.g., Kravis and Lipsey 1983, 11–16; Bhagwati 1984). We review it briefly here and offer a modification of past practice with respect to formulation of the openness variable.

The positive association between PL and r is attributable to higher prices of nontradables relative to tradables in higher-income countries. The explanation may be couched in terms of rich-country margins of superiority in productivity that are smaller for nontradables, especially services, than for tradables, or in terms of the tendency for nontradables to be labor intensive and for labor to be more costly relative to other factors of production in high-income countries than in low-income countries.

In general, we may expect high foreign trade/GDP ratios to reduce country-to-country divergences in price levels. Trade not only operates directly in pulling prices of tradables toward greater uniformity but affects the prices of nontradables by tending to raise the prices of relatively abundant factors and lowering the prices of relatively scarce ones. If poor countries tend to have abundant labor, and if nontradables (comprised largely of services) tend to be labor intensive, the effects of openness can be predicted. As between two countries with equal low incomes, the one with the higher level of openness should have higher prices for nontradables and for GDP as a whole. As between two countries with equal high incomes, the one with the higher level of openness should have lower prices.

The justification we give for the openness variable implies that the direction of its influence should vary with the factor abundance of the country involved. If we assume that the level of real income per capita is a good proxy for capital abundance (or labor scarcity), we could include a term for the combination of real income per capita (r) and openness (OP), and the coefficient for this cross-product term should be negative. Equations (1a) and (2a) correspond to equations (1) and (2) with the addition of this term:

$$PL(75) = 15.56 + 1.047r + 33.07OP - 0.27rOP, \tag{1a}$$
$$(1.72) \quad (7.01) \quad\quad (2.12) \quad\quad (1.18)$$

$$\bar{R}^2 = 0.855,$$

$$RMSE = 12.2,$$

No. Obs. = 25;

$$PL(75) = -5.88 + 0.725r + 16.38OP - 0.075rOP + 0.90SN, \tag{2a}$$
$$(0.44) \quad (3.44) \quad\quad (0.98) \quad\quad (0.32) \quad\quad (2.03)$$

$$\bar{R}^2 = 0.874,$$

$$RMSE = 11.3,$$

No. Obs. = 25.

The coefficient of the rOP term is negative, as we expect, but it is not statistically significant in this year.

The positive sign on the share coefficient, share being defined in terms of the current value of output in own prices, implies that given real GDP per capita and openness, high nontradables shares in final expenditures are associated with high nontradables prices. Such a relationship may be attributable to elasticities of substitution between tradables and non-tradables in final demand that are below 1.[12]

5.2   The Price Level for GDP

The Structural Equation for PL

The further explanation of comparative national price levels starts with the modification of equation (2) prior to fitting it to data for years other than

1975 in the period 1960–83. The formulation in equation (2) has the disadvantage that two of the independent variables, OP and SN, overlap. That is, OP may be regarded as the product of the share of tradables in GDP and the ratio of actually traded goods to tradables:

$$OP = \frac{X + M}{GDP} = \frac{X + M}{Tradables} \times \frac{Tradables}{GDP}. \tag{3}$$

An alternative way to decompose the independent variable is to substitute the two multiplicative components of OP for OP and SN. The results are

$$PL(75) = 87.84 + 0.666r + 5.71OPT - 0.90ST, \tag{4}$$
$$(3.06) \quad (5.65) \quad (1.70) \quad\quad (2.18)$$

$$\bar{R}^2 = 0.879,$$

RMSE = 11.1,

No. Obs. = 25;

$$PL(75) = 68.61 + 0.796r + 11.85OPT - 0.087rOPT - 0.69ST, \tag{4a}$$
$$(1.67) \quad (3.47) \quad\quad (1.20) \quad\quad\quad (0.66) \quad\quad\quad (1.32)$$

$$\bar{R}^2 = 0.876,$$

RMSE = 11.2,

No. Obs. = 25,

where $OPT = X + M/\text{Tradables}$ and $ST =$ the share of tradables in GDP. Equation (4a) again shows an attenuation of the influence of openness with higher levels of per capita income, but no reversal of direction.

There is no statistical basis for choosing between equations (2) or (2a), on the one hand, and (4) and (4a), on the other, but equations (4) and (4a) may be regarded as providing a slightly better classification of the factors at work on the right side of the equation. The same rationale can be offered for OPT that was given for OP, and what was said about SN applies to ST with a changed sign.[13] It should be reported that the formulations of equations (2) and (4) were reached after an investigation of a larger number of structural variables (e.g., relative productivity in traded and nontraded goods), different functional forms (log versus arithmetic), and different formulations of the variables finally chosen (e.g., defining OP in terms of merchandise trade only). Although the choices were not always clear-cut, some less than thorough investigation of the alternatives led us to believe that the results described below would not be very different if the alternative choices had been made.

A problem encountered in the use of equations (2) and (4) as prototypes for the investigation of long-run trends is that the ICP estimate of the share of tradables, used to form *OPT* and *ST*, is defined in terms of final products (i.e., goods purchased for final use and not for use as intermediate products) and is not readily available for other years.[14] This difficulty is not insuperable because a rough estimate of the tradables component of GDP can be derived from data, available in national accounts, on the share of GDP accounted for by different industries, each of which produces both final and intermediate products. For this purpose, as noted earlier, tradables have been defined as the output of agriculture, mining, and manufacturing, leaving the output of construction and of the service industries to be regarded as nontradables. The modified *OPT* and *ST* variables, *OPTI* and *STI*, respectively, produce similar results when substituted in equations (4) and (4a).

$$PL(75) = 56.42 + 0.718r + 6.03OPTI - 0.60STI, \qquad (4b)$$
$$ (2.75) \quad (6.29) \qquad (2.50) \qquad\quad (1.52)$$

$$\bar{R}^2 = 0.872,$$

$$RMSE = 11.4,$$

No. Obs. = 25;

$$PL(75) = 36.06 + 0.953r + 17.00OPTI - 0.16rOPTI - 0.45STI, \quad (4ab)$$
$$ (1.64) \quad (5.87) \qquad (2.78) \qquad\quad (1.93) \qquad\quad (1.18)$$

$$\bar{R}^2 = 0.886,$$

$$RMSE = 10.8,$$

No. Obs. = 25.

Even this version of the two trade exposure variables is available as far back as 1960 for only 25 countries, and this was one of the facts that determined the restriction of the analysis to these countries.

Trends in the Key Variables

Since we are interested primarily in price level trends, we have recast the annual data into a series of nonoverlapping three-year averages. These reduce the influence of short-term fluctuations and make the trends in the underlying data stand out more clearly.

The behavior of the four variables used in equation (4b) and the openness variable used in equations (1) and (2) is presented in table 5.1. One of the major changes over the whole period is that the average price level relative to the United States, after remaining in the range of 56 to 59 percent of the U.S. level during the fixed exchange rate period, climbed to nearly 80 percent in 1978–80 before falling back to 65 percent in 1981–83. It rose particularly during the two periods when there were major increases in petroleum prices (column 1). The dispersion of country price levels around their average increased (column 2); that is, deviations from the law of one price became larger. There was a particularly large jump in dispersion between the fixed exchange rate period and the floating exchange rate period, but the trend toward larger deviations began during the fixed rate period.

The two decades witnessed a great expansion in the world economy, but of course not all countries gained at the same rate: the United States lagged behind the average of the others, for example (column 3). The dispersion of country incomes around the mean remained almost constant (column 4).

The share of tradables in total GDP drifted downward (column 9), as service industry output grew relative to goods output, but the ratio of goods actually traded to tradables output rose sharply, especially in the 1970s (column 7). That rise in the trade ratio was partly a direct reflection of the increase in the price of oil, a heavily traded commodity, but was not confined to that group. It was evident also within manufactured goods (see Lipsey 1984).

Trends in the Structural Relationships

Table 5.2 shows the results of fitting equations like (4b) to each of the eight cross sections. It is evident that there were marked secular trends in the coefficients of real per capita GDP and openness. In each case the coefficient tends to rise through time, with the increases tending to be larger in the early 1970s at about the time that the Bretton Woods regime ended. That is, the price levels of the countries became more sharply differentiated according to their income levels and the extent of their participation in the international economy. At the same time the explanatory power of the independent variables increased markedly; the t-statistics and the $\bar{R}^2$s are clearly higher in the later periods. The "unexplained"

Table 5.1
Relative price levels, real GDP per capita, and trade exposure: means for 25 countries, for three-year periods, 1960–1983

	Price level (PL)		Real GDP per capita (r)		Trade relative to total output (OP)		Trade relative to tradables output (OPTI)		Tradables output relative to GDP (STI)	
	Mean[a,b]	Coefficient of variation	Mean[a,b]	Coefficient of variation	Mean[a]	Coefficient of variation	Mean[a]	Coefficient of variation	Mean[a]	Coefficient of variation
	(1)	(2)	(3)	(4)	(5)	(6)	(7)	(8)	(9)	(10)
1960–62	57.6	28	35.7	80	0.47	73	1.03	71	0.46	19
1963–65	59.1	30	35.9	80	0.46	72	1.04	71	0.45	19
1966–68	58.6	33	35.6	80	0.46	67	1.08	67	0.43	19
1969–71	56.4	35	38.8	79	0.48	70	1.15	67	0.42	20
1972–74	64.4	42	40.1	79	0.52	64	1.27	66	0.42	21
1975–77	70.0	45	41.0	78	0.55	59	1.44	71	0.40	22
1978–80	78.7	48	41.2	79	0.59	58	1.59[c]	70[c]	0.39[c]	22[c]
1981–83	64.8	41	42.6	78	0.60	61	1.77[c]	75[c]	0.37[c]	23[c]

Note: Data are for Austria, Belgium, Brazil, Colombia, Denmark, France, Germany (F.R.), India, Italy, Jamaica, Japan, Kenya, Korea, Luxembourg, Malawi, Malaysia, Mexico, Pakistan, Philippines, Sri Lanka, Thailand, United Kingdom, United States, Uruguay, Zambia, except as indicated.

a. Means are simple averages of values for the 25 countries.

b. U. S. = 100 in each period.

c. Excluding Malawi.

Table 5.2
Price level as a function of real per capita GDP (r), openness (OPTI), and share of tradables output in GDP (STI): 25 countries, three-year periods, 1960–1983

	Intercept	r	OPTI	STI	$\bar{R}^2$
	(1)	(2)	(3)	(4)	(5)
1960–62	60.70	0.389	0.25	−0.38	0.642
	(3.92)	(4.48)	(0.09)	(1.31)	(9.6)
1963–65	57.49	0.456	0.56	−0.34	0.700
	(3.40)	(4.77)	(0.20)	(1.09)	(9.8)
1966–68	48.91	0.537	1.54	−0.26	0.747
	(2.90)	(5.53)	(0.54)	(0.79)	(9.7)
1969–71	40.36	0.567	0.64	−0.16	0.836
	(3.25)	(7.90)	(0.29)	(0.65)	(8.0)
1972–74	39.09	0.714	3.96	−0.20	0.856
	(2.29)	(7.32)	(1.46)	(0.60)	(10.3)
1975–77	57.48	0.673	6.12	−0.59	0.842
	(2.50)	(5.14)	(2.16)	(1.31)	(12.6)
1978–80	43.76	0.913	6.79	−0.34	0.846
	(1.55)	(5.88)	(2.16)	(0.60)	(15.0)
1981–83	61.56	0.605	0.29	−0.62	0.831
	(3.28)	(6.03)	(0.15)	(1.55)	(10.7)

Notes: The dependent variable is PL with the U.S. = 100 in each period. All variables are three-year averages. There are 25 observations in each period, except 1978–80 and 1981–83 when Malawi is missing. The omission of Malawi has virtually no effect on the coefficients for the period before 1978.

PL = PPP/Exchange rate.

Figures in parentheses are t-statistics in columns 1–4 and root mean square errors in column 5.

Independent variables:

   r = real per capita GDP with the U.S. = 100 in each period.

OPTI = $(X + M)$/Tradables, based on national accounts data. Tradables based on shares of agriculture, mining, and manufacturing components of GDP.

   STI = Tradables as percent of GDP, with tradables based on national accounts data for agriculture, mining, and manufacturing.

$\bar{R}^2$s, intercept terms, and standard errors are the same whether the absolute or relative values of the variables are used (i.e., whether per capita GDP is expressed in dollars or, as is done, as an index with U.S. = 100).

Table 5.3
Price level as a function of real per capita GDP(r), openness ($OPTI$), share of tradables output in GDP (STI) and $rOPTI$: 25 countries, three-year periods, 1960–1983

	Intercept	r	$OPTI$	$rOPTI$	STI	$\bar{R}^2$
1960–62	51.38	0.506	5.23	−0.100	−0.29	0.646
	(2.94)	(3.76)	(1.00)	(1.12)	(0.97)	(9.5)
1963–65	46.80	0.582	6.39	−0.105	−0.24	0.704
	(2.44)	(4.02)	(1.10)	(1.15)	(0.74)	(9.7)
1966–68	40.64	0.664	8.10	−0.121	−0.21	0.753
	(2.27)	(4.74)	(1.36)	(1.25)	(0.66)	(9.6)
1969–71	31.24	0.690	6.98	−0.106	−0.10	0.845
	(2.30)	(6.32)	(1.44)	(1.46)	(0.40)	(7.8)
1972–74	19.95	0.933	14.89	−0.167	−0.04	0.873
	(1.06)	(6.38)	(2.39)	(1.92)	(0.12)	(9.7)
1975–77	37.22	0.916	19.64	−0.183	−0.49	0.862
	(1.57)	(5.32)	(2.71)	(2.00)	(1.15)	(11.8)
1978–80	36.29	1.017	12.03	−0.072	−0.33	0.842
	(1.19)	(4.72)	(1.50)	(0.71)	(0.56)	(15.2)
1981–83	45.87	0.758	6.67	−0.084	−0.46	0.839
	(2.13)	(5.14)	(1.34)	(1.39)	(1.13)	(10.5)

For notes, see table 5.2.

deviations from the law of one price therefore increased much less than the deviations themselves.

The degree to which our equations explain price levels, as measured by the $\bar{R}^2$s, increases monotonically from the early 1950s to the 1960s and, in fact, through the early 1970s, after which it changes only slightly.[15] For a good part of the period, up to the end of the era of "fixed" exchange rates, the standard error of the equations declines almost continuously. In the 1950s, the decline represented a fall in the variance of price levels, that is, a move toward aligning exchange rates with the purchasing power of currencies. Particularly during the era of floating exchange rates, price levels came to be explained more and more by per capita income and openness, until the last period, when the openness variable suddenly vanished.[16]

If we add the cross-product term $rOPTI$ to the equations of table 5.2 to permit the direction of the openness effect to vary with income level, we get the set of coefficients displayed in table 5.3. The degrees of explanation and the standard errors are quite similar to those of the earlier table, but the openness coefficients are very different and show the expected interrelation with income levels. In the last equation, for example, the coefficients imply that the effect of a greater degree of openness on the price level is positive for any country with real income per capita less than 81 percent of the U.S. level but negative for any country above that income. The latter group included Denmark, France, and Germany in that year. The 52 percent dividing line in 1960–62 suggested negative coefficients for the United States and all the European countries except Italy. The coefficient for Japan was always positive. There was considerable variation in the borderline over time, but in four of the eight periods the dividing line was between 52 and 67 percent of the U.S. income level. The equations suggest that openness had a positive effect on price levels for all countries in the 1970s, particularly 1975–80. That result confirms the failure to find any negative openness effect in the earlier single-year equations for 1975 and 1980.[17]

Aside from the increasing explanatory power of the equations, it is clear in all the sets of equations that the slope of the relationship between per capita income and price level was rising over most of the period. The coefficients for openness had a different history. In equations without a cross-product term (table 5.2), they played no role at all for the period of fixed exchange rates, increased in importance afterward, and virtually disappeared in the last period. When the cross-product term $rOPTI$ was added (table 5.3), both its coefficient and that of the OP term were more stable than the OP or $OPTI$ terms in table 5.2.[18]

The most likely explanation for the shifts in the coefficients over time is that there are important variables omitted from the analysis. One candidate for this role is capital movements. Since a capital importer is running a current account deficit, we might think of a high price level as part of the mechanism producing such a deficit, or of a low price level as part of the process that produces a current account surplus. This variable would be appropriate if we thought of shifts in the capital account as exogenous, reflecting forces in capital markets to which the current account must accommodate. It would be less appropriate if we thought of the capital account as accommodating changes in the determinants of the current account or of the two being determined simultaneously.[19]

Over the last 15 or 20 years the changing institutional background has continually brought new or newly important influences into the determination of exchange rates and price levels. The shift from fixed to floating rates and the enormous rise in the importance of capital movements, mentioned earlier, are only two of many. These changes are difficult to capture in econometric formulations. We have made no effort to measure the factors affecting exchange rates separately from domestic price levels or short-term effects on international price levels, and little effort to measure the effects of changes in the institutional climate. What is attempted here is to identify and take systematic account of certain permanent factors: those that tend to remain in play continuously. Some important factors that are relatively new and often difficult to quantify appear only as factors changing our coefficients or are left to be explained, possibly in more qualitative terms, as part of large and economically significant residuals.

Alternative Norms for Price Levels

The differences between the price levels implicit in one set of equations and those implicit in the purchasing power parity theory of exchange rates are described in table 5.4. We compare the deviations from the price levels implied by the absolute form of the theory (all PL $= 100$) with the residuals from the equations of table 5.2 (PL $- \widehat{\text{PL}}$). The results of the comparison are of course a foregone conclusion, given the high $\bar{R}^2$s of table 5.2. Any significant relation between the price level and our independent variables implies that our equations fit better than the purchasing power parity assumption, whose absolute form implies identity of price levels.

This comparison is not a test of the predictive power of our structural equations, since they have been fitted to the price levels of each period. Even so, it is of some interest that the fit can be so good using a common set of independent variables for all the periods, without taking into account the many short-term factors that can cause price levels to change if

Table 5.4
Measures of closeness of fit to actual country price levels (PL_i): structural equations compared with absolute version of purchasing power parity theory

	PPP theory[a]	Table 5.2 equation[b]
	(1)	(2)
Mean absolute deviation		
All periods	21.4	7.6
First four periods[c]	15.4	6.3
Last four periods[d]	27.4	8.8
Mean squared deviation		
All periods	625	99
First four periods[c]	322	73
Last four periods[d]	927	126

a. $PL_i -$ Average PL.
b. $PL_i - \widehat{PL_i}$.
c. 1960–62, 1963–65, 1966–68, and 1969–71.
d. 1972–74, 1975–77, 1978–80, and 1981–83.

own-price inflation rates and changes in exchange rates are not exactly offsetting.

Predictive power can be better assessed by asking how well our structural variables forecast *changes* in price levels. The relative form of PPP theory implies that there should be no changes.

Several tests could be constructed. Our tests asks how well the estimated cross-sectional equation for one period and the observed values of the structural variables for the next period predict the next period's price levels. The way we do the test is first to estimate a predicted price level $(\widehat{PL})_t$ using equations of the form (4ab), fitted to period $t-1$ but with values of the independent variables for period t substituted in the equation. We then use $\widehat{PL}_t$ and the deviations from the structural equation in period $t-1$ (because we know the deviations tend to be persistent) to predict the price level of period t (PL_t). The result for all eight cross sections combined is shown in equation (5):

$$PL_t = 4.22 + 0.93(\widehat{PL})_t + 0.78RES_{t-1}, \tag{5}$$
$$(1.63)\ (25.10) \qquad (8.10)$$

$$\bar{R}^2 = 0.801,$$

$$RMSE = 12.1,$$

No. Obs. = 173,

where

$(\widehat{PL})_t$ = estimated price level for period t based on structural equation (4ab) fitted for period $t-1$ and values of r, *OPTI*, *rOPTI*, and *STI* in period t,

RES_{t-1} = residual from $t-1$ structural equation.

Despite the shifts over time in the estimated cross-sectional equations recorded in table 5.3, each period's price level was very well estimated from that period's structural variables in combination with the previous period's equation and the residuals from that equation. The coefficient on the residual implies that these deviations from the structural relationships tended to persist but were reduced in size by about 20 percent from one period to the next.

The corresponding equations for individual periods are given in table 5.5 The predictions are quite good; all but one $\bar{R}^2$ are about 0.92 or over. The coefficient for the previous period's residual is always significant and generally below 1, reflecting the persistence of the residuals but some tendency for them to decline over time.

Table 5.5
Estimation of price levels from current period r, $OPTI$, and STI, and coefficients and residuals from previous period equations

	Intercept	Coefficient of $\widehat{PL_t^a}$	Residual$_{t-1}$	$\bar{R}^2$ (RMSE)
1963–65	−5.61	1.12	0.86	0.918
	(1.24)	(14.68)	(7.16)	(5.1)
1966–68	−8.01	1.12	0.91	0.967
	(2.79)	(23.94)	(11.40)	(3.5)
1969–71	−5.33	1.02	0.71	0.964
	(2.00)	(24.18)	(8.19)	(3.7)
1972–74	−12.62	1.35	0.88	0.928
	(2.67)	(17.12)	(4.23)	(7.3)
1975–77	−6.61	1.16	1.01	0.943
	(1.55)	(19.23)	(5.80)	(7.5)
1978–80	−9.98	1.23	0.96	0.919
	(1.62)	(15.64)	(4.64)	(10.9)
1981–83	12.46	0.64	0.49	0.890
	(2.82)	(13.18)	(3.71)	(8.7)

a. $\widehat{PL_t}$ is calculated using the coefficients from the equation $PL_{t-1} = f(r_{t-1}, OPTI_{t-1}, r_{t-1}OPTI_{t-1}STI_{t-1})$ together with the values of r_t, $OPTI_t$, and STI_t.

These equations, however, do not do much better in predicting price levels than the PPP-based prediction of no change. Relative price levels are so strongly related to relative real income per capita, which changes very slowly, that it is hard to beat the no-change prediction by much. However, these equations provide at least some estimates of changes in price levels, given changes in the independent variables. These estimated changes in price levels are correlated with the actual changes, as can be seen in equation (6), where ΔPL_t is $PL_t - PL_{t-1}$ and $\widehat{\Delta PL_t}$ is the difference between the estimated PL_t of equation (5) and the actual PL_{t-1}:

$$\Delta PL_t = 0.050 + 0.95\,(\widehat{\Delta PL_t}) \tag{6}$$
$$(0.10)\quad(18.60)$$

$$\bar{R}^2 = 0.667,$$

$$\text{RMSE} = 6.7,$$

No. Obs. = 173.

In other words, the structural variables of our equations do contribute to explaining changes in price levels or real exchange rates.

Price Levels for Tradables and Nontradables

The discussion up to this point has assumed that market forces operate on aggregate GDP price levels, price levels relative to those implied by structural equations, or changes in them, across countries. An alternative hypothesis is that these forces operate on traded goods prices but not, or to a much smaller extent, on nontradables prices. To test whether that is the case, we will perform the same comparisons and tests on PLTR, the price level for tradables, as on the aggregate price level.

The likelihood of large deviations from international equality of price levels is more readily acceptable for nontradables than for tradables, as is the possibility that price levels should be related to income or other variables. A number of theoretical analyses of price levels take account of this difference, as was pointed out in our earlier study (Kravis and Lipsey 1983). It was also pointed out there that although the relationship was not quite as strong, the variables that explained aggregate price levels also went a long way in explaining price levels for tradables. That result does not necessarily contradict the theories that imply the equalization of prices of some type of "pure" tradables, but it limits their empirical applicability. The measured prices of tradables inevitably incorporate some nontradable inputs, such as wholesale or retail services, and would differ among countries even if "pure" tradable prices were equalized.

There is a particular interest in the determinants of the two sets of prices separately, since we might expect that departures of tradables prices from equilibrium might be more quickly erased by changes in exchange rates than those of the total price level. They are also likely to the better indicators of any deliberate efforts by governments to influence trade flows and to be more influential in determining trade flows.

For the benchmark year 1975, the equations for the price levels for GDP as a whole (PL) and for tradables (PLTR) and nontradables (PLNT), based on data for the 25 countries of tables 5.1 and 5.2, are as follows:

$$PL(75) = 25.94 + 0.842r + 6.74OPTI, \tag{7}$$
$$ (5.69) \ (10.31) \quad (2.76)$$

$$\bar{R}^2 = 0.864,$$

$$RMSE = 11.8;$$

$$PLTR(75) = 46.94 + 0.673r + 8.39OPTI, \tag{8}$$
$$ (7.77) \ (6.22) \quad (2.60)$$

$$\bar{R}^2 = 0.726,$$

$$\text{RMSE} = 15.6;$$

$$\text{PLNT}(75) = 9.18 + 0.946r + 5.35OPTI, \tag{9}$$
$$\quad\quad\quad (2.45) \ (14.10) \quad\ (2.67)$$

$$\bar{R}^2 = 0.917,$$

$$\text{RMSE} = 9.7.$$

As we might expect, the levels for nontradables prices are better explained than those for tradables prices, and the coefficient for r is considerably higher. That seems reasonable in view of the explanations we have given for the relationship between income per capita and price levels. The coefficient for openness is larger in the equation for tradables, suggesting that the influence of competition with other countries plays more of a role for these products than for nontradables, in addition to effects of trade on factor prices.

In table 5.6, similar equations for tradables and nontradables, but including the interaction term $rOPTI$, are fitted to data for our successive three-year nonoverlapping periods.[20] As in the benchmark year equations, the prices of nontradables, viewed across countries, rise more sharply with increasing per capita incomes (r) than the prices of tradables.[21] The coefficients for openness, the ratio of goods actually traded to tradables output, are similar in the two sets of equations, but the interaction between per capita income and openness is much stronger for nontradables. In 1978–80, when the U.S. price level was very low, the coefficient for the interaction between real per capita income and openness is not only insignificant but even has the wrong sign.

5.3   The Deviations from the Structural Equations and Their Significance

The Pattern of Residuals

There are a number of ways to interpret the deviations of price levels from those predicted by our equations and to think about their consequences. If we regard the equations as representing estimates of equilibrium price levels, we might expect that deviations from them would be ephemeral. They might be quickly erased by movements of exchange rates, especially

Table 5.6
Price levels for tradables and nontradables as functions of real per capita GDP (r), openness (*OPTI*), and *rOPTI*: 19 countries, three-year periods, 1960–62 to 1981–83

	Tradables					Nontradables				
	Intercept	Coefficients of			$\bar{R}^2$ (RMSE)	Intercept	Coefficients of			$\bar{R}^2$ (RMSE)
		r	OPTI	rOPTI			r	OPTI	rOPTI	
1960–62	41.14 (5.64)	0.572 (3.69)	14.16 (1.82)	−0.157 (0.99)	0.590 (11.4)	13.18 (2.43)	0.812 (7.05)	11.29 (1.95)	−0.267 (2.26)	0.809 (8.5)
1963–65	44.06 (5.01)	0.551 (3.08)	11.33 (1.18)	−0.047 (0.26)	0.590 (12.9)	8.42 (1.57)	8.91 (8.17)	13.47 (2.29)	−0.251 (2.27)	0.867 (7.9)
1966–68	39.41 (4.48)	0.596 (3.49)	13.30 (1.36)	−0.065 (0.37)	0.671 (11.8)	6.45 (1.12)	0.912 (8.16)	12.43 (1.94)	−0.195 (1.71)	0.886 7.8
1969–71	39.46 (5.52)	0.575 (4.43)	9.79 (1.22)	−0.037 (.29)	0.792 (9.3)	6.24 (1.41)	0.867 (10.75)	8.00 (1.60)	−0.133 (1.67)	0.940 (5.8)
1972–74	44.08 (5.36)	0.642 (4.36)	4.63 (0.54)	0.096 (0.73)	0.862 (10.4)	2.98 (0.74)	0.974 (13.49)	6.83 (1.62)	−0.038 (0.59)	0.972 (5.1)
1975–77	24.43 (1.74)	0.851 (3.65)	28.97 (2.14)	−0.199 (1.02)	0.758 (15.6)	−1.23 (0.15)	1.017 (7.40)	12.00 (1.50)	−0.038 (0.33)	0.932 (9.2)
1978–80	40.09 (2.96)	0.828 (3.60)	10.01 (0.94)	0.027 (0.17)	0.791 (16.2)	7.56 (0.84)	1.026 (6.69)	1.35 (0.19)	0.142 (1.35)	0.936 (10.8)
1981–83	36.19 (3.23)	0.730 (3.90)	11.42 (1.46)	−0.15 (1.30)	0.599 (14.4)	1.09 (0.17)	1.065 (9.73)	9.04 (1.98)	−0.111 (1.71)	0.927 (8.4)

Note: Based on data for 19 countries, those listed in table 5.1 with the exception of Luxembourg, Kenya, Malaysia, Malawi, Brazil, and Zambia. The 1975 PPPs for tradables and nontradables, derived from ICP exchange rates and price levels (Kravis, Heston, and Summers 1982, pp. 10 and 196), were extrapolated to other years by the use of implicit deflators. The implicit deflator for tradables was derived by taking the ratio of GDP originating in agriculture, mining and manufacturing at current prices to the GDP originating in these industries at constant prices (data from IBRD, 1984 Economic Data Sheet 1). The implicit deflator for nontradables was formed in a similar way on the basis of GDP originating in other sectors. r and *OPTI* were the same as in table 5.2.

in the floating exchange rate period, or by price movements, especially in the fixed exchange rate era. If the deviations are long-lasting, they might reflect the omission from our equations of significant structural variables, such as the inflow or outflow of capital. They might, on the other hand, reflect government policies that sustain disequilibrium price levels for long periods, for example, by maintaining overvalued exchange rates and exchange controls or by maintaining undervalued rates to promote exports.[22]

One way of analyzing the persistence of residuals is by measuring whether the countries that have high price levels (PL), relative to those predicted by the equations ($\widehat{PL}$), in one period tend to have high price levels in preceding or following periods. An answer to this question is given in table 5.7, which shows the correlations among residuals in different periods for the structural equations found in table 5.3. Similar results are obtained when other structural equations such as those of table 5.2 are used.

There is clearly a strong tendency for the deviations to be similar for a country in the different periods. Although the association atrophies with time, the correlation coefficients are all positive and are usually significant at the 5 percent level ($r \geq 0.40$) between a given period and each of three or four prior and three or four subsequent periods.

The 25 countries included in the analysis are grouped in table 5.8 according to their long-run tendency to have low, intermediate or high price levels after the price levels have been purged of structural influences as measured by equation (4ab), that is, after levels of real income per capita, openness, and the share of nontradables in output have been taken into account. For the most part countries with actual PLs falling far short of the PLs estimated by the equation tended to have such shortfalls (negative residuals) consistently across the seven periods.[23] Similarly countries with actual PLs far exceeding estimated PLs tended to have positive residuals that also appeared rather consistently. Trends in the residuals characterized several countries, as noted in the table. One of the pronounced ones was for the United States; the U.S. residual moved almost monotonically from $+9.2$ in 1960–62 to -31.4 in 1978–80 but then declined sharply in absolute terms in the last period.

The behavior of price residuals for developed countries was somewhat different from that for developing countries. In particular, all the seven countries with consistent low residual price levels (negative residuals in six, seven, or eight periods) were developing countries.

Table 5.7
Correlation matrix for residuals from equations estimating price levels: 25 countries, 1960–1983

	1960–62	1963–65	1966–68	1969–71	1972–74	1975–77	1978–80	1981–83
1960–62	1.00							
1963–65	0.84	1.00						
1966–68	0.83	0.93	1.00					
1969–71	0.58	0.72	0.87	1.00				
1972–74	0.30	0.54	0.70	0.71	1.00			
1975–77	0.35	0.48	0.60	0.52	0.83	1.00		
1978–80	0.09	0.28	0.45	0.46	0.79	0.75	1.00	
1981–83	0.25	0.33	0.46	0.50	0.55	0.46	0.72	1.00

Notes: Residuals for each period equal actual PL minus PL estimated from equation ($\widehat{PL}$). The equation used here is (4ab): $PL = f(r, OPTI, rOPTI, STI)$. Malawi is omitted in the correlations for 1978–80 and 1981–83.

Table 5.8
Countries arrayed by residual price level after allowing for structural PL determinants: 1960 to 1983 (low to high)

Countries with low price levels			Countries with intermediate price levels			Countries with high price levels		
Country	Rank[a]	Periods with + residual	Country	Rank	Periods with + residual	Country	Rank	Periods with + residual
Uruguay	1	0	Mexico	9	2	Kenya	17	7
Sri Lanka[b]	2	3	Austria[c]	10	3	United Kingdom	18	6
Korea	3	0	Pakistan	11	2	Philippines	19	6
Malaysia[c]	4	0	India	12	4	Germany	20	4
United States[b]	5	4	Belgium	13	7	Denmark	21	6
Colombia	6	1	Japan	14	4	Italy	22	8
Thailand	7	0	Jamaica	15	5	Zambia[c]	23	8
Luxembourg	8	3	France[b]	16	6	Brazil	24	8

a. Based on residuals from equations of the form (4ab): $PL = f(r, OPTI, rOPTI, STI)$. The equation was fitted to each of eight nonoverlapping three-year periods, beginning with 1960–62 and ending with 1981–83. The residuals were averaged and the countries ranked, beginning with the one with the largest negative average residual. Malawi was omitted from the ranking because its price level was not available for all periods.

b. There was a negative trend in the residuals. The criterion was a 5 percent significance level for the coefficient of time (T) in the equation:

$$Residual = a + bT.$$

c. There was a positive trend in the residuals.

Since the structural equations come closer than identity of price levels to a representation of equilibrium price levels, the residuals from identical price levels should be more persistent. Table 5.9 shows the persistence of deviations from purchasing power parity, as measured by the correlations between PLs in different periods.[24] As we hypothesized, these deviations are more persistent than those from the structural equations of table 5.7. The differences between the two sets of deviations can be summarized as follows:

Length of span (periods)	Number of Observations	Average of correlation coefficients	
		Price levels	Price-level residuals
1	7	0.96	0.81
2	6	0.94	0.67
3	5	0.89	0.55
4	4	0.84	0.43
5	3	0.80	0.36
6	2	0.76	0.21
7	1	0.76	0.25
All spans	28	0.89	0.57

Each correlation is between two sets of average PLs or two sets of PL residuals for 25 countries, each set relating to a difference three-year period. The price level was obtained from table 5.9 and the price level residuals from equation (4ab) (table 5.7). The correlations between price levels (i.e., deviations from purchasing power parity) in one period and those in succeeding periods are higher than those for the residuals from the structural equations for every length of span, but the differences are much greater for the longer spans. In other words, a country with a high price level in one year is likely to have a high price level 20 years later. On the other hand, a country with a high price level relative to its structural characteristics, though it will be likely to still have a high price level three years later, is not particularly likely to have such a price level 15 or 20 years later. Our interpretation of this difference is that the deviations from the levels predicted by the structural equations represent something more like departures from long-run equilibrium price levels than the departures from purchasing power parity (equality of price levels). The latter represent not only deviations from equilibrium but also long-run structural characteristics of the economies.

Table 5.9
Correlation matrix for price levels in eight three-year periods

	1960–62	1963–65	1966–68	1969–71	1972–74	1975–77	1978–80	1981–83
1960–62	1.00							
1963–65	0.95	1.00						
1966–68	0.94	0.98	1.00					
1969–71	0.87	0.93	0.97	1.00				
1972–74	0.79	0.88	0.93	0.95	1.00			
1975–77	0.75	0.83	0.88	0.91	0.98	1.00		
1978–80	0.69	0.79	0.84	0.88	0.96	0.97	1.00	
1981–83	0.76	0.84	0.87	0.92	0.95	0.94	0.95	1.00

Note: (PL − 100) for each period (i.e., deviations from the identity of price levels implied by the absolute form of the purchasing power parity theory).

Residuals for Tradables and Nontradables

If equilibrium is more likely to be attained for tradables prices than for PL as a whole, and if exchange rates are not too greatly affected by intervention, deviations from the tradables equations might be expected to be less persistent than those for PL. That proposition is tested in table 5.10, a companion to table 5.7, but based on deviations of tradables prices from their structural equations.

Within the fixed rate era there was little difference in persistence between tradables residuals and those for the aggregate price level, as can be seen as follows:

	Number of Pairs	Average correlation coefficients between residuals for PLs for different periods	
		PL for tradables	PL for aggregate GDP
Within the Bretton Woods regime	6	0.81	0.80
Within the floating rate regime	6	0.63	0.68
Between the two regimes	16	0.38	0.44

The figures for the tradables prices were derived from table 5.10; those for the aggregate GDP prices differ from those derived earlier from table 5.7 because they refer to only 19 countries, to match the data for the price levels of tradables. Within the floating rate period, the residuals for tradables were a little less persistent than those for nontradables and the same was true for intervals spanning the two periods.

To the extent that persistently high or low price levels relative to those predicted by our equations represent policies of raising or depressing exchange rates rather than unaccounted-for characteristics of the economies, we might expect that they will operate equally on both tradable and nontradable price levels. Also from a purely statistical standpoint, the shared importance of tradables and nontradables in constituting GDP makes it unsurprising that countries that tend to have high predicted price levels for aggregate GDP generally tend to have high predicted price levels also for the tradable and nontradable components of GDP.[25] However, the connections were not so close that there was not room for a variety of patterns; the coefficient of correlation linking the PLTR and PLNT residuals was only 0.52. Thus some countries had higher price levels for tradables

Table 5.10
Correlation matrix for residuals from structural equations estimating tradables price levels: 19 countries, for eight three-year periods, 1960 to 1983

	1960–62	1963–65	1966–68	1969–71	1972–74	1975–77	1978–80	1981–83
1960–62	1.00							
1963–65	0.82	1.00						
1966–68	0.86	0.90	1.00					
1969–71	0.66	0.72	0.88	1.00				
1972–74	0.21	0.41	0.45	0.54	1.00			
1975–77	0.36	0.50	0.60	0.68	0.82	1.00		
1978–80	0.17	0.26	0.28	0.41	0.71	0.72	1.00	
1981–83	0.31	0.33	0.26	0.36	0.31	0.47	0.73	1.00

Residuals for each period equal actual tradable price level (PLTR) minus PLTR estimated from equation ($\widehat{PLTR}$). The equation used here is PLTR = $f(r, OPTI, rOPTI)$. See table 5.11 for the list of countries.

relative to nontradables than would be expected on the basis of the equations, and others exhibited the opposite relationship. The prices of tradables were substantially higher in these terms in Mexico, India, France, and Uruguay and substantially lower in Belgium, Korea, Thailand, and Japan (table 5.11).[26] Japan had, on the average, the highest price level for nontradables relative to the levels implied by the structural equations, among the 19 countries. Japanese tradables prices, on the other hand, were relatively low compared with those implied by the equations. This relationship probably reflects the exceptional decline in prices of tradables relative to nontradables discussed by Marston (chapter 4 in this volume).

Price Level Deviations and the Current-Account Balance

If the deviations from our equations represent departures from some sort of long-term relationship, we might expect them to have effects on subsequent flows of exports and imports of goods and services. A high price level relative to this norm (i.e., a large value for $PL - \widehat{PL}$) should reduce, and a low price level should increase, exports relative to imports. This possibility is tested in table 5.12, in which we relate the price level deviations in the first and fourth periods to changes in the export/import ratio between those periods and the seventh and eighth periods, the longest spans for which we have data.

The results give consistent, but weak, support for the idea that some such long-term relationships exist. A high price level in 1969–71 relative to that predicted by our equations from a country's real income per capita, degree of openness, and share of tradables in output was associated with a decline in exports relative to imports over the period to 1978–80, but the relationship was much weaker with the period ending in 1981–83. However, equations with fewer variables (not shown) produced significant correlations over three of the five spans.

Over shorter periods the coefficients were quite erratic and only one was significant at the 1 percent level: a high price level in 1969–71 was associated with declines in the export/import ratio in the next period.

Given all that we know about the factors determining trade flows, it is obvious that we have not specified a trade equation here. The most we might say is that there is some indication that it may be worth including some such measures of general price *levels* in more completely specified trade equations, in addition to the usual measures of price change for specific products or groups of products.

Table 5.11
Ranks of countries according to size of residuals from equations explaining PL, PLTR, and PLNT

Low price levels			Intermediate price levels			High price levels		
$PL - \widehat{PL}$	$PLTR - \widehat{PLTR}$	$PLNT - \widehat{PLNT}$	$PL - \widehat{PL}$	$PLTR - \widehat{PLTR}$	$PLNT - \widehat{PLNT}$	$PL - \widehat{PL}$	$PLTR - \widehat{PLTR}$	$PLNT - \widehat{PLNT}$
1 Uruguay[a]	1	1	7 Colombia	9	8	14 Pakistan	13	18
2 Sri Lanka[a]	4	2	8 Austria[a]	7	15	15 Japan	8	19
3 Korea[a]	3	6	9 Germany	11	5	16 United Kingdom[a]	15	13
4 United States[a]	5	9	10 Mexico[a]	10	3	17 Philippines[a]	14	12
5 Belgium	6	11	11 India[a]	16	10	18 Jamaica	19	17
6 Thailand[a]	2	14	12 France[a]	17	7	19 Italy[a]	18	16
			13 Denmark	12	4			

Note: The caret (ˆ) represents an estimate from the equation. PL = price level for GDP; PLTR = price level for tradables; PLNT = price level for nontradables. Countries are ranked from large negative values of the residuals to high positive ones. The residuals are averages of those from the seven equations, one for each period. For equations with PL as the dependent variable, r, OPTI, rOPTI, and STI were the independent variables. For the equations explaining PLTR and PLNT, r, OPTI, and rOPTI were the independent variables.

a. This country is classified in same price level group (i.e., low, intermediate, or high) in table 5.8.

Table 5.12
Relation of price level residuals to subsequent long-term changes in the balance on trade and nonfactor services

Period of independent variable (price level residual)	Period of dependent variable (change in balance on trade and nonfactor services)	Coefficient of independent variable (price level residual)	$\bar{R}^2$ (RMSE)
1960–62	1960–62 to 1981–83	−0.76 (1.29)	0.027 (25.0)
1960–62	1960–62 to 1978–80	−0.57 (1.49)	0.049 (16.3)
1960–62	1960–62 to 1969–71	−0.41 (1.54)	0.054 (11.4)
1969–71	1969–71 to 1981–83	−0.43 (0.64)	−0.025 (23.7)
1969–71	1969–71 to 1978–80	−0.87 (2.24)	0.144[a] (13.6)

Note: Price level residual is $PL - \widehat{PL}$, where $\widehat{PL}$ is estimated from equation (4ab): $PL = f(r, OPTI, rOPTI, STI)$. Change in balance on trade and nonfactor services is $[(x/M)_{t+n} - (x/M)_t] \times 100$.
a. Significant at 5 percent level.

5.4   Summary and Agenda for Future Research

This chapter starts from the fact that neither the absolute nor the relative version of purchasing power parity theory provides an adequate explanation for differences in national price levels. The former assumes that all price levels are equal and the latter that they all change by identical proportions. We have tried to find explanations for the price level differences that exist and for changes in relative levels that would be superior to those assumptions. From these explanations we attempt to derive some norms for national price levels.

The structural determinants of national price levels discovered in previous studies of data for 1975 and earlier years were still evident in the latest and much broader survey covering 55 countries in 1980. We fitted similar cross sections to a number of subperiods over 23 years, relating price levels to real income per capita, the openness of the economy, and the share of tradables in total output.

These equations suggested that since 1960, or even 1950, there has been a movement toward a more "orderly" alignment of price levels. That is, national price levels came to be explained to an increasing degree by our structural variables. Most of that increase in orderliness took place before the 1970s. The degree to which these structural variables explained price levels remained roughly constant after that and even declined a bit in the last period, 1981–83.

The higher the real income per capita of a country, the higher was its price level. In general, a greater degree of openness of an economy is also associated with a higher price level, but there are indications that that relationship varies by income level. In poor countries more openness is associated with higher price levels; in rich countries with lower price levels.

The coefficients of the structural equations changed substantially over time, the most important change being a gradual increase in the coefficient for real income per capita, at least through the end of the 1970s. We have not so far been able to explain the changes in coefficients.

Various tests suggest that equations that include variables such as these provide better explanations of price levels than the assumption of equality of levels and better explanations of changes in price levels than the assumption of identical changes. Furthermore deviations of price levels from the norms provided by these equations are associated with movements back toward the norms over intervals of several years and even over periods of one or two decades.

If the price level norms estimated from our equations are a better approximation to long-term equilibrium levels than those implied by purchasing power parity theory, the deviations of actual PLs from their estimated values should tend to be less persistent over time. This does prove to be the case. The correlation between deviations from PPP in one period and in other periods was still above 0.75 after 20 years or more, whereas that for deviations from the structural equations were lower than that after five years, and only about 0.20 after two decades. However, even in terms of deviations from the structural equations, some countries were persistently high priced and some, all developing countries, persistently low priced. By the measure of these deviations, the U.S. position was not stable. The United States moved from a high price level in the early 1960s to a very low price level in 1978–80, and then back toward a higher level in 1981–83. In general, the persistence of deviations from the equations seemed to be less under floating exchange rates than under fixed exchange rates and least across the change in regimes.

Our structural variables explained the price levels for nontradables considerably better than that for tradables, although the latter were explained fairly well. The effect of openness in reducing prices in higher-income countries was much stronger for nontradables than for tradables, and in fact was never significant for tradables prices. Countries with high or low prices for nontradables relative to those predicted by the structural equations were more likely than not to have deviations in the same direction for their tradables goods price levels. However, there were exceptions. In Thailand and Japan the deviations from predicted levels were in different directions for tradables and nontradables. Their price levels for tradables were low relative to those implied by the structural equations, while their price levels for nontradables were high relative to the predicted ones. That might suggest a bias in their economies or in their economic policies toward keeping tradable goods prices low at the expense of consumers of nontradables.

To the extent that the deviations from our structural relationships represent departures from sustainable long-term relationships, they might be expected to influence trade flows. We find that in fact a high price level, relative to the norm, was consistently associated with a decline in exports relative to imports over the next decade or two, although many of the coefficients were not significant. The relationship was much weaker and more erratic, however, over three-year intervals.

We do not imagine that the last word has been said on the specification of the structural equation. The next steps should include a search for explanations of the residuals to the structural equations. As suggested, short-run influences may be expected to account for some of the deviations of actual PLs from those predicted by the structural equations. Their inclusion might improve the estimates of the structural equations as well as help to explain the deviations from them. The deviations that persist over many years, found in this chapter for a number of countries, may prove to be explicable in terms of long-run characteristics of the economy that we have not yet identified or of government policies that affect price levels by restricting or promoting trade, or that affect the relationship between tradables and nontradables prices. Finally, the residuals appear to have economic consequences, such as those on trade flows, that deserve to be investigated further.

5.5. Appendix

Table 5.A1
Price level as a function of r, OPTI, rOPTI, and STI: 24 countries, three-year periods, 1960–1983

	Intercept	r	OPTI	rOPTI	STI
1960–62	56.49	0.541	4.67	−0.125	−0.40
	(5.11)	(5.26)	(1.16)	(1.74)	(2.17)
1963–65	51.90	0.607	3.96	−0.110	−0.32
	(4.43)	(5.71)	(.90)	(1.54)	(1.71)
1966–68	51.24	0.657	5.44	−0.124	−0.39
	(4.93)	(6.34)	(1.20)	(1.64)	(2.18)
1969–71	40.34	0.663	3.95	−0.092	−0.23
	(4.16)	(7.46)	(.99)	(1.52)	(1.35)
1972–74	29.88	0.877	8.70	−0.114	−0.12
	(2.36)	(7.76)	(1.80)	(1.65)	(0.58)
1975–77	52.17	0.831	14.37	−0.135	−0.67
	(2.89)	(5.66)	(2.35)	(1.74)	(2.17)
1978–80	49.73	0.951	7.58	−0.038	−0.49
	(2.27)	(5.35)	(1.18)	(.45)	(1.22)
1981–83	54.80	0.754	6.56	−0.097	−0.66
	(3.03)	(5.73)	(1.49)	(1.78)	(1.95)

Note: Results based on seemingly unrelated regression procedure.

Notes

1. We are indebted for valuable suggestions to the participants in two meetings of the AEI-NBER project on Real-Financial Linkages in Open Economics, particularly Robert Feenstra, Peter Hooper, Paul Krugman, and David Richardson, and also to participants in a session at the annual meeting of the Western Economic Association in 1985 and a seminar at the Graduate Center of the City University of New York. We are grateful to Linda Molinari and David Robinson for programming and statistical work and to Nancy Bonsall, James Hayes, and Rosa Schupbach for preparation of the manuscript.

This research was done mainly as part of the National Bureau of Economic Research studies of U.S. Trade Policy, Competitiveness, and Capital Mobility in the World Economy (NSF Grant No. PRA-8116459) and is part of the NBER program in International Studies. Any opinions expressed are those of the authors and do not represent those of the NBER or the sponsoring agency.

2. "Purchasing power parity" in this sentence is used in the sense of Cassel's theory holding that price levels will be *equal* after conversion to a common currency via exchange rates. Elsewhere (e.g., Kravis, Heston, and Summers 1982; Kravis and Lipsey 1983; Kravis 1984), the term has been used in an empirical sense to denote

the number of currency units having the same purchasing power as a unit of a numeraire currency, usually the U.S. dollar. The term is employed in both senses in this chapter; the context should make it clear which meaning is intended.

3. For example, a recent report by Peter Hill (1985) of work by the OECD showed the 1984 price levels of 18 member countries varying from 52 percent of the United States (Spain) to 97 percent (Finland). Another study, this one carried out by the Statistical Office of the European Community covering 15 African countries, found 1980 price levels varying from 56 percent of the average for the 15 (Ethiopia) to 126 percent (Nigeria).

4. For references on the influence of prices on trade flows, see Goldstein and Khan (1985), and for a current example, see Bushe, Kravis, and Lipsey (1986).

5. For example, the purchasing power parity of the Japanese yen in 1975 was 271 per U.S. dollar, and the exchange rate 297/$. Thus, with the U.S. dollar as the numeraire set equal to 100, the Japanese price level in 1975 was 91.

6. Kravis, Heston, and Summers (1982). Since that time, data for 1980 have become available from the fourth round of the ICP.

7. The 25 countries are listed in table 5.1. The exclusions that reduce the list to 19 are noted in table 5.6.

8. We work with two different sets of definitions of tradables and nontradables, one based on a subdivision of expenditures on GDP into various categories of final demand (e.g., shoes), and the other based on a subdivision of GDP according to its industrial origins (the leather industry, the shoe industry, etc.). The final demand categories—representing purchases not intended for resale—are used in the UN International Comparison Project and are followed here when equations based directly on ICP data are presented. The final demand classification is not available for other years on a comparable basis. Use has therefore been made of a definition of tradables based on more widely available industry-originating data: the output of agricultural, mining, and manufacturing industries has been regarded as tradable and the rest of GDP as nontradable. The industry-originating classification of course includes both final and intermediate goods directly; the final demand classification includes intermediate goods only as part of the value of final goods. Although the dividing line between tradables and nontradables in the industry-originating classification is somewhat arbitrary, it does distinguish groups of industries that in the aggregate differ a great deal with respect to the importance of trade. For the group of industries we include under tradables, the ratios of exports to output and imports to output in the United States in 1976 were each around 9 to 10 percent. For the group we include under nontradables, aside from general government, the ratios were under 2 percent (Young and Planting 1983, table 1).

9. The real exchange rate is sometimes defined in theoretical literature as the change in the price of tradables relative to that of nontradables (e.g., Berglas and Razin). This definition is appropriate only if the price of tradables is the same at

home and abroad (or if not the same, in a constant relationship). Among 25 ICP countries (15 developing and 10 developed) the price level for tradables varied in 1975 from 46 percent (Pakistan) to 144 percent (Denmark) of the U.S. level. ICP data are from Kravis, Heston, and Summers (1982). The classification used in that work groups construction with commodities rather than with services. However, for the tradables-nontradables dichotomy, as already noted, commodities excluding construction are regarded as tradables and services plus construction as nontradable.

10. The variables are scaled differently in the present equations; the United States is set equal to 100 for PL and r; OP is entered as a ratio and SN as a percentage. The mean PL for the 25 countries is 70.2. Some minor corrections in the price levels have also been made. t-values are in parentheses below the coefficients.

11. The latest round of the ICP, for 1980, covers a much larger number of countries, but at this point data are available only for the variables of equation (1). For 55 countries in 1980, the corresponding equation is

$$PL(80) = 42.56 + 0.662r + 17.54OP,$$
$$ (7.27) \quad (8.50) \qquad (2.00)$$

$$\bar{R}^2 = 0.623,$$

RMSE = 17.4,

No. Obs. = 55.

The explanatory power is much lower in the 1980 equation and the coefficient for r is also much lower. The explanation for the difference is that the additional countries, mainly developing, added in the broader survey did not exhibit the same relationship between price level and the other variables as the smaller group. When we run the equation with 1980 data for those countries (25) for which 1975 data were also available, the result is

$$PL(80) = 32.11 + 0.856r + 17.36OP,$$
$$ (4.43) \quad (8.55) \qquad (1.93)$$

$$\bar{R}^2 = 0.785,$$

RMSE = 16.0,

No. Obs. = 25.

The equation is very close to equation (1) with respect to the size of the constant term, the coefficients of r and OP and the $\bar{R}^2$. Thus it seems safe to say that there was no major change in the relationship from the substitution of 1980 relative prices and quantities for those of 1975. However, the addition of more countries did blur the relationship considerably, particularly because three newly added low-income African countries, Cameroon, Nigeria, and the Ivory Coast, had extremely high price levels, two even above that for the United States.

12. Since tradables prices are more nearly set by world prices, PL for GDP as a whole will be high when nontradables are dear, if the elasticity of substitution between tradables and nontradables in internal consumption is below 1. The Phase III ICP data yield an elasticity of substitution between tradables and nontradables of −0.44 (calculated from data in Kravis, Heston, and Summers 1982, p. 12, col. 5; p. 194, cols. 8 and 9; and p. 196, cols. 8 and 9 for 30 countries).

13. When ST is substituted for SN, its coefficient is the same but with the opposite sign. The intercept term is altered.

14. See note 8.

15. Changes in these relationships back to the 1950s can be traced only with equation (1) and only for 23 countries. The major finding is that the movement toward a more "orderly" alignment of PLs was very substantial then also, as can be seen from the coefficients of r and the $\bar{R}^2$s (t-ratios and root mean square errors in parentheses).

	r	$\bar{R}^2$
1950−52	0.245	−0.032
	(1.1)	(25.8)
1953−55	0.305	0.039
	(1.7)	(20.4)
1956−58	0.345	0.148
	(2.4)	(16.9)
1959−61	0.393	0.366
	(3.7)	(12.7)
1960−62	0.427	0.525
	(4.9)	(10.8)

See Kravis and Lipsey (1986, 15−16).

16. We should note, however, an alternative to the suggestion that the structure of price levels became more rational in some sense over time. It is conceivable that the price level estimates for the 1950s are very poor because they are extrapolated so far from the 1975 base. They do, however, match fairly well ($\bar{r}^2 = 0.73$ and the average absolute difference is only about 5 percent) the independent estimates made for that period by Gilbert and Kravis (1954) and Gilbert and Associates (1958) for the same countries, as can be seen from the comparison in Summers, Kravis, and Heston (1980, 30).

17. Since the deviations from the regressions are highly correlated with each other across periods, as is discussed later, and the same variables are used in each regression, we used Zellner's "seemingly unrelated regression" procedure to estimate the whole set of cross-sectional equations simultaneously. The results, given in appendix table 5.A1, are coefficients for per capita income and openness quite

similar to those of table 5.3. The *t*-statistics for the *r* and *STI* variables increased, and the coefficients were slightly higher as well, but both were lower for the *OPTI* variable. Many of the *OPTI* coefficients were actually negative, although not statistically significant, in the earlier periods. Since the per capita income variable is so dominant and the changes in its coefficients were not large, we did not substitute the reestimated coefficients in our analysis.

18. An alternative to the interpretation of these changes as representing shifts in the structural coefficients might be that the basic relationship is constant through time but curvilinear. In this case the higher coefficients for *r* and *OPT* in the equations for the more recent periods could be due to their being fitted to a steeper part of the function. That seems an unlikely explanation for the most important explanatory variable, real GDP per capita as a percent of the United States, since it increased only from 36 percent in 1960–68 to 42 percent in 1981–83 (see table 5.1). Of the other independent variables, the *OP* and *OPTI* measures, particularly the latter, increased substantially, while the share of tradable goods in GDP edged downward, but these variables account for only a small fraction of the estimated price level.

A preliminary test of the 1980 data for a larger sample of countries from ICP Phase IV did not suggest curvilinearity in the relationships between PL and either *r* or *OP*. Squared terms for these two variables did not have significant coefficients, and their introduction only reduced the significance of the other variables.

19. We did perform some preliminary experiments that involved adding to the equations of table 5.2 a variable for the ratio of the net current balance to GDP. The coefficients were never statistically significant and often had the wrong sign. The addition of this variable did not affect the coefficients of the other variables.

20. Only 19 countries were included in the table 5.6 regressions, because time series on GDP originating in different sectors in current and constant prices, necessary to derive implicit deflators for tradables and nontradables, were not available for the others. See notes to table 5.6. It should be added to those notes that the constant price series for the different economic sectors are in many instances subject to large margins of error and to country-to-country differences arising out of the use of different methods. We do not see any reason to believe that these incomparabilities bias the nineteen-country data in ways that invalidate our uses of them.

21. Tradables were defined as final expenditures on commodities other than construction in the benchmark year and as the output of agriculture, mining, and manufacturing in the table 5.6 equations.

22. In this case we might have to consider the possibility that our openness variable should be treated as partly endogenous. For example, an artificially sustained high exchange rate that produced a large positive deviation from the structural price level would reduce exports and perhaps force the country to cut imports as well. It might be appropriate to examine this possibility by substituting for openness itself a variable that represents the permanent determinants of openness, such as country size and population density.

23. The identification of the countries with low purged (or residual) price levels (i.e., PL − $\widehat{PL}$) or high ones is fairly robust to small changes in the specification of the structural equation, such as the use of OP or OPT instead of OPTI or the substitution of logs for arithmetic values. There is, however, the possibility that errors in the 1975 benchmark measures of PL are simply being extrapolated to other years. Some assurance that is not the case is given by a comparison of the 1980 PLs for ten industrial countries extrapolated from our 1975 benchmark with the 1980 PLs produced by a new OECD benchmark study (Hill 1985), most of the data representing comparisons carried out by the Statistical Office of the European Communities (1983). The coefficient of rank correlation was 0.78. The three countries with the lowest PLs were identical and so were the three with the highest PLs, though within neither set of three were the rankings identical and a fourth country was in a tie for the eighth rank (from low to high) in our estimates. The possibility remains, of course, that the statistical system of the country, which provides the basic data for the international comparisons, produces prices or expenditures that are biased relative to those produced by other countries. The reasonableness of the conformances of the benchmark series does not provide proof against this untoward outcome.

24. It is conceivable that the correlations are high because of nonpersistent variations in PL, but the frequent persistence of high or low deviations (table 5.8) makes this unlikely.

25. For the 19 countries in table 5.11, the coefficient of correlation between the residuals from the PL equations and those from the PLTR equations was 0.87; that between the residuals of the PL equations and the PLNT equations was 0.72. The residuals in these correlations were those obtained by averaging seven sets of residuals, one relating to each of the seven periods.

26. It would be interesting to investigate both the causes and consequences of these differing price relationships, but that must remain a matter for future research. (See, however, Kravis, Heston, and Summers 1983 and Kravis and Lipsey 1983 for the role of service prices that comprise the bulk of nontradables.)

References

Berglas, Eitan, and Assaf Razin. 1973. Real Exchange Rate and Devaluation. *Journal of International Economics* 3 (May): 179–192.

Bhagwati, Jagdish, N. 1984. Why are Services Cheaper in Poor Countries? *Economic Journal* 94 (June): 279–286.

Bushe, Dennis, Irving B. Kravis, and Robert E. Lipsey. 1986. Prices, Activity, and Machinery Exports: An Analysis Based on New Price Data. *Review of Economics and Statistics* 67 (May): 248–255.

Clague, Christopher. 1986. Determinants of the National Price Level: Some Empirical Results. *Review of Economics and Statistics* 68 (May): 320–323.

Gilbert, Milton, and Irving B. Kravis. 1954. *An International Comparison of National Products and Purchasing Power of Currencies: A Study of the U.S., the U.K., France, Germany, and Italy.* Paris: OEEC.

Gilbert, Milton, and Associates. 1958. *Comparative National Products and Price Levels.* Paris: OEEC.

Goldstein, Morris, and Mohsin S. Khan. 1985. Income and Price Effects in Foreign Trade. In Ronald W. Jones and Peter B. Kenen (eds), *Handbook of International Economics.* Amsterdam: Elsevier Science.

Hill, Peter. 1984. Real Gross Product in OECD Countries and Associated Purchasing Power Parities. OECD Economics and Statistics Department working paper no. 17.

Kravis, Irving B. 1984. Comparative Studies of National Income and Prices. *Journal of Economic Literature* 22 (March): 1–39.

Kravis, Irving B., Alan Heston, and Robert Summers. 1982. *World Product and Income: International Comparisons of Real GDP.* Baltimore: Johns Hopkins Press.

Kravis, Irving B., Alan Heston, and Robert Summers. 1983. The Share of Services in Economic Growth. In F. G. Adams and Bert Hickman (eds), *Global Econometrics: Essays in Honor of Lawrence R. Klein,* Cambridge: MIT Press.

Kravis, Irving B., Zoltan Kenessey, Alan Heston, and Robert Summers. 1975. *A System of International Comparisons of Gross Product and Purchasing Power.* Baltimore: Johns Hopkins University Press.

Kravis, Irving B., and Robert E. Lipsey. 1983. *Toward an Explanation of National Price Levels.* Princeton Studies in International Finance, no. 52.

Kravis, Irving B., and Robert E. Lipsey. 1986. The Assessment of National Price Levels. National Bureau of Economic Research working paper no. 1912.

Lipsey, Robert E. 1984. Recent Trends in U.S. Trade and Investment. In Nagasada Miyawaki (ed.), *Problems of Advanced Economies.* Proceedings of the Third Conference on Advanced Societies. Berlin and Heidelberg: Springer Verlag.

Statistical Office of the European Communities (Eurostat). 1983. *Comparison in Real Values of the Aggregates of ESA, 1980.* Luxembourg.

Statistical Office of the European Communities (Eurostat). 1985. *Comparison of Price Levels and Economic Aggregates: The Results for Fifteen African Countries, 1980.* Luxembourg.

Summers, Robert, Irving B. Kravis, and Alan Heston. 1980. International Comparisons of Real Product and its Composition: 1950–77. *The Review of Income and Wealth,* series 26, no. 1 (March): 19–66.

Young, Paula C., and Mark A. Planting. 1983. *Summary Input-Output Tables of the U.S. Economy: 1976, 1978, and 1979.* Bureau of Economic Analysis Staff Paper 39. U.S. Department of Commerce.

Zellner, Arnold. 1962. An Efficient Method of Estimating Seemingly Unrelated Regressions and Tests for Aggregation Bias. *Journal of the American Statistical Association* 57 (June): 298.

Zellner, Arnold. 1963. Estimates for Seemingly Unrelated Regression Equations: Some Exact Finite Sample Results. *Journal of the American Statistical Association* 58 (December): 304.

III

Intertemporal Sources of
Real-Financial Linkages

Introduction to Part III

This part contains three empirical studies of real-financial sector linkages, including the effects of fiscal expansion on interest rates, exchange rates and balances of payments, the consequences for trade and payments of the internationalization of the yen, and the effect of exchange rate volatility on international trade.

In chapter 6 Hutchison and Pigott examine the effects of budget policies in ten industrial countries on exchange rates, interest rates, and the balance of payments. In particular, changes in budget deficits and the means by which they are financed are studied with a view to determining the effect of the real expenditure shock on the financial sector and the effect of the financial shock implicit in deficit financing on real variables. The economy's adjustment depends on substitutability between home and foreign goods and between home and foreign assets, as well as the proportion of the expenditure that falls on domestic goods and the proportions of additional government debt or money that must be absorbed by private portfolios.

A broad review of the empirical evidence reveals two major shifts in fiscal stance, one after 1974, the other in the 1980s. For the United States, at least, the evidence shows a fiscal surplus combined with dollar depreciation, falling real interest rates, and a shrinking trade deficit in the first period, and a fiscal deficit, associated with a rising dollar, rising real interest rates and a worsening trade deficit in the second. The formal statistical analysis confirms these impressions for the United States, for the other countries as a group, and for Japan and several European countries taken individually.

In chapter 7 Hamada and Horiuchi study the internationalization of the yen, which they interpret as a monetary phenomenon, but one conditioned by real factors such as trade structure and trade openness and by financial factors such as financial market deregulation and exchange market decontrol. This suggests a wide variety of linkages and interactions, which are examined in terms of the main functions of money.

Chapter 8 by De Grauwe and de Bellefroid studies the effects of exchange rate variability on international trade, not, as has been done in past studies, by means of short-run time-series analysis, but in terms of a cross-sectional analysis of two broad periods that allows for the effect of other structural variables. The focus is on the effects of uncertainty created by sustained departures from purchasing power parity.

The authors conclude that exchange rate variability does engender some decline in trade. They estimate that GDP growth accounts for roughly 50 percent, trade integration for roughly 30 percent, and exchange rate volatility for 20 percent of the observed decline in trade.

6

Real and Financial Linkages in the Macroeconomic Response to Budget Deficits: An Empirical Investigation

Michael M. Hutchison
Charles A. Pigott

The September 1985 joint communique of the Group of Five countries expressed broad agreement that exchange rate and external balance misalignments were at least partly attributable to divergent budget policies. Controversy continues, however, both about the consequences of these policies for growth, investment, and sectoral balances, as well as the appropriate policy responses. In particular, there remains broad disagreement over whether an appropriate response is for Europe and Japan to follow a more expansionary budget policy stance, while U.S. budget policy becomes more restrictive.

This controversy reflects our limited knowledge about the way financial and real variables, such as interest and exchange rates and the trade balance, are likely to react following a policy-induced rise in domestic budget deficits. In this regard recent theoretical models of fiscal policy in open economies have identified more issues than empiricists have yet been able to resolve. There is an extensive literature on the theoretical importance of both real and financial sectors, and linkages between these sectors, in the adjustment process. Empirical evidence guiding policymakers on the relative importance of these linkages in influencing the adjustment of the economy to changes in budget policy is at present quite limited, however.

In this chapter we attempt to shed empirical light on the controversy over the effects of budget policy by examining the experiences of the major industrial countries with budget deficits since the beginning of flexible exchange rates in 1971. In particular, we investigate empirically the effects of budget deficits on real interest rates, real exchange rates, and current accounts for ten industrial countries. We begin by identifying the most important real and financial factors that in theory determine the adjustment pattern to a policy-induced rise in the domestic budget deficit (section 6.2). We argue that for a given country, the observed pattern of response of real interest rates, the real exchange rate, and the current account provides important information about which combination of the fundamental factors—real or financial—is playing a dominant role in shaping the economy's adjustment.

The theoretical discussion serves as the basis for the empirical analysis in section 6.3. There the responses of real exchange rates, real interest rates, and current accounts associated with changes in structural budget deficits and their financing are examined statistically for the ten major industrial countries. Given the approximate nature of the estimated relations, the results must be taken as highly tentative and suggestive. Nevertheless, they are consistent with the view that fiscal deficits lead to real exchange rate appreciation and current account deterioration for the United States, as well as for several other—although not all—foreign industrial economies. The conclusions we draw for policy from these findings are discussed in section 6.4.

6.1 Budget Deficits under Floating Exchange Rates

A rise in the government budget deficit represents a direct disturbance to both real and financial sectors. The financial shock arises from the debt or money creation issued to finance the deficit. The tax and expenditure policies underlying the deficits, which directly affect commodity and factor markets, constitute the real shocks. The dual, real and financial, character of deficits is central to the controversy surrounding the likely impacts of a fiscal expansion in Europe and Japan, with some arguing that it is the financing that dominates the economy's pattern of adjustment while others contend that real-sector impacts are paramount.

Real Linkages

The direct real impact of a rise in the government budget deficit is to cause an excess demand for home-produced goods relative to foreign-produced goods. This channel of transmission is emphasized in several recent models, including Dornbusch and Fischer (1984), Blanchard and Dornbusch (1984), Giovannini (1984), and Hutchison and Pigott (1985). This literature argues that the rise in domestic aggregate demand tends both to worsen the current account balance and to place upward pressure on both domestic nominal and real interest rates and the real exchange rate. The current account deterioration, as well as the increase in real interest rates, represents the economy's response to increased domestic absorption relative to current (and future) output capacity. The appreciation of the real exchange rate reflects the increase in demand for home-produced goods relative to foreign goods.[1] These patterns are similar to those implied by the traditional Mundell-Fleming model.

Several factors play a role in shaping the economy's medium-term adjustment to the direct real impact of a rise in the government budget deficit.[2] Particularly important are the mobility of international capital flows, the degree of substitutability between domestic and foreign goods, and the extent to which either the government expenditure rise or tax cut generating the budget deficit increases demand for home- relative to foreign-produced goods.

Barriers to international capital mobility tend to reduce the current account deterioration and real appreciation arising from a budget deficit increase, while magnifying the attendent rise in real interest rates. In the limiting case, where international borrowing or lending is not possible at the margin, the fiscal deficit must be entirely financed out of the excess of domestic saving over investment and the real exchange rate must be consistent with an unchanged current account balance. The real interest rate rise needed to meet the public sector's increased demand for savings will almost certainly be greater than when borrowing from abroad is possible.

A high degree of substitutability between domestic and foreign goods may limit the range of real exchange rate (and real interest rate) movements resulting from fiscal or other shocks. An appreciation of the real exchange rate represents a rise in the price of home-produced goods relative to foreign-produced goods. The greater is the substitutability in consumption between these two national outputs, therefore the less their relative price—and the less the real exchange rate—will shift in response to aggregate demand pressures. In the case of perfect goods substitutability, a rise in domestic aggregate demand associated with an increase in the budget deficit would cause the current account balance to deteriorate (by increasing domestic absorption) but would generally not have any significant persistent effect on the real exchange rate.[3] With limited goods substitutability, on the other hand, real exchange rate effects of a given fiscal stimulus are likely to be more pronounced.

The pattern of aggregate demand associated with an increased budget deficit also plays a potentially important role in the adjustment process. The greater the degree to which the rise in government expenditures or fall in taxes creates excess demand for home-produced goods relative to foreign-produced goods, the greater will be the pressure for the home currency to appreciate in real terms. This is emphasized by Buiter (1984).

For example, a government expenditure rise directed entirely toward home-produced goods would generally create greater excess demand for home output relative to abroad—and thereby put more upward pressure on the domestic real exchange rate—than would a tax cut on consumption expenditures (which directly generates additional demand for both home-produced goods and imports).

Generally, only when the rise in the budget deficit has the unlikely effect of lowering domestic demand for home output relative to abroad would the direct goods market impact of the fiscal shift tend to depreciate the real exchange rate. This could occur, for example, if a large proportion of a rise in government spending is directed toward imports and the private marginal propensity to import is very high. The imposition of trade barriers could also distort the typical adjustment pattern by restricting import availability or distorting relative prices.

Financial Linkages

Budget deficits must of course be financed—by money creation and/or issuance of interest-bearing debt ("bonds"). An ongoing deficit implies a rising stock of public obligations that directly influence domestic interest rates and exchange rates, which in turn affect the real sector. These impacts may increase over time as the debt stocks accumulate and debt-sevice payments rise. Indeed recent models incorporating a time-consistent government budget constraint suggest that these financing effects may modify, and even eventually reverse, the goods market influences of the tax and spending policies underlying the deficit (e.g., see Sachs and Wyplosz 1984; Oudiz and Sachs 1984; Branson 1985; Dornbusch and Fisher 1984).[4] Furthermore the size of these impacts also depends on the extent to which government debt is viewed as net wealth by private agents.

The exact impacts of the financing of deficits depend on a variety of factors, among the most important of which are the form of the financing (money versus bonds) and the degree of substitutability between domestic and foreign assets. When asset substitutability is imperfect, the accumulation of domestic debt to finance a deficit is apt to raise the differential between domestic interest rates (real and nominal, short-term and long-term) and the ex ante yield of their foreign counterparts, allowing for expected exchange rate changes; this differential is normally termed the exchange "risk premium" since in most models it is associated with the currency denomination of government debt.[5] The risk premium will normally be manifest in higher domestic (real) interest rates and a greater (real) currency depreciation than would otherwise occur. The depreciation itself helps to restore portfolio balance, possibly by altering the distribution of wealth between domestic and foreign investors and by lowering the share of domestic currency-denominated debt in the world portfolio (e.g., Branson et al. 1977).

The risk premium is most directly related to asset and wealth *stocks*. Thus the accumulation of government bond stocks from financing recurrent fiscal deficits is apt to put increasing upward pressure on domestic real interest rates and downward pressure on the real exchange rate. In effect, bond financing of a fiscal stimulus tends to reinforce its real interest rate impacts but offsets, at least partly, its effect on the real exchange rate. These effects from the financing will of course tend to be greater, the lower is the degree of asset substitutability, and they are likely to increase over time as the debt increases.[6]

Monetary "accommodation" of budget deficits is apt to modify substantially the adjustments to budget deficits and their financing over the short-medium term (e.g., see Branson and Buiter 1984), although perhaps not in the long run. Money increases raise liquidity in the near term and place upward pressure on domestic prices and wages. Thus money finance of deficits is likely to lead to smaller increases (possibly even declines) in real interest rates and real exchange rates than bond finance; the effect on the current account is less clear since money growth also stimulates domestic spending. Furthermore, as money stocks grow and prices increase, the nominal exchange rate is very likely to depreciate even if the real exchange rate rises.

Real and Financial Interactions

As the preceding discussion illustrates, the tax/spending impacts associated with a deficit are not confined to goods markets, any more than the financing affects financial markets only. Effects that begin in one sector inevitably propagate to others. Indeed, the linkages between the real sector and the financial sector play a central role in the economy's adjustment to a policy-induced rise in the government budget deficit. In particular, the real goods and factor market impacts on the economy arising from government expenditure and tax policies are dependent on financial factors associated with government debt financing, and vice versa.

The terms on which the government can finance additional debt issues, for example, is determined by the degree of capital mobility and asset substitutability and the size of the economy relative to the rest of the world (i.e., a large country might influence the world interest rate, thereby increasing domestic interest rates with new debt issues regardless of whether an exchange risk premium exists or not). Debt financing, although impacting financial markets directly, influences interest rates and thereby the pattern of fiscal "crowding out" in the real sector (i.e., the extent to which crowding out is felt in domestic interest-sensitive sectors—investment and consumption—as opposed to export- and import-competing—tradable—goods sectors).

As indicated earlier, the lower the degree of capital mobility and/or asset substitutability, the greater will be the rise in domestic interest rates associated with a bond-financed fiscal expansion. With a large risk premium the rise in aggregate demand for home-produced goods relative to foreign goods (associated with either the rise in government expenditures or the fall in taxes) is partly offset by the fall in domestic interest-sensitive expenditures. Consequently total absorption rises less than in the case of no risk premium. The net result is that the real exchange rate will appreciate less (there will be less excess demand for home output relative to foreign output) and the current account will fall less than would otherwise have been the case.

Real factors may also exert an important influence on adjustments in the financial sector. For example, consider the degree to which the rise in aggregate demand generated by a fiscal expansion falls on home output relative to foreign output. The greater the stimulus to home output, the greater the likely upward pressures on domestic real interest rates and the real exchange rate. A fiscal expansion could conceivably, however, entail the opposite—that is, policies that shift demand away from home goods and toward foreign goods. In this instance foreign interest rates conceivably could rise (absolutely and relative to domestic rates) and the domestic real exchange rate could depreciate (to absorb excess supply of home output). This in turn would tend to stimulate—rather than "crowd out"— the export sector. Such an outcome would have qualitatively different wealth and portfolio impacts and risk premium implications from the more "normal" case where fiscal stimulus falls mainly on home output.

Moreover the way expectations are formed can play an important role in the paths real and financial variables follow in their adjustments to long-run values. The more forward-looking are expectations and accurate in their assessment of long-run outcomes (i.e. "rational"), the more rapid are adjustments likely to be in both financial and real sectors. Furthermore, because financial market prices are generally more flexible than those in goods and factor markets, forward-looking expectations are much more likely to lead to overshooting of interest and exchange rates than when expectations are backward-looking (e.g., "adaptive").

6.2   Empirical Analysis

As our theoretical discussion suggests, the potential range of effects of budget deficits on real and financial variables is wide but not unlimited. Normally the direct goods market impact of an increase in spending relative to taxes will raise the demand for home output, tending to push up real interest rates and the real exchange rate and depress the current account surplus. The financing of the deficit may alter these effects, however. In particular, a deficit is most likely to lead to real depreciation over the medium-term primarily under two circumstances: when debt financing significantly raises exchange risk premia, or when the deficit is substantially accommodated by money growth. Thus accurate assessment of the real and financial impacts of budget deficits entails a clear distinction between their direct goods market and their financing dimensions.

Data Trends

Table 6.1 lists two (OECD staff) measures of public sector structural (full employment) budget surpluses as a share of GNP for the major industrial countries, one with and one without adjustment for the inflation component of interest payments on (net) public sector debt. The data suggest several major shifts in fiscal stances, the most pronounced coming after the first oil shock in 1974. Prior to 1974, the U.S. structural budget surplus (share of GNP) rose moderately relative to abroad. This trend accelerated over the 1976 to 1979 recovery, as Germany, Japan, and other foreign industrial nations incurred sharply increased budget deficits in attempting to stimulate their economies. The 1980s brought a dramatic reversal of this pattern, however, as the U.S. budget moved sharply into deficit while deficits in several major foreign nations fell considerably from their 1979 to 1980 peaks. Over the period as a whole the U.S. budget deficit reached its lowest level relative to abroad in 1979, and is presently at its highest level since the mid-1970s.[7]

Shifts in fiscal stance over the past decade, together with movements in other real and financial variables over the same period, lend some support to the hypothesis that budget deficits lead to real exchange rate appreciation and current account deterioration, at least for the U.S. (tables 6.2 and 6.3). The real value of the dollar reached a period low in 1979 to 1980, and

Table 6.1
Alternative structural budget measures

	Unadjusted surplus					Inflation-adjusted surplus				
	United States	West Germany	Japan	United Kingdom	World[a]	United States	West Germany	Japan	United Kingdom	World[a]
1971	-0.5	-0.2	1.7	1.6	0.0	0.6	-0.6	1.3	7.4	0.9
1972	0.0	0.0	0.6	-0.8	-0.3	0.8	-0.4	0.3	3.3	0.4
1973	-0.2	1.3	0.3	-3.6	-0.4	1.2	0.8	-0.5	1.4	0.6
1974	0.7	-0.5	0.7	-3.7	-0.2	2.9	-0.9	-0.6	3.9	1.5
1975	-0.9	-3.4	-1.9	-3.2	-1.9	1.0	-3.6	-2.3	7.6	0.0
1976	0.4	-2.2	-2.9	-3.4	-1.3	1.6	-2.1	-2.8	4.6	0.3
1977	0.6	-1.3	-3.1	-1.7	-1.0	1.9	-1.1	-2.8	5.9	0.6
1978	0.9	-1.7	-4.9	-3.8	-1.7	2.3	-1.5	-4.5	0.2	-0.4
1979	1.2	-2.3	-4.3	-3.2	-1.5	3.1	-1.9	-3.5	2.9	0.4
1980	0.7	-2.5	-4.1	-1.1	-1.9	2.8	-1.9	-2.5	5.3	1.0
1981	1.6	-2.4	-3.5	1.8	-1.0	3.2	-1.7	-2.3	5.7	0.9
1982	0.3	-0.9	-2.8	3.3	-1.1	1.7	-0.5	-2.3	5.9	0.4
1983	-0.2	0.5	-2.2	1.6	-1.0	0.7	0.6	-1.9	3.3	0.1
1984	-0.5	1.7	-1.3	2.0	-0.8	0.0	1.0	-1.2	2.9	0.0

Source: OECD staff measures of the *structural* public sector surplus as percentage of potential GNP.
Note: The "inflation-adjusted" structural surplus is the unadjusted surplus less the inflation-premium component of interest paid on public sector debt.
a. Refers to the (1978 GNP-weighted) average of ten major OECD nations.

Table 6.2
Long-term real interest rate proxies and real exchange rates

	Real interest rates[a]				Real exchange rates[b]			
	United States	West Germany	Japan	United Kingdom	United States	West Germany	Japan	United Kingdom
1971	0.9	0.3	1.0	0.5	146	90	116	75
1972	1.4	1.3	1.5	0.0	131	90	124	76
1973	2.1	3.3	−1.3	3.0	113	99	136	68
1974	0.7	3.7	−7.0	3.7	111	100	137	65
1975	−0.8	2.0	−5.0	−6.7	112	95	116	70
1976	0.6	3.0	1.6	−6.6	117	96	117	64
1977	2.1	2.6	1.2	−1.6	116	100	120	67
1978	1.8	1.8	0.9	0.0	105	104	138	73
1979	1.3	3.2	4.0	0.2	100	105	116	81
1980	2.4	4.2	6.4	−3.3	100	100	100	100
1981	4.3	6.0	5.8	−1.0	116	90	110	103
1982	5.0	4.5	5.8	3.3	122	94	98	100
1983	6.4	3.9	6.2	4.5	126	96	102	92
1984	8.6	5.2	5.4	5.9	136	92	104	90

Source: IMF.
a. The long-term real interest rate is a rough proxy measured by the nominal long-term government bond rate less average of past two year's (GNP deflator) inflation rate.
b. Trade-weighted average of bilateral exchange rates, adjusted for relative manufacturing value-added deflators.

Table 6.3
Current account surpluses (percent of GNP)

	United States	West Germany	Japan	United Kingdom
1970	0.2	0.5	1.0	1.6
1971	−0.1	0.4	2.5	1.9
1972	−0.5	−0.3	2.2	0.4
1973	0.5	1.4	−0.0	−1.4
1974	0.1	2.7	−1.0	−3.9
1975	1.2	1.0	−0.1	−1.5
1976	0.2	0.9	0.7	−0.7
1977	−0.7	0.8	1.6	0.0
1978	−0.7	1.4	1.8	0.7
1979	−0.0	−0.8	−0.9	−0.2
1980	0.1	−2.0	−1.0	1.6
1981	0.2	−0.8	0.4	2.8
1982	−0.3	0.5	0.6	1.7
1983	−1.2	0.6	1.8	1.1
1984	−2.8	1.0	2.8	0.1

a high in 1984, while the reverse was the case for Germany. Relative to abroad, U.S. long-term real interest rates were also quite low during the 1970s but climbed appreciably after 1980. Similarly, the U.S. current account deficit fell during the 1970s, while those abroad generally rose; during the 1980s, the U.S. external deficit has grown to its highest level in history, while current account balances abroad have moved into large surplus positions.

This evidence is suggestive, but neither conclusive nor comprehensive, partly because other factors influenced these patterns as well. Expansionary U.S. monetary policy over 1976 to 1979, leading to an acceleration in U.S. inflation relative to abroad, likely played a substantial role in the dollar's decline in both real and nominal terms over this period; conversely, the sharp tightening of U.S. monetary policy beginning in 1980 was presumably a major factor in the dollar's rise during 1980 to 1982 (table 6.4).

Furthermore the relations among fiscal deficits, exchange rates, real interest rates, and the current account are less clear-cut for several other countries. The average real value of the German mark during 1971 to 1973 was nearly the same as during 1982 to 1984, even though Germany's budget surplus relative to abroad was significantly higher in the later period. Moreover Japan's current account surplus rose sharply over 1976 to 1978, despite a significant rise in its structural budget deficit relative to abroad.

The influence of the stocks of net public sector debt associated with changing fiscal deficits is also somewhat ambiguous. As shown in table 6.5,

Table 6.4
Money growth rates (year/year percentage growth)

	United States	United Kingdom	West Germany	Japan
1971	6.6	15.1	12.7	24.7
1972	9.3	14.2	14.1	24.7
1973	5.2	5.1	1.7	16.8
1974	4.3	10.8	10.7	11.5
1975	4.9	18.6	14.3	11.2
1976	6.7	11.3	3.3	12.5
1977	8.0	20.8	12.0	8.2
1978	8.3	16.3	14.6	13.4
1979	6.7	9.1	2.9	3.0
1980	6.9	4.0	4.0	−2.0
1981	6.4	17.7	−1.6	10.0
1982	8.8	11.3	7.1	5.7
1983	9.4	11.2	8.4	−0.1
1984	5.7	15.4	6.0	6.9

Note: Refers to "narrow" money, generally M1 or its equivalent.

Table 6.5
Net public sector debt (percent of GNP)

	United States	West Germany	Japan	United Kingdom	World[a]
1970	28.4	−8.2	−6.6	75.3	18.2
1971	28.4	−7.1	−7.3	70.6	18.0
1972	26.3	−5.8	−6.5	65.8	17.2
1973	23.5	−6.7	−6.1	58.5	15.4
1974	22.9	−4.7	−5.4	55.5	15.1
1975	25.6	1.0	−2.1	57.3	18.5
1976	25.6	4.6	1.9	56.7	19.7
1977	24.7	7.0	5.4	55.7	20.3
1978	22.5	9.4	11.3	53.4	21.2
1979	20.5	11.5	15.0	48.6	21.2
1980	20.4	14.3	17.5	48.3	21.8
1981	19.7	17.4	21.0	47.6	23.2
1982	22.8	19.8	23.5	46.6	26.0
1983	25.4	21.8	26.3	47.2	29.2
1984	26.8	23.0	27.4	49.2	31.3

Source: OECD.
Note: Debt of public sector excluding that held by other public entities.
a. See note to table 6.1.

the ratio of U.S. net public sector debt to GNP declined steadily from 1971 to 1981, and then rose sharply. However, because foreign debt-to-GNP ratios have climbed steadily since the early 1970s, U.S. debt relative to abroad in 1984 was significantly lower than in 1971. Despite this trend U.S. real interest rates generally increased during this period, both absolutely and relative to abroad. Thus the movement in relative debt levels does not suggest that the financing of the deficits has dominated their impact on exchange rates, interest rates, or the current account. Conceivably, however, the general rise in the public sector debt-GNP ratio in the industrial economies may help explain why the average level of real interest rates has been considerably higher in the 1980s than the previous decade. (In any case the general rise in real interest rates during the 1980s is not easily explained by trends in budget deficits; indeed, the average budget deficit/GNP ratio for the industrial countries was nearly as high during the late 1970s as in 1984.)

Statistical Analysis

We now turn to a more systematic statistical analysis of the relation between budget deficits and their financing and three key financial and real variables—the real exchange rate, a proxy for the long-term real interest rate, and the current account—for ten major industrial countries over the 1971 to 1984 period of flexible exchange rates. One objective is to distinguish empirically between the effects associated with the shift in expenditure relative to taxes underlying a deficit (the "fiscal thrust") from those of its financing. Does the financing dominate the overall effect of a deficit, and how different are the impacts associated with bond versus money financing? Another objective is to see if foreigners' deficits have a qualitatively different impact on their real exchange rates and current accounts than U.S. deficits seem to have on the dollar and our current account. Our hope is that in examining several relations, consistent patterns—ones that are at least suggestive about the underlying structural linkages—will emerge.

The estimated equations are

E1: $\quad RLRF(j, t) = a1(j) + b1(j)BSRF(j, t) + c1(j)DRF(j, t)$

$$+ \; d1(j)MF(j, t) + U1(j, t),$$

E2: $\quad RXR(j, t) = a2(j) + b2(j)BSRF(j, t) + c2(j)DRF(j, t)$

$$+ \; d2(j)MF(j, t) + e2(j)PO(t) + U2(j, t),$$

$$E3: \quad CA(j,t) \ = a3(j) + b3(j)BSRF(j,t) + c3(j)DRF(j,t)$$

$$+ \ d3(j)MF(j,t) + e3(j)YGAP(j,t) + U3(j,t),$$

where (also see the data appendix)

$RLRF =$ proxy for real long-term government bond rate (domestic nominal rate less average of past two years of domestic inflation) *less* that of abroad,

$RXR \ =$ real exchange rate index (using value-added deflators),

$CA \ =$ current account surplus as share of GNP,

$BSRF =$ structural budget surplus as percent of GNP, *less* that of abroad,

$DRF \ =$ net public sector debt as percent of GNP, *less* that of abroad,

$MF \ =$ acceleration in (M1) growth, expressed as the difference between the current and the past two year's average growth, and *less* that of abroad,

$PO \ =$ relative price of oil, expressed as index of dollar oil price deflated by U.S. CPI,

$YGAP =$ a proxy for the deviation of actual from potential output, calculated as the difference between the actual and structural budget deficit/GNP ratios,

$U \ =$ a random disturbance term, assumed uncorrelated across time but correlated across countries.

The structural or full employment budget surplus contained (in relative form) in *BSRF* is essentially a measure of "fiscal thrust," that is, of spending relative to taxes. The financing of deficits is represented by the *stock* of government bonds held by the public (*DRF*) and by the relative money growth proxy (*MF*). We also attempt to "control" for other potentially important influences, by including the relative price of oil in the real exchange rate equation and a proxy for the influence of cyclical fluctuations on trade flows in the current account relation.[8]

The equations were estimated for the ten major industrial countries over the 1971 to 1984 period. Because of the difficulties of capturing dynamic relations among the variables, annual data was used. The "seemingly unrelated regressions" procedure (SUR) was used for the estimation since there are strong reasons to suspect that errors in the real exchange rate, real interest rate, and current account equations may be closely related across countries.[9] If so, the SUR procedures could significantly increase the efficiency of the estimates, particularly given the limited data.

The estimated relations are best regarded as measuring the historical association between the "endogenous" (left-hand-side) and the budget variables over the medium term. They are at least consistent with relations implied by recent two-country versions of a (revised) Mundell-Fleming framework (e.g., Oudiz and Sachs 1984; Weiller 1985) and will hopefully provide some indication, if indirect, of the underlying structure. The approach necessarily involves several approximations. Expressing the variables relative to their foreign counterparts (calculated as a 1978-GNP weighted average across all foreign countries *except* the focus) is not perfectly general, but perhaps reasonable given the data limitations. Similarly, without direct measures on long-term inflation expectations, we must rely on a very rough proxy for the long-term real interest rate.

Possibly more restrictive is the combining of expenditures and taxes into a single measure of fiscal stimulus. In principle, increases in government spending on goods and services and reductions in taxes may have different impacts, although simulations of several large econometric models suggest that the differences are often fairly modest; if so, combining the two may not be an unreasonable approximation.[10]

There are also reasons for doubting that increases in interest payments on public debt that effectively "compensate" for inflation have nearly the same impact as equal increases in goods/services spending on tax reductions.[11] For this reason we consider results using two budget measures, one including the inflation portion of interest payments (the unadjusted surplus) and the second excluding that portion (the adjusted surplus); we generally take the latter as providing the more reliable basis for conclusions.

Pooled Estimates

Tables 6.6 and 6.7 present estimates of the three equations for the U.S. and "pooled" results for the other nine countries in the sample. These estimates are derived using SUR on the group of ten countries (for each equation) with each of the deficit, debt, and money coefficients constrained to be equal across the nine countries in the "abroad" category. (Coefficients of the PO and YGAP variables are allowed to vary across the foreign countries, as are the intercepts.) The results are qualitatively very similar using either the inflation-adjusted or unadjusted structural budget surplus measure, although, for the reason given earlier, we focus our attention on the former (table 6.6).

The results in table 6.6 suggest that, ceteris paribus, an increase in government spending relative to revenue is highly associated with both

Table 6.6
U.S. and pooled foreign results: inflation-adjusted deficits

Equation[a]	Independent variables			R^2	MSE
	Budget surplus	Debt	Money		
1. Relative real interest rate					
United States	−0.20[b]	−0.05[b]	−0.01[c]	0.96	3.51
Abroad	−0.40[b]	−0.30[b]	−0.01[d]		
2. Real exchange rate[e]					
United States	−5.21[b]	−0.03[f]	−0.70[b]	0.72	9.44
Abroad	−1.17[b]	−0.23[b]	−0.04[f]		
3. Current account surplus[e]					
United States	0.39[b]	0.15[b]	0.01[c]	0.58	3.11
Abroad	0.28[b]	0.01[c]	0.03[b]		

Note: Inflation adjusted deficits refer to the structural general government deficit to GNP ratio, excluding that part of public debt service payments reflecting the erosion of purchasing power due to inflation.
a. Estimates are derived using a seemingly unrelated regression procedure (SUR) on the group of ten countries with budget surplus, debt, and money variables constrained to be equal across the nine countries in "abroad".
b. t-statistic is not less than 2.0 in absolute value.
c. t-statistic is less than 1.0 in absolute value.
d. t-statistic is between 1.0 and 1.5 in absolute value.
e. Coefficients of the relative price of oil in the real exchange rate equations, and of the income gap ("cycle") variable in the current account equation were allowed to vary across the foreign countries. Space prevents listing them here, but they will be provided on request.
f. t-statistic is between 1.5 and 2.0 in absolute value.

Table 6.7
U.S. and pooled foreign results with unadjusted deficits

Equation[a]	Independent variables			R^2	MSE
	Budget surplus	Debt	Money		
1. Relative real interest rate					
United States	−0.040[b]	−0.018[b]	−0.014[d]	0.95	5.11
Abroad	−0.268[b]	−0.019[b]	0.00[c]		
2. Real exchange rate[e]					
United States	−4.12[b]	−2.77[b]	−1.18[b]	0.82	12.39
Abroad	0.15[d]	−0.33[b]	−0.0[c]		
3. Current account surplus[e]					
United States	0.76[b]	0.21[b]	0.01[c]	0.66	2.53
Abroad	0.39[b]	0.03[f]	0.04[b]		

Note: See notes in table 6.6. The unadjusted deficit is the structural balance including all (net) interest payments on government debt.

rising long-term real interest rates (relative to those abroad) and appreciating real exchange rates. The estimated coefficients are generally significant at the 5 percent level of confidence. Increases in the stock of government debt, on the other hand, are associated with real exchange rate depreciation and current account surpluses. Debt is also negatively associated with real interest rates. Quantatively, a bond-financed 1 percent rise in the ratio of the U.S. budget deficit to GNP is associated with a roughly 5 percent real dollar appreciation, and a current account deficit increase of about 0.25 percent of GNP, after the first year (i.e., allowing for the first year's debt accumulation).[12] If the deficit is maintained, further rises in the debt stock are associated with a decline in the real exchange rate (of about 0.3 percent per year) and in the external deficit (of about 0.15 percent of GNP per year). The impacts for the foreign group of countries are qualitatively the same as for the United States but generally smaller in magnitude and statistical significance.

The estimates also suggest that *complete* financing of a deficit increase by money growth could at least partly offset the direct impact on the real value of the dollar. A rise in the monetary base to finance a 1 percent increase in the ratio of debt to GNP would imply an acceleration of money growth of nearly 8 to 10 percent in the first year; multiplied by its coefficient in the estimated relation, this impact actually exceeds the direct effect of the deficit.

While these results provide an indication of the "average" associations abroad, other studies suggest considerable diversity in responses to deficits among foreign countries (e.g., Hutchison and Pigott 1985; Weiller 1985; Amano 1985). If so, constraining the coefficients to be the same for all these nations (as in tables 6.6 and 6.7) is inappropriate; indeed, these restrictions are strongly rejected statistically in the subsequent analysis. Results allowing all the parameters to differ among the countries (except for the three small European countries) are given in tables 6.8 and 6.9, where we again focus on the estimates using the adjusted budget measure (table 6.8).[13]

Unconstrained Estimates

The results suggest substantial differences in the association between budget deficits and real exchange rates across countries, although the pattern for several foreign nations is fairly similar to that for the United States. The budget measure itself usually has a statistically significant coefficient of the expected sign in the interest rate and current account relations (i.e., negative and positive respectively) but varies in sign across countries in the

Table 6.8
Unconstrained estimates with inflation-adjusted budget surpluses

	(Relative) real interest rate			Real exchange rate				Current account surplus			
	Budget surplus	Debt	Money	Budget surplus	Debt	Money	Oil price	Budget surplus	Debt	Money	Cycle
United States	−0.34[a]	−0.07[a]	−0.06[b]	−8.09[a]	0.15[d]	−0.45[b]	0.04[c]	0.36[a]	0.11[a]	0.05[b]	−0.35[a]
Canada	0.11[d]	0.29[a]	−0.04[d]	2.25[b]	0.88[a]	−0.29[a]	0.04[c]	0.87[a]	0.20[a]	0.03[b]	−0.42[a]
Japan	−0.51[c]	0.15[a]	−0.06[d]	−11.90[a]	0.85[a]	−0.00[d]	−0.38[a]	0.30[a]	−0.02[d]	0.06[a]	−1.38[a]
Germany	−0.98[a]	−0.05[a]	−0.06[a]	0.46[d]	0.86[a]	0.00[d]	−0.06[b]	0.11[d]	−0.07[b]	0.04[d]	−0.10[d]
United Kingdom	−0.94[a]	0.14[a]	0.12[c]	2.93[a]	0.60[a]	−1.00[a]	0.19[a]	0.19[c]	0.04[d]	−0.07[d]	−0.51[b]
France	0.09[d]	0.29[a]	0.07[c]	1.08[b]	1.02[a]	−0.52[a]	0.05[a]	0.37[d]	0.02[d]	−0.10[b]	0.47[b]
Italy	−0.39[a]	−0.03[b]	0.02[c]	−1.03[a]	0.13[c]	−0.32[a]	0.04[a]	−0.10[d]	−0.08[a]	0.08[a]	−0.68[c]
"Small European"	−0.24[a]	−0.06[a]	0.08[a]	−1.66[a]	−0.72[a]	0.31[a]	[e]	0.60[a]	0.08[a]	0.08[b]	[f]
	$R^2 = 0.98$			$R^2 = 0.88$				$R^2 = 0.82$			
	MSE = 2.16			MSE = 4.67				MSE = 1.49			
	DF = 106			DF = 96				DF = 96			

a. t-statistic is no less than 2 in absolute value.
b. t-statistic is between 1.5 and 2.0 in absolute value.
c. t-statistic is between 1.0 and 1.5 in absolute value.
d. t-statistic is less than 1.0 in absolute value.
e. Coefficient for Belgium, Sweden, and Norway are −1.81[b], +0.83[d], and −9.32[a].
f. Coefficients for Belgium, Sweden, and Norway are 0.68[a], 0.60[a], and 1.29[b].

Table 6.9
Unconstrained estimates with unadjusted budget surpluses

	(Relative) real interest rate			Real exchange rate				Current account surplus			
	Budget surplus	Debt	Money	Budget surplus	Debt	Money	Oil price	Budget surplus	Debt	Money	Cycle
United States	-0.56[a]	-0.09[a]	-0.04[a]	-4.86	-0.58[a]	-1.33[a]	-0.03[d]	0.38[a]	0.12[a]	0.02[d]	-0.25[b]
Canada	-0.04[d]	-0.39[a]	-0.06[a]	-0.58[d]	-0.23[d]	-0.17[b]	-0.02[d]	0.82[a]	0.33[a]	0.02[d]	-0.28[a]
Japan	-1.14[a]	0.09[c]	-0.21[a]	-7.87[a]	-0.91[a]	-0.41[a]	-0.12[a]	-0.09[d]	-0.07[a]	0.06[a]	-1.34[a]
Germany	-1.19[a]	-0.09[a]	-0.00[d]	1.76[a]	-0.23[d]	0.00[d]	0.04[c]	0.31[b]	-0.05[c]	0.06[b]	-0.05[d]
United Kingdom	0.31[c]	0.14[a]	-0.16[a]	5.70[a]	0.06[d]	-1.57[a]	0.08[c]	0.78[a]	-0.04[d]	-0.04[d]	0.42[d]
France	0.12[d]	0.19[a]	0.20[a]	-0.98[c]	0.25[d]	-1.16[a]	0.02[c]	0.29[d]	0.06[d]	-0.09[c]	0.41[c]
Italy	-0.40[a]	-0.01[d]	0.05[a]	-0.28[c]	0.28[a]	-0.17[a]	0.02[d]	0.46[c]	-0.12[c]	0.08[c]	-0.55[d]
"Small European"	-0.44[a]	-0.09[a]	0.08[a]	-0.42[a]	-0.71[a]	0.00[d]	[e]	0.74[a]	0.13[a]	0.12[a]	[f]
	$R^2 = 0.97$			$R^2 = 0.96$				$R^2 = 0.85$			
	MSE = 3.44			MSE = 2.95				MSE = 1.28			
	DF = 100			DF = 96				DF = 96			

a. t-statistic is no less than 2 in absolute value.
b. t-statistic is between 1.5 and 2.0 in absolute value.
c. t-statistic is between 1.0 and 1.5 in absolute value.
d. t-statistic is less than 1.0 in absolute value.
e. Coefficient for Belgium, Sweden, and Norway are -0.93[d], 4.88[a], and 9.66[a].
f. Coefficients for Belgium, Sweden, and Norway are 0.71[a], 0.49[a], and 1.08[a].

exchange rate equations. The bond-debt measure is generally (and significantly) associated with real depreciation, although it has the "wrong" sign in several of the real interest rate relations. On the whole, money growth has the expected (negative) effect in the exchange rate and (less often) interest rate relations.

On the whole, the results for the United States, as well as Japan and several European countries, suggest that increased fiscal deficits, including their financing impacts, are associated with higher domestic real interest rates, real exchange rate appreciation, and current account deterioration. The impact of the (bond) debt associated with a deficit, even where statistically significant, is dominated (at least for the first several years) by that of the stimulus to goods markets from the rise in spending relative to taxes. In contrast, deficits do seem to be associated with real depreciation for the major European countries, notably Germany, France, and the United Kingdom. Even in these cases, however, fiscal deficits are generally associated with current account deterioration and relatively higher real interest rates.

U.S. results most closely accord with the standard case outlined in our theoretical discussion, as well as the findings of prior studies (e.g., Hutchison and Pigott 1984, 1985). As expected, a rise in the U.S. structural budget deficit tends to raise real long-term interest rates (by about 35 to 55 basis points for a 1 percent increase in the deficit/GNP ratio). (The debt variable has the "wrong" sign in the U.S. interest rate relation, but its effect is overwhelmed by the goods market influence of the deficit.) The exchange rate impacts are equally unambiguous. U.S. debt appears to play a very limited role, so that the goods-market impact dominates: according to the table 6.8 results, the real exchange rate appreciates 8.1 percent for each one percentage point increase in the deficit/GNP ratio. Increased fiscal deficits also appear to raise the current account deficit, the direct goods-market impact again dominating the debt influence. Moreover, although these results suggest that the bond financing element of a U.S. fiscal stimulus play a role, it may still be important. In particular, the current account relation suggests that risk factors associated with U.S. debt are potentially significant.

More surprising is that the impacts associated with fiscal deficits in Japan, the small European countries, and Italy are fairly similar to those found for the United States. Increased budget deficits are associated with higher real interest rates and real exchange rate appreciation in all three cases. As with the United States, the stimulus from a deficit typically dominates its financing (whose effect appears generally insignificant for Italy and significant for Japan). In Japan, for example, a 1 percent rise in the deficit/GNP ratio that is debt financed leads to approximately 7 to 11 percent real exchange rate appreciation in the first year. Moreover in both Japan and the small European country group a fiscal stimulus leads to a current account decline. (The current account impacts of the budget surplus and debt are insignificant for Italy, however.) The results for these countries are of particular note since they differ significantly from earlier analyses (e.g., Amano 1985) suggesting that foreign countries generally differ sharply from the United States in their reactions to fiscal policies.

The results for the three major European countries (Germany, the United Kingdom, and France), as well as for Canada, are consistent with these earlier analyses, however. In particular, budget deficits appear to lead to real exchange rate depreciation for these countries. Note however that budget deficits do continue to be (generally) associated with higher real interest rates and current account declines, as in the U.S. case. Furthermore the fiscal stimulus, rather than the financing, remain the determining factor in the real exchange and interest rate equations, with debt playing a relatively minor role. This pattern is difficult to interpret since it suggests that the tax and spending policies underlying a deficit shift demand away from home output, (e.g., a disproportionate share of government spending is directed toward imports), that is, fiscal expansion has a net *contractionary* effect on the economy. In any case the fact that fiscal deficits generally are associated with current account deterioration even in these cases may be more significant from a policy perspective than their apparent association with real depreciation.[14] Note that this evidence is consistent with a number of recent empirical studies, such as Knight and Mason (1985) and van Wijnbergen (1985).

Conclusions and Policy Implications

A major objective of this chapter is to provide evidence on two questions now the source of much controversy: Will a fall in the U.S. budget deficit, and/or a rise in deficits abroad, lead to a further real decline in the dollar versus other currencies? And will such a fiscal "realignment" also lower the external imbalances of the United States and its foreign trading partners?

Fiscal deficits have several distinct dimensions that need to be recognized in conceptual and empirical analyses. A rise in government spending relative to taxes normally raises aggregate demand and increases domestic real interest rates. This induces real exchange rate appreciation and a current account deterioration. But the financing of the deficit, and the form it takes, will generally modify these effects and may even reverse them. In particular, real depreciation is most likely to result from a deficit (over the medium term) if the rising debt stock to finance it requires a fairly large increase in the expected yield on domestic versus foreign assets. In this case the financing may dominate the direct effects of the goods market stimulus from the deficit. Moreover the various impacts of budget deficits and their financing may vary significantly among countries, depending on the degree of substitutability of home goods and assets for their foreign counterparts and other factors.

The empirical analysis has sought to examine historical associations between budget deficits and their financing and the real interest rate, the real exchange rate and current account. These patterns should provide a rough indication of underlying structural linkages. Our approach is subject to clear limitations in both data and approximations in specification. Partly to compensate, we have departed from most recent studies by examining the relations between budget deficits and several real and financial variables to see if a consistent pattern emerges. Furthermore, the estimates have been derived in an explicitly multicountry context, and with very few prior restrictions placed on the parameters. By comparing and examining patterns of adjustment to budget deficits of several real and financial variables, the approach taken here adds significantly to evidence from earlier studies that have focused exclusively on linkages between fiscal policy and real interest rates (e.g., Hutchison and Pyle 1984; Muller and Price 1984), or the real exchange rate (e.g., Weiller 1985).

Our results are consistent with "conventional wisdom" and prior studies in certain respects but depart in others. For the United States, budget deficit increases seem fairly clearly associated with real appreciation, current account deterioration, *and* real interest rate increases—the latter in contrast to findings of several earlier studies of the U.S. experience (U.S. Treasury 1984; Evans 1985). However, our results are consistent with more indirect evidence derived from the macroeconomic model simulations reported in other studies (Knight and Mason 1985; McKibbin and Sachs 1985; van Wijnbergen 1985). Essentially the same pattern also seems to apply to Japan and several European countries, including Italy, suggesting that there may be no general tendency for foreign deficits' impacts to be qualitatively different from those found for the United States. As for the United States, it is the fiscal stimulus from a deficit that seems to largely dominate the outcome for these countries.

What implications then can be drawn from these findings for the present debate over fiscal policy between the United States and its major economic partners? Reducing the U.S. fiscal deficit would likely improve the U.S. current account imbalance and further lower the value of the dollar. Furthermore fiscal expansion by Japan would likely put additional upward pressure on the yen. The fiscal realignment and resulting yen appreciation could also significantly lower Japan's trade surplus. In Europe, however, there *may* be merit to policymakers' concerns that a fiscal expansion could lead to modest real exchange depreciation, with relatively little shift in current account positions.

Finally, it is worth noting that even if budget deficits do lead to exchange depreciation in major European countries, the reason does not appear to be the one most often advanced, namely, that the financing of the deficit dominates the outcome by substantially increasing international risk premia on these nations' assets. Our results suggest that debt is not the major influence on the real and financial variables examined here, even for Europe. Furthermore it seems implausible that risk premia would be much less important for Japan, whose currency is less widely used than the mark, or the smaller European nations, than for Germany or the United Kingdom. Nevertheless, the evidence indicates that budget deficits do lead to real exchange rate appreciation for Japan and the small European countries. These results, admitting their tentative character, suggest that the diversity of fiscal policy impacts across countries may derive primarily from factors other than those of pure portfolio balance.

6.4   Appendix: Data Sources and Variable Definitions

RLRF   Real long-term government bond rate relative to foreign.

The nominal long-term government bond rate is drawn from the *International Financial Statistics* (IFS) of the IMF, line 61. The two-year moving average of the rate of change of the GNP deflator, also drawn from IFS, is subtracted to arrive at the real rate. The real rate relative to foreign is the difference between the country's real rate and a weighted average of the remaining countries' real rates.

BSRF/BIRF   Budget surplus of general government as percentage of GNP less that of the rest of the world.

BSRF refers to the structural budget surplus; *BIRF* to the structural budget surplus adjusted for the inflation component of net interest payments by general government. The data are from Price and Muller (1984) and have been updated from the OECD *Economic Outlook*, no. 38 (December 1985). The rest-of-world budget surplus is a weighted average of the remaining countries' budget surpluses.

---

*This appendix was prepared by Allan Malz.

Unadjusted structural budget surpluses measured both at midcycle and at the cycle peak are presented by Price and Muller. The two meausres differ by a constant for each country. Inflation-adjusted structural budget surpluses presented the Price and Muller are measured only at midcycle. The constant difference between peak- and midcycle measures of the unadjusted surplus has been added to the adjusted surplus in order to arrive at peak-cycle measures of both.

DRF   Net debt of general government as a percentage of GNP less that of rest of world.

     The data are from Price and Muller (1984). The rest-of-world debt is a weighted average of the remaining countries' net debts.

MRF   Acceleration in M1 growth.

     The narrow-definition money supply data are from IFS, line 34. A two-year moving average of the rate of change of M1 was calculated. The difference between the current value and the average of the past two years' values of this moving average yields a measure of the acceleration in a country's M1 growth. It is set in relation to rest-of-world acceleration by subtracting from it a weighted average of the remaining countries' M1 acceleration measures.

PO   Relative price of oil.

     The dollar price of Saudi Arabian oil is drawn from the IFS *Yearbook* (line 76aa of the Commodity Prices table). The variable is defined as the log of 100 times the dollar oil price divided by the U.S. GNP deflator.

YGAP   Deviation of actual from potential output.

     YGAP is a proxy for this variable, defined as the difference between actual and structural budget surpluses. The actual budget surpluses, like the structural, are drawn from Price and Muller (1984).

RXR   Real exchange rate index.

     This variable is the log of the relative value-added deflator (base year 1980) and is drawn from IFS *Yearbook* (line 99 by 110 of the Cost and Price Comparisons for Manufacture table)

CA   Current account surplus as a percentage of GNP.

     Current account data are taken from various country sources. The GNP figures are from the IFS.

GNP/GDP data are from IFS, lines 99A.R, 99A.P, 99B.R or 99B.P.

The GNP/GDP deflators are from IFS, line 99AIR, 99AIP, 99BIR or 99BIP.

1978 GNP weights are used in calculating rest-of-world and relative-to-foreign variables.

Notes

The opinions expressed in this paper are those of the authors and do not necessarily reflect the views of the Federal Reserve Bank of New York or of the Federal Reserve Bank of San Francisco. We thank Allan Malz for providing research assistance in carrying out the empirical work and for preparing the data appendix. We wish to acknowledge helpful comments from Sven Arndt, Michael Darby, J. David Richardson, and other participants in the AEI/NBER Conference.

1. In models with perfectly flexible prices and continuous full employment, the rise in the real exchange rate (which amounts to an improvement in the terms of trade) can be viewed as reflecting an increased demand for home goods relative to their supply (see Hutchison and Pigott 1985). In models with unemployment due to "inflexible" prices, fiscal stimulus that raised demand for home goods is apt to lead to real appreciation via increases in domestic real interest rates; the increases in real income *and* the real exchange rate are then the proximate "causes" of the current account deterioration.

2. Beyond the initial responses the further changes in taxes and spending needed to maintain a fiscal deficit at a given level will also affect the economy's adjustment. A rise in government spending *excluding* debt-service payments relative to revenues is generally *not* ultimately sustainable. For example, a rise in spending initially financed by borrowing will eventually require a rise in taxes or fall in (noninterest) expenditure to maintain a sustainable equilibrium. Thus it is perhaps reasonable to consider (as we do here) responses to a fiscal shift over the first several years, but this becomes somewhat ambiguous over the full-adjustment path.

3. In the short-run there could be deviations from a fixed real exchange rate if prices are sluggish to adjust to real and financial shocks, while asset markets clear continuously. This asymmetry generates the well-known exchange rate "overshooting" result (Dornbusch 1976).

4. Generally, the long-run effects of a budget deficit are apt to differ in important ways from its impact and medium-term effects. A rise in spending ultimately requires a rise in revenues if it is to be sustained; the amount of the tax increase can actually exceed the rise in spending if the real interest rate paid exceeds the economy's real growth rate (e.g., Darby 1984). Hence the long-run "goods-market" aspect of a deficit may be quite different from its initial appearance. In addition, where domestic assets are regarded as poor substitutes for foreign counterparts, financing of deficits could raise domestic interest rates enough to more than offset the stimulus to demand for home output from the deficit itself. For a more complete discussion of long-run consequences, see also Hutchison and Pigott 1984.

5. Actually the differential may arise from two broad sets of factors: institutional impediments to free financial flows among countries (imperfect capital mobility) and perceived risks associated with the currency denomination (or other characteristics) of domestic versus foreign debt (imperfect substitutability).

6. Of course, if expectations were forward-looking, the prospect of higher future debt stocks may immediately push up interest rates, and lower exchange rates.

7. The data appendix describes the data and sources in more detail. Note that the inflation-adjusted deficit measure shows an even more pronounced swing in the U.S. position over 1979 to 1984 than the unadjusted measures. The main reason is that the "inflation premium" portion of the interest paid on the U.S. debt fell sharply as U.S. inflation declined over this period.

8. Increases in the relative price of oil should tend to lower real currency values for countries relatively dependent on oil imports and raise currency values for net oil exporters or those relatively little dependent on its import. The experience of the last decade suggests that these effects can be sizable.

9. Indeed, the correlations in the disturbances across countries are often substantial.

10. The expenditure and tax multipliers on GNP for the United States, for example, in the Fair, and Federal Reserve Board's Multicountry model are very close after one year. For a comparison, see Weiller (1986).

11. In theory, a "rational" public is likely to save any increase in interest payments received on government debt arising simply from higher inflation. If so, the inflation-adjusted measure may be the better measure of fiscal stimulus. See Darby (1984).

12. A rise in the deficit/GNP ratio of one percentage point raises the debt/GNP ratio by slightly less than 1 percent over the subsequent year. Thus the first-year impact of a debt-financed expenditure increase is approximately the difference between the debt and budget (surplus) coefficients listed in the table. Eventually, of course, the debt/GNP ratio will rise considerably further if the deficit increase is sustained. In particular, a permanent 1 percent rise in the deficit/GNP ratio will raise the debt/GNP ratio by $1/g$, where g is the economy's nominal growth rate expressed in decimals. In many of the results discussed in the text, the "permanent" impact of the debt calculated in this way does dominate that of the deficit itself. However, it is doubtful that such long-term implications drawn from these equations should be given much weight.

13. The intercepts and coefficients of the oil and cyclical variable (in the current account equation) were allowed to vary among the three small European countries.

14. This point is particularly relevant for the present policy debate. U.S. officials have recommended fiscal expansion to several foreign countries as a means of reducing external imbalances, with a fall in the real value of the dollar viewed largely (although certainly not entirely) as a means to that end.

References

Amano, A. 1986. Exchange Rate Simulations: A Comparative Study *European Economic Review* 30 (February): 137–148.

Blanchard, O., and R. Dornbusch. 1984. U.S. Deficits, the Dollar and Europe. *Banca Nazionale del Lavoro* 148 (March):89–113.

Branson, W. H. 1985. Causes of Appreciation and Volatility of the Dollar. In *The U.S. Dollar—Recent Developments, Outlook, and Policy Options.* Proceedings of a Symposium sponsored by The Federal Reserve Bank of Kansas City, pp. 33–52.

Branson, W. H., and W. Buiter. 1983. Monetary and Fiscal Policy with Flexible Exchange Rates. In J. Bhandari and B. Putnam (eds.), *Economic Interdependence and Flexible Exchange Rates.* Cambridge: MIT Press, pp. 251–285.

Branson, W. H., H. Halttunen, and P. Masson. 1977. Exchange Rates in the Short Run: The Dollar-Deutschemark Rate. *European Economic Review* 10:303–324.

Buiter, W. H. 1984. Fiscal Policy in Open, Interdependent Economies. NBER working paper no. 1429. August.

Danker, D., R. Hass, D. Henderson, S. Symansky, and R. Tyron. 1984. Small Empirical Models of Exchange Rate Intervention: Applications to Canada, Germany and Japan. Staff studies no. 135. Board of Governors of the Federal Reserve System.

Darby, M. 1984. Some Pleasant Monetarist Arithmetic. Federal Reserve Bank of Minneapolis *Quarterly Review* 8 (Spring):15–20.

Dornbusch, R. 1980. *Open Economy Macroeconomics.* New York: Basic Books.

Dornbusch, R., and S. Fischer. 1984. The Open Economy: Implications for Monetary and Fiscal Policy. NBER working paper no. 1422. August.

Evans, P. 1985. Do Large Deficits Prouduce High Interest Rates? *American Economic Review* 75:68–87.

Feldstein, M. 1983. Domestic Saving and International Capital Movements in the Long Run and the Short Run. *European Economic Review* 21 (March–April): 129–151.

Feldstein, M., and C. Horioka. 1980. Domestic Savings and International Capital Flows. *The Economic Journal* 90 (June):324–329.

Furstenberg, G. M. von 1980. Domestic Determinants of Net U.S. Foreign Investment. IMF *Staff Papers* 27 (December): 637–677.

Giovannini, A. 1984. The Exchange Rate, the Capital Stock, and Fiscal Policy. Working paper no. FB-84-13. First Boston Bank. June.

Harberger, A. C. 1980. Vignettes on the World Capital Market. *American Economic Review* 70 (May):331–337.

Hoelscher, G. 1983. Federal Borrowing and Short-Term Interest Rates. *Southern Journal of Economics* 50 (October):319–333.

Hutchison, M. M. 1984. Intervention, Deficit Finance and Real Exchange Rates: The Case of Japan. Federal Reserve Bank of San Francisco *Economic Review*, no. 1 (Winter): 27–44.

Hutchison, M. M., and C. A. Pigott. 1984. Budget Deficits, Exchange Rates and the Current Account: Theory and U.S. Evidence. Federal Reserve Bank of San Francisco *Economic Review*, no. 4 (Fall): 5–25.

Hutchison, M. M., and C. A. Pigott. 1985. Real and Financial Adjustments to Fiscal Deficits in Growing Open Economies. Working paper no. 85–03. Federal Reserve Bank of San Francisco. May.

Hutchison, M., and D. Pyle. 1984. The Real Interest Rate/Budget Deficit Link: International Evidence, 1973–82. Federal Reserve Bank of San Francisco *Economic Review*, no. 4 (Fall): 26–35.

Knight, M., and P. Masson. 1985. Fiscal Policies, Net Savings and Real Exchange Rates. Presented at the NBER Conference on International Aspects of Fiscal Policies, Cambridge, Mass., December 13–14.

McKibbin, W., and J. Sachs. 1985. Coordination of Monetary and Fiscal Policies in the OECD. Presented at the NBER Conference on International Aspects of Fiscal Policies, Cambridge, Mass., December 13–14.

Motley, B. 1983. Real Interest Rates, Money and Government Deficits. Federal Reserve Bank of San Francisco *Economic Review*, no. 3 (Summer): 31–45.

Oudiz, G., and J. Sachs. 1984. Macroeconomic Policy Coordination among the Industrial Countries. *Brookings Papers on Economic Activity* 1: 1–65.

Niehans, J. 1984. *International Monetary Economics*. Baltimore: John Hopkins Press.

Penati, A. (1983). Expansionary Fiscal Policy and the Exchange Rate: A Review. IMF *Staff Papers* 30 (September): 543–569.

Price, R. W. R., and P. Muller. 1984. Structural Budget Indicators and the Interpretation of Fiscal Policy Stance in OECD Economics. *OECD Economic Studies* 3 (Autumn): 28–72.

Sachs, J. D. 1981. The Current Account and Macroeconomic Adjustment in the 1970s. *Brookings Papers on Economic Activity* 1: 201–268.

Sachs, J. D. 1983. Aspects of Current Account Behavior of OECD Economies. In E. Claasen and P. Salin (eds.), *Recent Issues in the Theory of Flexible Exchange Rates*. Amsterdam: North Holland, pp. 101–122.

Sachs, J. D., and C. Wyplosz. 1984. Real Exchange Rate Effects of Fiscal Policy. NBER working paper no. 1255. January.

U.S. Treasury Department. The Office of the Assistant Secretary for Economic Policy (1984). The Effects of Deficits on Prices of Financial Assets: Theory and Evidence. Monograph. March.

Weiller, K. J. 1985. Government Deficits, Debt and the Real Exchange Rate in a Two Country Model: Theory and Evidence. Ph. D. dissertation. Harvard University. February.

Weiller, K. J. 1986. The Effects of Using Consumption in the Money Demand Function. Working paper no. 8603. Federal Reserve Bank of New York. March.

Wijnbergen, S. van. 1985. Fiscal Policy and World Real Interest Rates: An Empirical Analysis. Presented at the NBER Conference on International Aspects of Fiscal Policy, Cambridge, Mass., December 13–14.

7 Monetary, Financial, and Real Effects of Yen Internationalization

Koichi Hamada
Akiyoshi Horiuchi

The internationalization of a national currency—that is, the increasingly international use of a national currency—can be regarded as a monetary phenomenon. This process, however, is conditioned by real factors such as the structure of trade and by financial factors such as the degree of deregulation in capital markets and the degree of decontrol in the exchange market. At the same time, the internationalization of a national currency gives rise to various real and financial repurcussions. Thus the internationalization of a currency is certainly a suitable topic as a study of the interaction of real, financial and monetary phenomena in the world economy.

Taking the yen's internationalization as an example, we will discuss real-monetary and real-financial linkages that are interwoven in the process of internationalization. In the real-monetary linkage we focus on the structural and behavioral conditions for the use of the yen as a unit of account and medium of exchange and, in turn, some real effects of such uses of the yen. In the real-financial linkage we focus on the structural and behavioral conditions for the use of yen assets as a store of value and, in turn, real effects of such use of yen assets.

In section 7.1 we survey briefly the current status of the yen as an international currency and the openness of the Japanese economy in its real as well as in its financial side. In section 7.2 we discuss the factors that affect the international use of the yen as a unit of account and a medium of exchange. We describe this real-monetary linkage emphasizing the role of the structure of trade. In section 7.3 we discuss the factors that affect the international use of the yen as a store of value. We describe this real-financial linkage, emphasizing the role of deregulation in Japan's financial markets.

In section 7.4 we discuss some real effects of the yen's internationalization. In particular, we trace the transmission of nominal exchange rate movements to various price levels and real exchange rates calculated by alternative price indexes. We ask how the internationalization of the yen affected this transmission process.

In section 7.5 we discuss the macroeconomic aspect of the real effects of yen internationalization, relying on the currency substitution model incorporating real balance effects. An important effect of the internationalization of the yen is to change the asset preference of foreigners toward holding more assets or more liabilities denominated in yen. The effect on the value of the yen depends on the relative strength of these counteracting forces. The observed sluggishness of the adjustment of the Japanese balance of payments may stem from the effect of slow price movements that prevents the real balance effect from working smoothly.

7.1   An Overview on the Openness of Japan's Economy and the Status of the Yen as an International Currency

The rapid postwar growth of Japan took place in a relatively closed system. If we define "openness" of a national economy by the ratio of exports and imports to GNP, table 7.1 shows that both ratios were around 9 percent in Japan during the 1960s and are only a little higher today.[1] This is true even though exports have been essential to a Japan that depends crucially on foreign energy sources.

On the other hand, from the global perspective, the Japanese economy has remarkably increased its relative share in world trade since 1970, surpassing the United Kingdom in the beginning of the 1970s and now catching up to West Germany (table 7.2). In this sense the real side of the Japanese economy has been rapidly internationalized.

On the financial side, Japan was closed during the high growth era. The high rate of investment for economic growth was almost totally financed by abundant domestic savings. Most financial markets have been regulated to considerable degrees. In the 1950s and the early 1960s, almost all interest rates were directly controlled in order to reduce capital costs for business borrowers. However, restraints on financial markets hardly troubled the Japanese financial system, because the main suppliers of savings in those days were a multitude of small savers whose portfolio choices were severely restricted by transactions costs and regulations. Despite regulated low interest rates those small savers were given little opportunity to transfer their assets from domestic markets to underground markets or foreign markets. Therefore financial markets in Japan did not seem to

Table 7.1
Ratios of exports and imports to GNP (percent)

	1960–69	1970–79	1980	1981	1982	1983	1984
Japan							
Export (1)	9.0	10.2	11.0	13.1	12.2	12.2	—
Import (2)	9.9	9.8	11.9	12.4	11.6	10.5	—
(1) + (2)	19.9	19.9	22.9	25.5	23.8	22.8	—
United States							
Export (1)	3.9	5.9	8.4	7.9	6.9	6.1	5.9
Import (2)	3.2	6.2	9.2	8.8	7.9	7.8	8.9
(1) + (2)	7.1	12.1	17.5	16.7	14.9	13.9	14.8
Germany							
Export (1)	16.3	20.9	23.6	25.7	26.7	25.8	27.9
Import (2)	14.4	17.9	23.0	23.9	23.5	23.3	24.8
(1) + (2)	30.7	38.8	46.6	49.6	50.3	49.1	52.7
United Kingdom							
Export (1)	16.2	21.4	23.8	23.4	23.6	23.6	25.8
Import (2)	19.1	25.2	25.0	23.5	24.2	25.7	28.8
(1) + (2)	35.3	46.6	48.8	47.0	47.8	49.3	54.6
France							
Export (1)	10.2	15.2	17.0	17.7	16.9	17.5	19.9
Import (2)	10.7	16.3	20.5	21.1	21.2	20.3	21.2
(1) + (2)	20.9	31.5	37.5	38.8	38.1	37.8	41.1

Source: Bank of Japan.

Table 7.2
Relative shares of main countries in the world exports and imports (percent)

	1960–64	1965–69	1970–74	1975–79	1980–84
Exports					
Japan	4.0	5.3	6.7	7.1	7.8
United States	17.0	16.0	12.7	11.9	11.4
United Kingdom	8.9	7.7	5.8	5.2	5.2
West Germany	10.5	11.4	11.3	10.9	9.3
Imports					
Japan	4.5	5.0	6.2	6.6	6.9
United States	12.0	13.6	12.5	12.6	13.5
United Kingdom	10.2	8.6	6.7	6.0	5.3
West Germany	8.9	9.4	9.3	9.3	8.2

Sources: UN, *Statistical Yearbook*, and Bank of Japan.

Table 7.3
External assets and liabilities of Japan (millions of dollars)

End of year	External assets (per GNP, percent)	External liabilities (per GNP, percent)
1971	32,753 (12.5)	22,980 (8.7)
1972	43,595 (13.7)	29,728 (9.3)
1973	47,595 (11.4)	34,535 (8.3)
1974	55,942 (12.7)	46,999 (10.6)
1975	58,334 (11.7)	51,316 (10.3)
1976	67,990 (11.7)	58,416 (10.1)
1977	80,860 (10.2)	58,080 (7.4)
1978	117,725 (11.2)	82,511 (7.8)
1979	135,369 (14.6)	106,588 (11.5)
1980	159,580 (13.7)	148,046 (11.9)
1981	209,257 (18.3)	198,339 (17.3)
1982	227,688 (20.8)	203,006 (18.6)
1983	271,956 (23.2)	234,697 (20.0)
1984	341,208 (27.3)	266,862 (21.3)

Sources: Bank of Japan, and Economic Planning Agency.

reveal the "financial repression" that McKinnon (1973) associates with direct restraints on financial mechanism.

Table 7.3 shows a possible measure of the degree of financial openness, the ratios of Japanese external assets and liabilities to GNP. (Unfortunately the data on external assets-liabilities before 1970 are not available.) This table implies that internationalization of Japanese financial markets did not proceed much during the 1970s, but started around 1980.

During the 1970s the Japanese monetary authorities alternated liberalization and restriction on capital flow in order to moderate fluctuations in exchange rates, though the general trend was directed toward more liberalization.[2] This unsteady policy stance prevented Japanese financial markets from becoming more internationalized. A new Foreign Exchange and Foreign Trade Control Law introduced in December 1980 testified to the Japanese authorities' intention for liberalization, however, and was reflected in the increased degree of financial openness after 1980.

Thus internationalization of Japanese financial markets has substantially lagged behind internationalization on the real side of the economy. However, structural changes in the domestic financial system that started in the early 1970s are now eroding the closedness of financial markets.[3]

First, Japanese firms now regard many restrictive practices in financial markets as substantial obstacles, although they once benefited from them. They need more financial services in international markets as they extend their overseas activities.

Second, the decline of investment relative to high savings after the first oil crisis brought about large net excess savings in private sectors. The government budget deficit that absorbed these net savings reached a peak because of political resistance by the end of the 1970s. Thus the large savings surplus has to be directed to foreign borrowers. This creates pressure to make Japanese financial markets more open.

Internationalization of financial markets is not to be confused, however, with internationalization of a currency. Financial internationalization of the Japanese economy may be a precondition for the yen's internationalization as a monetary medium, but it does not guarantee it. One way of clarifying these distinctions is to recall the three basic functions of money as a unit of account, a medium of exchange, and a store of value. Internationalization of the yen then might imply that the yen plays any one or all of these three functions internationally. (See Cohen 1971 for a systematic account of these three functions that consider differences between domestic and international transactions.) In section 7.2 we will concentrate on the role of the yen as a unit of account and a medium of exchange, and accordingly discuss the *real-monetary* linkage involved in the process of internationalization. In section 7.3 we will concentrate on the yen as a store of value and discuss *real-financial* linkage.

7.2   Real-Monetary Linkage: The Yen as a Unit of Account and a Medium of Exchange

As a unit of account the yen is still far short of international status. According to table 7.4 and some unpublished data from monetary authorities, about 33 percent of Japanese exports and only 3 percent of imports were invoiced in yen in 1984. As the ratios were only 0.9 and 0.3 percent in 1970, the yen made substantial progress. These ratios are still low, however, compared with those in most industrial countries: according to table 7.5, in 1978 the shares of exports invoiced in domestic currencies are all higher than 50 percent, and those of imports are, though somewhat lower than 50 percent, higher than 30 percent except in Japan.[4] Therefore the yen is far short of the status of "international currency" for vehicle currency). It does not play even the role of "symmetric nonvehicle currency" in Magee-Rao's sense but merely that of "minor nonvehicle currency."[5] This minor status of the yen in mediating international exchange stands in contrast to the significant role of real Japanese trade since 1970.[6]

These low ratios for Japan reflect its real trade structure, and thereby

Table 7.4
Percentage of Japanese total exports invoiced in yen and other currencies, 1970–1984.

Currency	1970	1975	1980	1982	1983	1984
Yen						
Export	0.9	17.5	29.4	32.2	34.5	33.7
Import	0.3	0.9	2.4	na	na	na
Dollar						
Export	90.4	78.0	65.7	62.3	60.4	61.4
Import	80.0	89.9	93.1	na	na	na
Pound sterling						
Export	7.1	1.9	1.1	1.4	1.0	0.9
Import	8.8	3.8	0.9	na	na	na
Mark						
Export	0.5	1.1	1.9	2.1	2.1	1.9
Import	2.8	1.5	1.4	na	na	na
Other						
Export	1.1	1.5	1.9	2.0	2.0	2.1
Import	8.1	3.9	2.2	na	na	na

Source: Ministry of Finance, *Annual Report of the International Finance Bureau*, 1985.

Table 7.5
Currency distribution of world trade (percent)

	Exports		Imports	
	U.S. dollar	National currency	U.S. dollar	National currency
United States	98	98	85	85
Japan	60.9	33.8	93.0	2.0
West Germany	7.2	82.3	33.1	42.8
United Kingdom	17	76	29	38
France	11.6	62.4	28.7	35.8
World total	54.8	—	54.3	—

Sources: NIESR, *National Institute Economic Review*, and Bank of Japan.
Note: Figures for Japan's exports are for 1982, and Japan's and Germany's imports for 1980. Figures for United Kingdom and France are for 1979. Figures for United States are estimated.

Table 7.6
Percentage of Japan's exports invoiced in yen (1983, percent)

	To United States	To Western Europe	To Oceania	Total
Textiles	0	61	65	31
Chemicals	—	—	20	12
Metals	1	15	13	14
Machinery	27	48	57	53
Electric apparatus	6	56	86	41
Tape recorders	2	33	86	32
Automobiles	18	68	94	46
Bicycles	—	21	99	26
Ships	—	66	—	90
Optical instrument	14	67	77	47
Total	13	51	68	40

Source: Ministry of Finance, *Annual Report of the International Finance Bureau*, 1985.

illustrate "linkage." With respect to imports, most are primary products such as materials and energy, what McKinnon (1979) calls Tradables II, and invoiced mostly in dollars. Moreover some Japanese exporting firms that depend heavily on imports of primary products, for example, steel and nonferrous products, may prefer invoicing in dollars in order to hedge exchange risks as simultaneous buyers and sellers.

With respect to exports, yen invoicing is much smaller than implied by McKinnon's hypothesis (1979, 68): resident firms view their domestic currency as the relatively riskless asset into which they want their profits translated, and they strive to stabilize the liquidity (realizable) value of their asset portfolios in terms of the domestic currency. One reason this hypothesis is not sustained for Japan is that there are remarkable differences across regions and individuals with respect to invoicing exports in yen. Table 7.6 shows shares of Japanese exports invoiced in yen, classified by sector and customer. According to this table, while the ratio of yen-denominated exports to the United States is extremely low (only 13 percent in 1983), that to western Europe (and, say, to Oceania) is on the average a little higher than 50 percent (with variations among exported commodities). These regional differences have contributed to lowering the ratio of total yen-denominated export, because Japanese exports have been heavily concentrated on the United States.[7]

Since the U.S. dollar is a vehicle currency, it tends to be intensively used for invoicing even in the case of the U.S. imports.[8] (More than 80 percent of the U.S. imports are in dollars, according to table 7.5.) Therefore the more heavily a national economy relies on exports to the United States, the lower will be the ratio of exports invoiced in its domestic currency. The low level of the Japanese yen-denominated exports reflects its reliance on exports to the United States.[9]

Invoicing may thus reflect the structure of trade; it may also influence it, illustrating another real-financial linkage. When costs of hedging exchange risk are not negligible, the choice of currencies in invoicing can be one means of nonprice competition. Japanese exporters may have tactically used currency invoicing to penetrate foreign markets, especially U.S. markets. Japanese exporters of automobiles and electric apparatus export mostly to their subsidiaries in the United States by invoicing in the U.S. dollar. The highly competitive U.S. subsidiaries need not bear the cost of hedging exchange risk, passing it back instead to the monopolistically competitive parent, which in turn passes some of it along to Japanese consumers.[10] According to a questionnaire survey by the Ministry of Finance made in the spring of 1984, Japanese firms report that a principal reason for foreign-currency-invoiced export contracts is the hard pressure from international competition. By way of contrast, if Japan had some product that gave it monopolistic or oligopolistic power, Japanese exporters might be able to force foreign importers to conclude yen-denominated contracts. In fact the overall shares of yen-invoiced exports of ships, automobiles, and VCRs to the rest of the world other than the United States during 1983 or 1984 exceeded 50 percent.

Financial factors, particularly the state of Japan's money market, may also explain these low ratios and illustrate what we could call a "financial-monetary linkage." Particularly, the past absence of any market for yen-denominated bankers' acceptance (BA) was often considered a barrier to the development of yen-denominated exports. Japan's trade finance depended almost completely on the dollar-denominated BA market. In June 1985 a yen-denominated BA market was established for the first time. The volume of transactions in the market remains quite low, contrary to most people's expectations. The stamp duty on BA transactions and lack of experience may have hindered development of the market.

In summary, although financial factors may have played some role, the low status of the yen as unit of account and medium of exchange can be explained importantly by the real trade structure, especially by the close trade relationship with the United States, whose currency has long been established as an international money, or vehicle currency. Japanese firms may choose the dollar as an invoicing currency tactically to compete in U.S. markets.

Table 7.7
Shares of major currencies in international bond issues (percent)

	Yen	Dollar	Mark	Pound sterling
1976	0.7 (—)	60.9 (64.1)	12.2 (18.7)	— (—)
1977	4.1 (0.6)	56.1 (65.4)	18.6 (23.2)	0.6 (1.2)
1978	11.5 (0.9)	38.2 (51.6)	26.3 (37.2)	0.7 (1.7)
1979	4.8 (0.6)	41.7 (67.1)	22.0 (19.4)	0.7 (1.6)
1980	3.3 (1.3)	47.4 (68.5)	20.1 (15.0)	2.7 (4.1)
1981	5.3 (1.2)	64.9 (84.9)	4.9 (4.0)	2.4 (1.6)
1982	4.2 (0.7)	63.9 (85.1)	7.1 (5.0)	2.5 (1.4)
1983	5.3 (0.4)	56.3 (79.2)	8.5 (7.9)	3.6 (4.0)
1984	5.4 (1.5)	64.3 (80.0)	6.4 (5.8)	4.9 (5.0)
1985 (January–September)	7.8 (4.4)	63.4 (73.6)	5.3 (5.0)	3.7 (3.8)

Source: Morgan Guaranty Trust Company of New York, *World Financial Markets.*
Note: Figures in parentheses present the relative shares of Eurocurrency bond issues in the Eurobond market.

7.3   Real-Financial Linkage: Liberalization and the Yen as a Store of Value

Internationalization of the yen would also generally imply that international credit arrangements would be denominated in terms of the yen. Here we can see again a *financial-monetary* linkage. These arrangements have two sides: yen claims on foreigners and yen liabilities to them.

Table 7.7 summarizes some of the fragmentary data on Japanese yen claims on foreigners. It shows the amount of funds that nonresidents obtained by issuing yen-denominated bonds in both the Japanese bond market and the Eurobond market. Though yen-denominated bonds had shown an upward trend since the beginning of the 1970s, they have experienced considerable fluctuations due partly to the changing attitude of the Japanese monetary authorities toward these markets. Yen-denominated bonds of all kinds did not increase their share substantially in overall international bond markets, accounting for 4 percent and 5 percent of the total amount of all international bonds issues respectively in 1973 and 1984. Euro-yen bonds had only a minor share in the Eurobond market, accounting for less than 2 percent of the total amount of Eurobond issues. This reflected the Japanese authorities' restrictive attitude toward the Euro-yen market. Until 1977 nonresidents were not allowed to issue Euro-yen bonds.

However, the Japanese authorities' stance toward Euro-yen has changed since 1984. Nonresidents have begun to issue substantial amounts of yen-

Table 7.8
Shares of nonresidents' selling and buying in Japanese security markets (millions of dollars, percent)

Year	Bond markets		Stock markets	
	Selling	Buying	Selling	Buying
1978	8,040 (1.8)	22,682 (5.0)	5,633 (3.6)	4,830 (3.1)
1979	14,469 (3.3)	20,011 (4.4)	6,171 (4.4)	5,486 (3.9)
1980	23,526 (4.2)	32,662 (5.8)	7,185 (4.1)	12,174 (7.0)
1981	40,944 (5.6)	49,520 (6.8)	21,452 (9.8)	24,971 (11.4)
1982	54,567 (5.8)	70,867 (7.6)	15,664 (10.8)	17,276 (11.9)
1983	138,810 (11.1)	148,965 (12.0)	26,941 (12.4)	31,061 (14.3)
1984	461,568 (16.8)	474,973 (17.5)	43,152 (16.1)	35,903 (13.4)

Sources: Nomura Research Institute, and Bank of Japan.
Note: Figures in parentheses give percentage of total selling and buying in respective markets.

denominated bonds in the Eurobond market. From January to September of 1985 nonresidents obtained $4.4 billion by this means. This figure is 3.6 times as large as the amount of Euro-yen bonds issued in the previous year.

In contrast to Eurobonds, Japanese bond markets have been relatively open to nonresident borrowers for some time. For example, yen-denominated bonds issued by nonresidents in Japan (i.e, samurai bonds) accounted for 17 percent and 24 percent of the total foreign bonds that were issued in various national markets (excluding Eurobonds) in 1984 and 1985 (January–September), respectively.

Table 7.8 shows the amount and relative share of nonresidents' sales and purchases of Japanese bonds in secondary markets. The relative importance of nonresident investors has been gradually increasing since the latter half of the 1970s, when the secondary markets started to develop due to a rapid increase in outstanding public bonds.

Nonresidents have also been influential participants in the Japanese stock market in recent years. Table 7.8 also shows that the relative share of nonresidents in stock-market transactions increased rapidly since the beginning of the 1980s.

With respect to Japan's yen liabilities to foreigners, Table 7.9 summarizes some fragmentary data. In May 1979 the Ministry of Finance permitted foreign investors to participate in the *gensaki* (bond trading with repurchase agreements) markets. Since that time nonresidents have become quite important in this market, particularly as lenders, holding up to 18 percent of the total *gensaki* outstanding. In the yen CD (certificate of

Table 7.9
Gensaki and CDs held by nonresidents (100 million yen, percent)

End of month	*Gensaki*	CDs
1979/6	898 (2.2)	na
/9	2,270 (5.4)	na
/12	739 (1.9)	na
1980/3	4,282 (8.3)	na
/6	1,110 (2.3)	na
/9	2,962 (6.2)	na
/12	1,139 (2.5)	na
1981/3	7,954 (13.9)	na
/6	2,129 (4.9)	498 (1.1)
/9	6,092 (14.7)	590 (2.0)
/12	8,117 (18.1)	635 (2.0)
1982/3	8,754 (18.0)	939 (3.6)
/6	5,483 (13.4)	715 (1.8)
/9	5,720 (12.9)	1,335 (3.3)
/12	5,505 (12.8)	1,836 (4.3)
1983/3	6,535 (13.7)	2,389 (6.4)
/6	3,626 (8.8)	2,575 (4.9)
/9	2,875 (7.4)	2,460 (4.2)
/12	3,249 (7.6)	1,630 (3.0)
1984/3	1,971 (4.8)	5,132 (9.4)
/6	2,250 (6.1)	3,084 (3.9)
/9	1,828 (5.6)	3,545 (4.6)
/12	2,198 (6.2)	3,048 (3.7)
1985/3	2,274 (5.8)	2,121 (2.7)

Source: Nomura Research Institute.
Note: Figures in parentheses give percentage of total outstanding stocks in respective markets.

Table 7.10
Share of national currencies in eurodeposit liabilities of BIS reporting banks (percent)

End of year	Yen	Dollar	Mark	Pound sterling	Swiss franc
1977	0.5(270)	77.3	13.2	1.3	4.4
1978	0.9(620)	75.1	14.1	1.5	4.2
1979	1.2(1030)	73.1	14.9	1.8	4.8
1980	1.1(1120)	74.9	12.2	2.3	5.3
1981	1.3(1610)	77.3	9.9	1.6	5.9
1982	1.3(1690)	78.6	9.3	1.3	5.0
1983	1.3(2170)	82.8	7.0	0.9	4.0
1984	1.3(2170)	83.2	6.8	1.0	3.4

Source: BIS International Banking Developments.
Note: Figures in parentheses give total amount of Euro-yen deposits (billions of yen).

deposits) market, foreign investors held nearly 10 percent of the outstanding CDs as of March 1984.

Table 7.10 summarizes a time series of the amount of Euro-yen time deposit liabilities of BIS (Bank for International Settlements) reporting banks. The share of Euro-yen in total Eurodeposits has remained minor, though the relative importance of Euro-yen deposits has been gradually increasing since the beginning of the 1980s. Japanese residents can hold neither Euro-yen deposits nor Euro-yen CDs without permission from the monetary authority. Euro-yen CDs with longer maturity than six months are not allowed. The minor position of the yen as a unit of account in international trade, explained in section 7.2, may also contribute to this situation because nonresident demand for liquidity in yen is limited by the amount of trade denominated in yen.

The yen could also serve as a medium of exchange for foreign monetary authorities who intervene in foreign exchange markets and as a store of value for the public purpose if foreign authorities hold a substantial proportion of their reserves in the form of yen-denominated assets. However, the amount of yen-denominated assets held by foreign authorities as reserves is not large either. In 1984 the share of yen reserves was only 5 percent of total official foreign reserves, though table 7.11 reveals a gradual increase.

In sum, the current role of the yen as a store of value is minor. Nonresidents have been admittedly important as investors in some yen-denominated assets. In general, however, the yen's internationalization as a store of value is very low relative to the internationalization of the Japanese real economy.

Until the early 1970s the yen was not internationalized at all. An important objective for Japanese macroeconomic policy was to maintain a suffi-

Table 7.11
Share of national currencies in total identified official holdings of foreign exchange (percent)

End of year	Yen	Dollar	Mark	Pound sterling	Swiss franc
1977	2.4	78.0	9.1	1.8	2.2
1978	3.3	75.6	10.9	1.7	2.1
1979	3.6	72.9	12.5	2.0	2.5
1980	4.4	66.8	15.0	3.0	3.2
1981	4.1	69.8	12.9	2.1	2.7
1982	4.5	68.7	12.3	2.4	2.7
1983	4.7	68.5	11.2	2.6	2.3
1984	5.2	65.4	12.0	2.9	2.0

Source: IMF, *Annual Report 1985*.

cient amount of foreign exchange reserves under the regime of fixed exchange rates. The instruments to meet that objective were severe controls on transactions in both foreign exchange markets and international capital movements.

As the Japanese current account tended into surplus in the beginning of the 70s, restrictive control on capital movements was gradually relaxed. The liberalization process reached a climax when the Law of Foreign Exchange Transaction was totally amended in December 1980.

The Japanese government, however, did not smoothly deregulate. The government occasionally strengthened the regulations as a means of restricting capital movements in order to prevent allegedly "undue" fluctuations in the yen rate. The government prohibited yen-denominated bond issues by foreigners from the end of 1973 to mid-1975 to regain the external balance. Also from 1979 to 1980, substantial restrictions were imposed upon yen bond issues and syndicated loans to nonresidents in order to prevent the yen from depreciating further. These restrictions were quite effective (table 7.12). The stop-and-go nature of these restrictions probably worked against the upward trend in the international use of the yen.

Since 1980 the Japanese government has been deregulating more smoothly. Although the promise of liberalizing Euro-yen markets made by the Working Group of the Joint Japan-U.S. Ad Hoc Group on Yen/Dollar Exchange Rate was directly a product of the strong pressure from the United States, it was consistent with the government's changing attitude toward deregulation and internationalization.

There still remains scope for further deregulation. First, there is no full-fledged short-term government securities (Treasury Bills, TB) market in

Table 7.12
Nonresidents' yen-denominated bond issues (100 million yen)

Fiscal year	Yen bonds issued in Japan		Euro-yen bonds	Total
	Publicly offered	Privately placed		
1972	700	238	—	938
1973	400	271	—	671
1974	—	—	—	—
1975	350	—	—	350
1976	620	—	—	620
1977	4,540	750	300	5,590
1978	6,570	820	150	7,540
1979	2,840	452	250	3,542
1980	2,800	175	750	3,725
1981	6,130	1,500	800	8,430
1982	6,900	1,870	1,100	9,870
1983	6,150	1,790	600	8,540

Sources: Koshasai Hikiuke Kyokai (Association of Bond Underwriters), and Nomura Research Institute.

Japan. In order for foreign private as well as public agents to hold more liquid, short-term yen-denominated assets in their portfolios, there must be safe, liquid and standardized short-term assets such as TBs. The Ministry of Finance still issues short-term securities with an interest rate slightly lower than the market-determined rate. Being unable to sell them on the open market, the Ministry sells almost all to the Bank of Japan. The Bank of Japan now engages in selling operations of the TBs in the open market, naturally with some capital loss, for the purpose of promoting the development of the TB's secondary market. Development of a less cumbersome market in short-term government bonds would contribute to the yen's internationalization.

Second, deregulation of Euromarket activities will help portfolio preferences shift toward yen-denominated assets, while also encouraging a shift toward more borrowing of yen-denominated funds in the Euromarket. Whether or not the first-shift dominates the second is considered in section 7.5, along with its consequent real effects.

Third, nonresidents' propensity to hold yen-denominated assets will surely increase with more solid prospects for Japanese political security and for prosperity and stability of the domestic Japanese economy.

Finally, accumulation of overhead facilities and human capital in the Tokyo market of provision of sophisticated financial service will be necessary conditions for the yen's internationalization.

The three functions of the yen as unit of account, medium of exchange, and store of value are, of course, related to each other; one function reinforces the other. If the yen is used as a unit of account and means of international payments, this will increase confidence in yen-denominated assets and make them more attractive as a store of value. If yen assets are held more widely, this will facilitate the writing and clearance of contracts denominated in yen. The circular logic inherent in money also applies to international money: a currency is held by economic agents because other agents accept it. Allowing the yen to internationalize can start this ball rolling, although it is wise to remember that economic agents will not necessarily hold more yen just because they are allowed to.

7.4   Effects of the Internationalization of the Yen on the Real-Financial Transmission Mechanism

What are the real effects of the yen's internationalization? Some obvious effects from the preceding discussion include alterations in the resource costs of hedging, currency conversion, and financial intermediation more generally.

What interests us more, however, is the effect of the yen's internationalization on the transmission process from nominal exchange rates to real exchange rates, and to absolute and relative prices.

During the period of yen internationalization and deregulation of the Japanese financial market, we observe volatile fluctuations in exchange rates. Figure 7.1 indicates the index of the value of yen in terms of the dollar, and the index of the effective exchange rate of yen calculated by the IMF's Multilateral Exchange Rate Model (MERM). Figure 7.2 indicates the movement of the current account of the balance of payments of Japan. These figures suggests that despite the volatile movements of the yen, the Japanese current account showed a distinct upward trend and that nominal exchange rates did not seem to dampen the movement of the current account.

In a sense this may not be unnatural because, as we will discuss in the next section, the current account is an expression of net asset accumulation by a country. At some stages a nation will desire to accumulate net foreign assets as a result of natural supplies of savings that exceed investment. It is interesting then to see why nominal exchange rates may not directly influence trade and current account balances. The underlying question in financial real linkage is by what channels nominal exchange rate fluctuations are transmitted to real adjustments, and how the yen's internationalization weakened or otherwise affected this transmission.

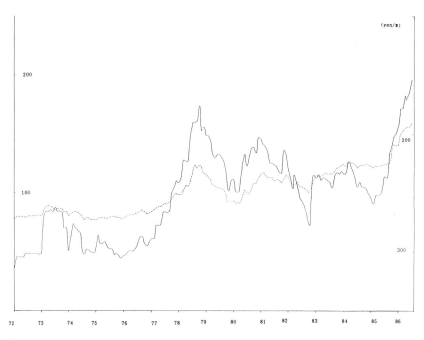

Figure 7.1
Nominal and effective exchange rates: 1970–1986. The solid line gives nominal exchange rates (yen/U.S. $, right scale); the dashed line effective exchange rates (MERM 1980 = 100, left scale). Source: IMF, *International Financial Statistics*.

There are several components of the linkage between the movement of nominal exchange rates, a monetary or financial factor, and real adjustments. First, there is a linkage between exchange rates and export or import prices. Suppose the value of the yen appreciates. The export price in terms of yen may stay the same, resulting in an increased price abroad of Japanese products in terms of foreign currency. Or the export price in terms of yens may go down in such a way as to keep the price of Japanese products constant in terms of foreign currency. There are of course many cases in between, or occasionally outside this range. Second, there is a linkage between exchange rates and domestic prices, including those of nontradables. This linkage and the first are in turn reflected in the relationship of exchange rates to general price levels such as the wholesale price index (WPI) and the consumer price index (CPI). We will very roughly examine these component linkages, and ask how progress in the yen's internationalization after 1980 could possibly affect the process of transmission at these stages.

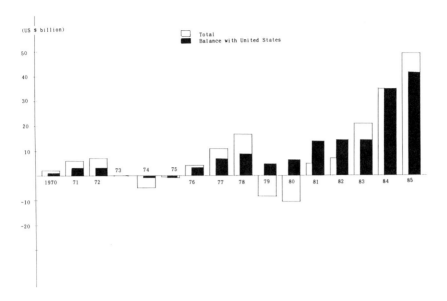

Figure 7.2
Japan's current account balances: 1970–1985 (U.S. $ billion). Source: Bank of Japan, *Balance of Payments Monthly*.

A useful benchmark is 1980, because in December 1980 the new Foreign Exchange Law was introduced. Also as an indicator of internationalization, various measures of covered interest parity became quite accurate around this time.

The Nominal Exchange Rate, Export and Import Prices

Figure 7.3 shows the nominal effective exchange rate (MERM) of the yen, an index of unit values of exports in yen, and the product of these two indexes. The index of unit values of exports in terms of yen moves much more smoothly than the effective exchange rate. This indicates that the unit value of exports has significant inertia, which is closer to the assumption that export prices are constant in terms of domestic prices of the exporting country. With yen internationalization, the ratio of exports invoiced in yen has increased. Thus a plausible hypothesis is that export prices in terms of yen will move even more stably when the yen is internationalized. If we neglect very recent movements in these values, figure 7.3 seems to support such a hypothesis weakly, though a decisive statement needs more statistical analysis.

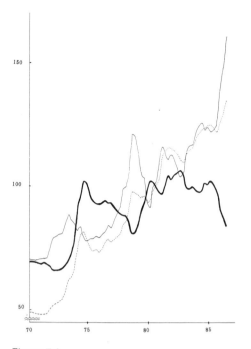

Figure 7.3
Indexes of Japan's exchange rates and export prices: 1970–1986 (1980 = 100). The solid line gives effective exchange rates (MERM); the heavy solid line the index of export prices in yen; the dashed line the index of export prices in foreign currencies. Source: IMF, *International Financial Statistics*.

On the other hand, import prices in yen move more drastically in the reverse direction to the MERM (figure 7.4). One has to take account of two oil price hikes around 1974 and 1979, and oil's decline starting in late 1985. Even with this qualification it seems that the import index obtained slightly more stability since 1980. Whether this is caused by slowly increasing yen invoicing still remains to be seen.

Nominal and Real Exchange Rates

Purchasing power parity (PPP) theory implies that nominal exchange rates ought to affect more than just export and import prices. One of its implications is that general price levels, such as the WPI and the CPI, ought to co-vary with exchange rates, even though general price indexes obviously include prices of nontradables as well as tradables. More pointedly, PPP implies that covariation ought to be such that real exchange rates are insensitive to exogenous changes in nominal exchange rates. Figure 7.5 is a

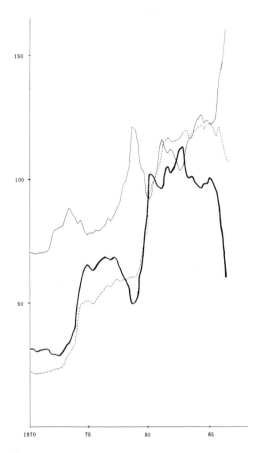

Figure 7.4
Index of Japan's exchange rates and import prices: 1970–1986 (1980 = 100). The solid
line gives effective exchange rates (MERM); the heavy solid line the index of import
prices in yen; the dashed line the index of import prices in foreign currencies. Source: IMF,
International Financial Statistics.

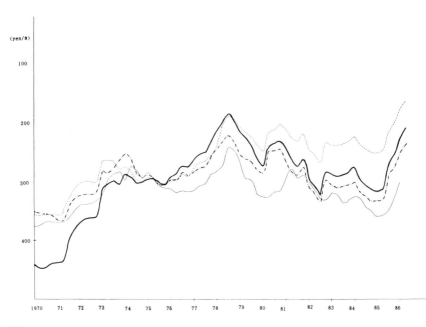

Figure 7.5
Japan's real exchange rates: 1970−1986 (yen/U.S. $). The solid line gives the real exchange rate index based on the unit labor cost; the dashed line nominal exchange rates; the heavy solid line the CPI-based real exchange rates; the heavy dashed line the WPI-based real exchange rates. The CPI, WPI, and the unit labor costs (relative normalized unit labor costs) are expressed using the base 1975 = 100. Sources: IMF, *International Financial Statistics*, and Bank of Japan, *Economic Statistics Annual*.

crude device for checking whether this might be so, and whether internationalization of the yen had any impact on the implied (lack of) transmission from nominal to real exchange rates.

Figure 7.5 shows the movement of the yen/dollar real exchange rates in terms of WPI and CPI. Neither real exchange rate seems to have a very definite trend or sharp movements. Although a large shift in the nominal exchange rate is quite often accompanied by the same in the real exchange rate in the short run, as time passes by, real exchange rates tend to return to the values calculated in 1975. In the long run the PPP relationship seems more or less restored.

If we compare the real exchange rate in terms of WPI to that in terms of CPI, the former almost always shows a smaller value. This reflects greater productivity growth in manufacturing sectors than in other sectors such as services (see Arndt and Richardson, section 1.7, this volume). This tendency had been quite distinct until the first peak of the yen's nominal value,

1977—79, but became less so recently. One could argue therefore that the narrowing of the discrepancy between these two series reflects the slow but gradual increase in openness in services, agriculture, and nontradables sectors.

Incidentally figure 7.5 also shows the comparison of relative labor unit cost (prepared by the IFS) between Japan and the United States.

In contrast to other real exchange rate indexes, this real exchange rate index in terms of labor cost exhibits a path that diverges from the nominal exchange rate in recent years. The relative unit cost for Japanese products that is translated into the dollar terms declined substantially since 1978 when it hit the peak. The law of one price has always been under the pressure of declining labor unit cost that is likely due to the higher productivity increase and moderate wage increases in Japan. In order to understand the relative competitiveness between countries, one has to take account of labor cost as well.

In sum, increased openness and progress in internationalization of the yen seem provisionally to have had some impact on the movement in various prices. Yet their implied further effects on balance-of-payments adjustment are mixed. Export prices seem to be stabilized in terms of yen. CPI-and WPI-based real exchange rates seem also slow to adjust, and seem not very well correlated with current account imbalance. Most of these tendencies seem to imply reasons for slow adjustment in the balance of payments to nominal exchange rates despite the progress in the yen's internationalization.

7.5   Effects of the Internationalization of the Yen on Real and International Balances

One reason for considering the impacts of yen internationalization on prices and real exchange rates is that these in turn create the real capital gains and losses that alter the current and capital accounts of a country's balance of payments through their effects on real wealth and real cash balances. We consider these effects in this section.

We could examine these effects in simple analytical models of cross-currency holdings, such as Henderson and Rogoff (1982) and Branson and Henderson (1985), where economic agents have saving behavior based on real balance (real wealth) effects. They aim a certain desired wealth-income ratio with some parametric adustment speed. The adjustment process is simply an accumulation or decumulation of net foreign wealth by the current deficit or surplus. Any change in preferences for the agents' own-currency assets or foreign-currency assets has a real effect because it changes the exchange rate and exerts real wealth effects on both countries.

Even though we would ideally prefer a model of savings and investment that is based on microeconomic foundation, these simple models are useful to attain intuition on the real effect of the internationalization of a currency. Comparative dynamics using the simple models seems to indicate the following. If the yen's internationalization increases the net global demand for yen-denominated assets, it will normally have a positive effect on the value of the yen. Then there will be a process accumulation and decumulation before both countries attain an equilibrium level of national wealth. The yen will likely appreciate by the shift in asset preference toward it, and the current account surplus will fall for a while so as to make room for a small capital account deficit. The terms of trade will improve temporarily, provided that each country has higher propensity to consume the goods produced in his own country than imported goods. On the other hand, if the yen's internationalization encourages the world on balance to hold more wealth in the form of dollar-denominated assets, then the opposite constellation of effects is likely.

When the Joint Japan-U.S. Ad Hoc Group on the Yen/Dollar Exchange Rate announced its agreement, the exchange rate of the yen depreciated. This suggests that the positive effect on the value of the yen due to expected increase in the demand for yen-denominated assets was dominated by the negative effect due to the shift of domestic preference toward dollar assets. In fact the deregulation of the Japanese financial markets proceeded in such a way that the effect of the decontrol of capital exports was stronger than that of capital imports, which had already been in progress.

The course of events after the G-Five intervention in September 1986 was in the opposite direction. The yen appreciated along with other European currencies, perhaps because official reserve-holding preferences were believed to have shifted away from the dollar. Yet the concomitant adjustment in the balance of payments seems to be very slow, possibly because prices are adjusting slowly, as explained in the last section. Accordingly the working of the real balance (real wealth) effect will also be sluggish.

Even as the value of the yen appreciates, the general price level, in particular, CPI, will not go down as much. Thus Japanese people may not desire to decumulate (or at least to slow down the pace of accumulation) of their national wealth quickly. Thus one may need a larger nominal appreciation of the yen in order to fill the savings-investment gap.

An interesting further issue is the effects is volatile exchange rate movements on intertemporal allocation of resources. In a classical world, money and exchange rates should be neutral, so that any exchange rate movements would imply invariant real rate of interest (or intertemporal commodity price structure) that governs the allocation of resources. However, suppose there is price or wage rigidity as in, say, Dornbusch (1976) but the financial linkage makes the exchange rate very volatile. What would be its effects on savings, investment, the capital stock, real wealth? what would be the intertemporal welfare consequences? These are questions worthy of further exploration.

The internationalization of the yen is a slow process. It depends on various real and financial factors, and it affects significantly mechanisms of microeconomic as well as macroeconomic adjustment. It is not clear, however, whether the ongoing yen internationalization will facilitate the adjustment of Japan's current account smoothly and as promptly.

Notes

We thank our many friends who helped us during the various stages of our research. We are grateful to John Makin, Donald Mathieson, Hirohiko Okumura for their comments, and to Shigeko Uchikomi for her research assistance. Without the encouragement and constructive criticisms by the editors of the volume, particularly by David Richardson, this version would not have been completed.

1. For example, see Tower and Willett (1976, 13−14).

2. See DECD (1984, 56−60).

3. See Horiuchi and Hamada (1985).

4. Grassman (1973) and Page (1977) also point out a general tendency that two-thirds of trade is denominated in the exporter's currency; one-fourth is denominated in the importer's currency.

5. According to Magee-Rao's definition, "nonvehicle currency pricing occurs when the currency of the exporter or the importer is used; vehicle currency pricing occurs when a third currency is used." For any pair of bilateral trading partners, one of the two currencies is defined as "major" if it is used as the dominant form of pricing for trade in both directions; the other currency is "minor." Bilateral trade between pairs of "symmetric currencies" occurs when one country's currency dominates trade in one direction while the other country's currency dominates trade in the other direction."

6. Krugman writes, "This may in part reflect a political decision on the part of Japan not to allow the yen to become an international currency." However, we do not know of any incidence where the Japanese government discouraged traders to invoice their imports or exports. Certainly such a policy does not exist at present.

7. Exports to the United States accounted for 28 percent of the Japanese exports during 1980—84, while those to Western Europe accounted for 16 percent. Some argue that relatively well-developed forward yen markets in western Europe are a reason why yen invoicing has been more common there. See Eken (1984, 528). It is, however, doubtful if this argument applies since 1980, because of the development of forward yen markets everywhere.

8. Direct trade with the center or Nth country is mainly invoiced in that country's currency. For example, 64.5 percent of Swedish exports to the United States (and Canada) were invoiced in U.S. dollars, and 94.3 percent of Swedish imports from the United States (and Canada) were also invoiced in U.S. dollars. (McKinnon 1979, 72)

9. In the period of 1980—84 the relative shares of exports to the United States in the total exports are 13.0 percent in the United Kingdom, 7.4 percent in West Germany, and 6.2 percent in France. These figures are significantly smaller than the 28.3 percent from Japan.

10. It is reported, however, that the recent rise in the ratio of yen-invoiced exports depicted in table 7.1 reflects increases in yen-denominated exports from Japanese firms to their foreign subsidiaries.

References

Bilson, J. F. O. 1983. The Choice of an Invoice Currency in International Transactions. In J. S. Bhandari and B. H. Putnam (eds.), *Economic Interdependence and Flexible Exchange Rates.* Cambridge: MIT Press, ch. 14.

Branson, W. H., and D. W. Henderson. 1985. The Specification and Influence of Asset Markets. In R. W. Jones and P. B. Kenen (eds.), *Handbook of International Economics.* Vol. 2. Amsterdam: Elsevier, ch. 15.

Cohen, B. J. 1971. *The Future of Sterling as an International Currency.* London: Macmillan.

Dornbusch, R. 1976. Expectations and Exchange Rate Dynamics. *Journal of Political Economy* 84:1161—1176.

Eken, S. 1984. Integration of Domestic and International Financial Markets: The Japanese Experience. *IMF Staff Papers* 31, no. 3:499—548.

Frankel, J. A. 1984. *The Yen/Dollar Agreement: Liberalizing Japanese Capital Markets.* Institute for International Economics, Policy Analyses in International Economics, 9.

Grassman, S. 1973. A Fundamental Symmetry in International Payment Patterns. *Journal of International Economics* 3:105—116.

Hamada, K., and F. Hayashi. 1985. Monetary Policy in Postwar Japan. In A. Ando, H. Eguchi, R. Farmer, and Y. Suzuki (eds.), *Monetary Policy of Our Time.* Cambridge: MIT Press.

Henderson, D. W., and K. Rogoff. 1982. Negative Net Foreign Asset Positions and Stability in a World Portfolio Balance Model. *Journal of International Economics* 13:85–104.

Horiuchi, A., and K. Hamada. 1985. The Political Economy of the Japanese Financial Markets. A paper presented to the Japan Political Economy Research Conference.

Kindleberger, C. P. 1965. *Balance-of-Payments Deficits and International Market for Liquidity*. Princeton Studies in International Finance, no. 46. Princeton: Princeton University Press.

Kindleberger, C. P. 1972. The Benefits of International Money. *Journal of International Economics* 2:425–442.

Krugman, P. 1980. Vehicle Currencies and the Structure of International Exchange. *Journal of Money, Credit, and Banking* 12, no. 3:511–526.

Krugman, P. 1984. The International Role of the Dollar: Theory and Prospect. In J. F. O. Bilson and R. C. Marston (eds.), *Exchange Rate Theory and Practice*. Chicago: University of Chicago Press, pp. 261–278.

Magee, S. P., and R. K. S. Rao. 1980. Vehicle and Nonvehicle Currencies in International Trade. *American Economic Review* 70, no. 2:368–373.

McKinnon, R. I. 1973. *Money and Capital in Economic Development*. Washington, D. C.: Brookings Institution.

McKinnon, R. I. 1979. *Money in International Exchange*. Oxford: Oxford University Press.

McKinnon, R. I. 1984. *An International Standard for Monetary Stabilization*. Policy Analyses in International Economics, B. Washington, D.C.: Institute for International Economics.

DECD. 1984. *Economic Surveys 1983–1984: Japan*. Paris: OECD.

Okumura, H. 1985. Internationalization of the Yen: Present Situation and Policy Choice. Paper presented at the NBER/NIPA Joint Study Group, August.

Page, S. A. B. 1977. The Currency of Invoicing in Merchandise Trade. *National Institute Economic Review*, no. 81:77–81.

Sakakibara, E., and A. Kondoh 1984. *Study on the Internationalization of Tokyo's Money Markets*. JCIF Policy Study Series, no. 1.

Shinkai, Y. 1984. Internationalization of Finance in Japan. Mimeo. Osaka University. Prepared for JPERC, Vol. 2.

Tower, E., and T. D. Willett 1976. *The Theory of Optimum Currency Areas and Exchange-Rate Flexibility*. Special Papers in International Economics, no. 11. Princeton: Princeton University Press.

8

Long-Run Exchange Rate Variability and International Trade

Paul De Grauwe
Bernard de Bellefroid

With the advent of flexible exchange rates, the issue of the effects of exchange rate variability on international trade has become an important one. Much of the research effort in this area has focused on the question of whether the greater exchange rate variability has negatively affected international trade. Researchers have tried to test the hypothesis that exchange rate variability is destructive for trade. On the whole, it can be said that a majority of studies have failed to find conclusive evidence supporting this hypothesis.[1]

The major criticism that can be formulated against these empirical studies is that by using time-series data of a relatively short period, they are compelled to analyze the effect of exchange rate variability measured on a daily or monthly basis. As a result they have failed to analyze the effects of exchange rate movements that occur over time horizons of several years.

It is now generally felt that the floating exchange rate regime may affect the international trading system, not so much because the exchange rates have become mre volatile on a monthly or even quarterly basis but rather because it makes it possible for currencies to deviate from their purchasing power parities during several years in a row (see Williamson 1983). It can be said that if the flexible exchange rate regime only leads to larger short-term exchange rate movements, it increases the degree of *risk*, against which insurance can be taken at relatively low cost. This risk therefore should not be expected to have significant effects on international trade. If, however, the floating exchange rate system leads to long swings in real exchange rates ("sustained misalignment"), it increases the degree of *uncertainty*.[2] A characteristic of these long-run movements of the real exchange rates is their low frequency. The dollar, for example, declined during the first six years of the flexible exchange rate period (1973–78) and moved up again during 1979–84. As a result economic agents lack sufficient observations to compute probability distributions of these exchange rate changes. It is generally very difficult to buy insurance against this uncertainty, since the pricing of this long-run risk is impossible. Thus, if the flexible exchange rate regime has affected international trade, it is most likely to come from these long swings in real exchange rates. The first contribution that this chapter makes is to outline a method that makes it possible to analyze the effects of exchange rate variability defined over longer periods than days or months.

The stylized facts of the 1970s and the early 1980s are that the growth rate of international trade has declined substantially and that this decline has coincided with the inception of the flexible exchange rate system. The issue here is whether this is pure coincidence (so that we have to find other factors that are responsible for the decline in the growth rate of trade), or whether there is a causal relation between exchange rate variability and the decline in the growth rate of trade. One major empirical problem here is to separate the effect of exchange rate variability from other shocks, in particular, the oil shock, that occured at about the time exchange rates became more volatile. The second contribution that this chapter makes is to use cross-sectional techniques that allow us to separate the effects of oil shocks, and trade integration, from the exchange rate effects.

8.1   Growth of Exports and Exchange Rate Variability

In this section we study the question of the extent to which increased real exchange rate variability, observed during the flexible exchange rate period, contributed to a reduced *growth* of trade. Most of the empirical literature on the subject has analyzed how exchange rate variability has affected the *levels* of international trade.[3] Thus a distinctive feature of the present study is that it concentrates on the factors that explain the decline in the growth rates of international trade.

A second feature of the present study is that, contrary to most of the empirical studies that have been conducted using time series, we will use cross-sectional techniques. The cross-sectional approach used here has the advantage of allowing us to exploit better the very different degrees of exchange rate variability that countries had during the same flexible exchange rate period. In addition, by using cross-sectional approaches it is possible to separate out the effects of shocks (e.g., oil shocks) that affected all countries simultaneously from the effects of exchange rate variability. Finally, the cross-sectional evidence enables us to isolate structural variables (in particular, differences in trade regime) from the exchange rate variable.

The most striking fact about the long-run growth rate of international trade is its substantial deceleration observed since the inception of the floating exchange rate system. On average the growth rate of trade during the post-1973 period was less than half the growth rate observed during the 1960s. This decline is even more pronounced for a subgroup of countries, the original EEC. Whereas the bilateral trade flows of the original EEC countries grew at an average yearly growth rate of 14 percent during the 1960s, this growth rate had dropped to 3 percent after 1973. This deceleration of the *intra*-EEC trade occurred despite the fact that *intra*-EEC exchange rates were not substantially more volatile after 1973 than before that date.

The model

In order to explain these striking phenomena, we propose a model that distinguishes between the effects of four types of variables: (1) trade integration (or disintegration) variables, (2) the growth of real income, (3) variables that proxy for exchange rate uncertainty, (4) systemwide shocks such as the oil shock.

The model is specified as follows:

$$X_{ijt} = b_t T_{ijt} + c_t Y_{jt} + e_t S_{ijt} + a_t + u_{ijt},$$ (1)

with $i, j = 1, \ldots, n, \quad t = 1, 2,$

where X_{ijt} is the average yearly growth rate of the exports of country i to country j, during period t. We distinguish two periods, the fixed exchange rate period 1960−69 and the flexible exchange rate period 1973−84. We leave out the period 1970−72 which can best be considered as a transition period between the two exchange rate regimes. Note that since X_{ijt} is defined as an average growth rate over a 10 and a 12-year period, the model aims at explaining why the *long-run* growth rates of trade differ both between the two subperiods and between countries within each subperiod.

The variable T_{ijt} represents the trade integration that has occurred between groups of countries. It is defined as a dummy variable in the following way. When a subgroup of countries ($i = 1, \ldots, k$ and $k < n$) form a customs union during subperiod t, all the observations on the bilateral trade flows of these countries are given a value 1, and a 0 otherwise. As there are several subgroups of countries that can be clustered together according to this criterion, we have more than one trade integration variable. We expect that if two countries form a customs union, this will increase the level of their trade flows. This then also implies that during the period of adjustment to the trade arrangement, the *growth rates* of trade among the members of the customs union will increase.[4]

The income variable is represented by Y_{jt}, which is defined as the average yearly growth rate of GDP of country j (the importing country) during the subperiod t. We expect that countries that have experienced a high growth rate of output during the subperiod t also experience a high growth rate of their imports from the other countries in the sample. There are two income variables, one for the fixed exchange rate period (Y_1) and one for the flexible exchange rate period (Y_2).

Exchange rate uncertainty is captured by the variable S_{ijt}.[5] The latter is defined as the variability (discussed more precisely later) of the yearly percentage changes of the bilateral exchange rate between currency i and currency j around the mean observed during subperiod t. Thus this variable reflects long-run (yearly) movements of the bilateral exchange rates around the mean changes observed during the fixed and the flexible exchange rate subperiods.

There are several reasons why an increase in exchange rate uncertainty might lower the growth rate of trade. One appeals to risk aversion and could be called the "risk premium effect." With more exchange rate uncertainty a risk premium will be added to the cost of international transactions, thereby reducing their size (see Hooper and Kohlhagen 1978). This then will lead to a reduction of the growth rates of trade, until economic agents have adjusted to the desired (lower) level of trade.

A second might be called the "political economy effect." Increased exchange rate movements lead to protectionist pressures in those countries whose real exchange rate appreciates. To the extent that the protectionist measures are left in place when the currency tends to depreciate again, exchange rate variability increases the level of protection over time and affects trade flows negatively. (see Williamson 1983). Here we expect that exchange rate variability leads to a trendwise increase in protectionist pressure and therefore to a permanent decline in the growth rates of trade. This contrasts with the risk premium effect which leads to a temporary decline in the growth rates of trade.

Several alternative definitions of variability are considered here. First, we distinguish between *nominal* and *real* exchange rate variability. The former measures the variability of the nominal exchange rates; the latter the variability of the nominal exchange rates corrected for inflation differentials (real exchange rates). We expect that movements of the real exchange rates generally lead to higher uncertainty in international trade than movements of the same magnitude in the nominal exchange rates. The reason can be explained as follows. When a currency depreciates by x percent, it is likely that the real exchange rate will change by less than x percent, because inflation differentials will in general offset the nominal depreciation, at least partially. Put the other way around, a given real exchange rate movement typically implies that the nominal exchange rate has changed by a larger amount. This difference between real and nominal exchange rate changes is typically very small when we consider short-term movements. It becomes more important when long-run movements are analyzed, as is done here.

Second, the statistical measures of variability which we use are the *standard deviation* of the yearly growth rates of the exchange rates around the mean (real and nominal), and the *mean absolute change* of the exchange rates (in percent). With these different definitions of variability we end up with four possible measures of exchange rate variability. More detail about the precise definition of these variables is presented in appendix B.

Note that we only consider measures of *ex post* exchange rate variability—that is, the observed variability of exchange rate changes. We have not attempted to estimate *ex ante* measures of exchange rate variability—that is, that forecasted over the future decision period. There are two reasons why we have not computed these ex ante measures here. First, since we are averaging over at least ten years, we expect the average of forecast errors over that long period to be zero. Second, from a practical point of view, it may not make much difference whether we use ex ante or ex post measures of variability. Empirical studies suggest that most of the observed changes in the exchange rates were unanticipated (see Mussa 1978; Frenkel 1981), so that the ex ante and ex post measures are highly correlated. Thus, when the observed exchange rate variability increases, we can be confident that the errors in forecasting the exchange rates also increase.

The final variable to be explained is a_t ($t = 1, 2$). a_1 is a constant term for the observations of the first period; a_2 is a constant term for the observations of the second period. Thus a_t measures the extent to which the average growth rates of trade were different during the two subperiods, where these differences are unrelated to the other explanatory variables in the model. Therefore this variable can be interpreted as measuring the effects of shocks (e.g., the oil shock) which occurred since 1973 and affected the trade flows of all the industrialized countries in the sample in the same way.

The reader may wonder why no relative price (or competitiveness) variables appear in the equation (1). The reason is that we concentrate here

on the determinants of the long-run growth rates of trade. We will apply
the model to explain the growth rates of trade during two periods of 10
and 12 years of duration. Typically relative price variables affect trade
flows in the short run (with lags of up to two or three years). Over very
long periods, as considered here, these relative price effects are likely to
have disappeared.

Empirical Results

The model was estimated using the bilateral trade flows between the ten
major industrialized countries (in terms of the size of their external trade).
These countries are Belgium, Canada, France, Germany, Italy, Japan, Neth-
erlands, Switzerland, United Kingdom, and United States. Together their
external trade amounts to 87 percent of the international trade of the
industrialized countries and 60 percent of world trade.

With ten countries we obtain 90 bilateral trade flows during the fixed
and the flexible exchange rate periods, so that we have 180 observations.
The result of estimating equation (1) is presented in table 8.1. Note that the
way we have specified the model implies that we do not restrict the income
and the exchange rate variable to have identical coefficients during the
fixed and the flexible exchange rate periods. Table 8.2 presents the results
where we impose such restrictions (also on the constant term).

We distinguish between several trade integration variables. One, called
EC-60, groups all the trade flows between the original EEC members in the
first subperiod. The second one, EC-70, has the same grouping during the
floating rate period. The third one, EC-new, brings together the trade flows
between the United Kingdom and the original EEC countries during the
second subperiod. This variable captures the effect of the admission of the
United Kingdom in the EEC. Finally, we have also added dummy variables
for the exports of Japan during the two subperiods (JAP-60 and JAP-70).
These variables capture the exceptional Japanese trade creation phenomenon during the two subperiods which we cannot explain by income
growth or by exchange rate variability.

The results can now be interpreted as follows. First, the constant term of
the second period tends to be somewhat smaller that the one of the first
period. However, the difference is not statistically significant. Thus the
shocks (other than those specified in the model) that occurred after 1973
and affected all industrial countries comparably do not seem to have significantly affected the trade flows *between* the industrialized countries.[6]

Second, the trade integration variables have a significant influence in the

Table 8.1
Estimation results, equation (1): 1960–69 and 1973–84

Explanatory variables	Coefficients			
	Nominal variability		Real variability	
	Standard deviation	Mean absolute change	Standard deviation	Mean absolute change
Constant-60 (a_1)	2.52	3.02	5.13	4.66
	(2.4)	(2.8)	(3.5)	(3.2)
Constant-70 (a_2)	3.31	2.62	3.95	3.60
	(2.4)	(1.9)	(2.9)	(2.6)
Trade integration				
EEC-60	6.18	6.10	6.08	5.97
	(9.2)	(9.0)	(9.3)	(8.9)
EEC-70	−1.32	−0.85	−1.59	−1.41
	(−1.5)	(−1.0)	(−1.8)	(−1.6)
EEC-new	4.74	4.67	5.57	5.21
	(5.2)	(5.0)	(6.0)	(5.7)
JAP-60	12.46	12.27	12.19	12.26
	(13.1)	(12.7)	(13.2)	(13.2)
JAP-70	4.19	3.90	4.20	3.89
	(4.2)	(4.0)	(4.4)	(4.1)
Income growth				
Y-60	1.02	0.99	0.97	0.99
	(6.9)	(6.5)	(6.7)	(6.8)
Y-70	1.14	1.00	1.10	1.02
	(3.1)	(2.8)	(3.2)	(3.0)
Exchange rate				
S-60	−0.04	−0.36	−0.82	−0.88
	(−0.2)	(−1.0)	(−2.3)	(−1.9)
S-70	−0.22	−0.15	−0.32	−0.32
	(−2.0)	(−1.3)	(−2.6)	(−2.2)
Coefficient of determination (R^2)	0.76	0.76	0.77	0.77

Note: The numbers in parenthesis are t-statistics.

Table 8.2
Estimation results, equation (1): 1960−69 and 1973−84 (restricted version)

Explanatory variables	Coefficients			
	Nominal variability		Real variability	
	Standard deviation	Mean absolute change	Standard deviation	Mean absolute change
Constant	2.90	2.72	3.66	3.44
	(3.7)	(3.5)	(4.4)	(4.1)
Trade integration				
EEC-60	6.20	6.13	6.02	6.02
	(9.5)	(9.3)	(9.3)	(9.2)
EEC-70	−1.03	−0.89	−1.28	−1.26
	(−1.5)	(−1.3)	(−1.9)	(−1.9)
EEC-new	4.76	4.66	5.54	5.26
	(5.4)	(5.3)	(6.2)	(5.9)
JAP-60	12.33	12.39	12.26	12.32
	(13.3)	(13.4)	(13.5)	(13.6)
JAP-70	4.01	3.93	4.19	3.94
	(4.2)	(4.1)	(4.5)	(4.2)
Income growth				
Y	1.01	1.01	0.97	0.98
	(8.3)	(8.1)	(8.1)	(8.2)
Exchange rate				
S	−0.16	−0.17	−0.28	−0.30
	(−3.0)	(−2.9)	(−3.9)	(−3.6)
Coefficient of determination (R^2)	0.76	0.76	0.77	0.77

Note: The numbers in parenthesis are t-statistics.

explanation of the bilateral trade flows. For example, during the fixed rate period the existence of a customs union among the EEC countries increased the yearly growth rate of the members' trade (relative to the other countries in the sample) by approximately 6 percent (see the row EEC-60 in table 8.1). During the flexible exchange rate system we observe the opposite phenomenon: the same group of countries now experience a small negative effect from their trade association (see row EEC-70). This negative trade integration effect could be due to trade diversion following the adhesion of new members in the EEC. During the same period we observe a positive and significant integration effect on the UK-EEC trade of approximately 5.0 percent per year. This reflects the positive effects of the adhesion of the United Kingdom to the EEC.

Third, we find that 1 percent higher GDP growth leads in the long run to approximately 1.0 percent higher growth of trade. This income elasticity of bilateral trade flows is not significantly different between the two subperiods.[7] These results may seem surprising to those accustomed to time-series studies of the income elasticities of international trade flows. In these studies one usually finds long-run income elasticities exceeding 1, which implies that in the long run people tend to spend their whole income on imports. These results are typically obtained for periods when countries experienced strong trade integration. To the extent that one ignores the trade integration effects (which is typical in time-series studies), these effects will show up in the income elasticity of the trade flows.[8] As a result one can say that time-series studies will tend to overestimate the long-run income elasticity of trade flows. In the results obtained here, where we have isolated the trade integration effects, we obtain the more plausible result of a unit (long-run) income elasticity of trade.

Fourth, it appears that the proxies of exchange rate uncertainty all have the expected negative sign. In addition they are usually significant. The size of the coefficients and the level of significance tend to be higher when we use measures of *real* exchange rate variability, than when we employ *nominal* measures, as we should expect since relative prices are what determine rational economic decisions. In addition the coefficients tend to be more significant, albeit smaller, for the period of flexible exchange rates (compare row S-70 with S-60).

Note also that the results of table 8.2, where we have restricted the coefficients of the constant terms, of the income and of the exchange rate variables to be the same over the two periods, are very similar to table 8.1. In addition an F-test leaves us unable to reject the hypothesis that these coefficients are the same for the two periods.

We can conclude that the variability of the exchange rates (especially of the *real* exchange rates) had a significant negative effect on the growth rates of bilateral trade flows among the major industrialized countries.

As noted earlier, most time-series studies have been unable to find such effects. The reason we find negative effects of exchange rate variability here are twofold. First, by using cross-sectional techniques, we are able to separate the effects of trade integration among groups of countries. This is quite important as the evidence concerning trade among the EEC countries testifies. The old EEC countries experienced a substantial deceleration of their bilateral trade in the 1970s despite low exchange rate variability. Thus studies that do not take these effects into account may lead to bias. Second, we have concentrated on the long-run exchange rate movements, which tend to lead to more pronounced uncertainty than short-term variations against which insurance can be taken relatively cheaply. To illustrate this point, we have estimated the same equation using measures of short-run exchange rate variability. The results are reported in appendix A. It appears that these short-term measures have no significant negative effect on trade flows. Thus, when we concentrate on short-term exchange rate variability, we also find, as in most empirical studies, that these have little effects on the growth rates of international trade.

The regression results contained in table 8.1 or table 8.2, allow us to quantify the contribution of the independent variables on average to the average deceleration of international trade since 1973. Since the constant term and the coefficients of the income and exchange rate variables are not significantly different between the two periods, we will use the regression results of table 8.2 (which restricts these coefficients to be equal in the two subperiods). To obtain these contributions, we multiply the coefficients of the income variable with the observed mean growth rates of income in the first and second periods.[9] The difference between these two numbers measures the contribution of the decline in the growth rate of output in explaining the decline in the growth rate of trade. A similar procedure allows us to compute the contribution of the observed (average) increase of the exchange rate variability from 1960−69 to 1973−84 in the explanation of the deceleration of international trade.[10] Finally, we obtain the contribution of the trade integration variables by multiplying the mean value of these variables with the respective coefficients. This yields average trade integration effects in the fixed and flexible exchange rate periods. By subtracting the latter from the former, we obtain a number that tells us by how much international trade flows have changed due to the changes which occurred in the trade regimes.

The results are presented in table 8.3. Since we have four different

Table 8.3
Explanation of the decline in the growth rate of international trade from 1960−69 to 1973−84 (using the results of table 8.2)

Observed decline: 6.4 percent			
Measure of exchange rate variability	Contribution of		
	Trade integration	Income growth	Exchange rates
Nominal			
Standard deviation	1.9	3.2	1.3
Absolute change	1.9	3.2	1.4
Real			
Standard deviation	1.8	3.0	1.7
Absolute change	1.9	3.1	1.5

definitions of exchange rate variability, we obtain four sets of estimates. It can be seen that the major part (about half) of the total decline in the growth rate of international trade among the major industrialized countries (6.4 percent) can be accounted for by the deceleration of the growth rate of output. About 30 percent can be explained by the trade integration effects—that is, by the substantial slowdown of trade integration among the original EEC countries during the second period (which was only partially offset by trade creation between these EEC countries and the United Kingdom) and the slowdown of the trade penetration of Japan in the industrialized world. Finally, the increase of the exchange rate variability observed since 1973 accounts for approximately 20 percent of the total decline in the growth rate of international trade among these countries (depending on the measure of variability we use).

We conclude that although the uncertainty generated by the large variability of (real) exchange rates since 1973 is less important than the other two factors (GDP growth rate and trade integration) as an explanation of the deceleration of international trade in the industrialized world, it has contributed significantly toward this phenomenon.

The results of table 8.3 explain the slowdown in international trade for the industrial countries as a whole. It is also useful to disaggregate these results. As stressed earlier, the decline of the bilateral trade flows among the original EEC countries was substantially larger than the other bilateral trade flows. Therefore we divide the sample of trade flows in two parts, the intra-EEC flows and all the others. We then compute tables similar to table 8.3.[11] The results are given in tables 8.4 and 8.5. They lead to the following interpretation. First, the trade integration variables explain the largest part

Table 8.4
Explanation of the decline in the growth rate of intra-EEC trade from 1960–69 to 1973–84 (using the results of table 8.2)

Observed decline: 11 percent

Measure of exchange rate variability	Contribution of		
	Trade integration	Income growth	Exchange rates
Nominal			
Standard deviation	7.2	3.2	0.6
Absolute change	7.0	3.2	0.8
Real			
Standard deviation	7.3	3.1	0.7
Absolute change	7.3	3.1	0.6

Table 8.5
Explanation of the decline in the growth rate of non-intra-EEC trade from 1960–69 to 1973–84 (using the results of table 8.2)

Observed decline: 5.1 percent

Measure of exchange rate variability	Contribution of		
	Trade integration	Income growth	Exchange rates
Nominal			
Standard deviation	0.4	3.2	1.5
Absolute change	0.4	3.2	1.6
Real			
Standard deviation	0.2	3.0	2.1
Absolute change	0.3	3.1	1.8

(two-thirds) of the spectacular decline of the yearly growth rate of intra-EEC trade flows, whereas the variability of the exchange rates does not contribute much in the explanation of this decline. Second, for the trade flows outside the original EEC, we find a completely different picture. The substantially smaller decline of the growth rates of these trade flows is explained to a larger degree by the increased exchange rate variability. Close to one-third of the decline in the growth rate of trade can be accounted for by the exchange rate variable. Conversely, a smaller part of this decline is due to trade integration effects. Thus one can say that the slowdown of the growth rate of international trade flows outside the EEC has been significantly affected by the increase in the degree of exchange rate variability.

8.2   Limitations and Extensions of the Analysis

There are at least two limitations inherent in the estimation of the previous sections. The first one is that the right-hand-side variables in our basic equation (1) may not be independent. This may then bias the results. In particular, the increase in the exchange rate variability since 1973 may have caused some decline in the growth rate of output observed since the same date. If this is the case, the procedure reported in the previous section underestimates the effect of exchange rate variability on the growth rates of international trade.

The same can be said about the effects of trade integration. The slowdown in the process of trade integration among the industrialized countries may also have contributed to the decline in the growth rate of output. As a result we may have underestimated the importance of trade integration variables in the explanation of the slowdown in international trade. We have not yet been able to model these interactions in a satisfactory way and will not pursue this matter here.

A second limitation of the analysis of the previous section is the assumption that it is uncertainty concerning the movements of the bilateral exchange rates only which affects the long-run growth rates of the bilateral trade flows. It may be, however, that the systemwide exchange rate uncertainty is an important contributing factor too. For example, bilateral exchange rate variability within the original EEC has not increased substantially during the flexible rate period. However, the exchange rate uncertainty facing the EEC may have increased nevertheless because of the large exchange rate variations outside this trading bloc. If this is the case, we underestimate the importance of exchange rate uncertainty by only looking at the bilateral exchange rate movements.

In order to take this point into account, we extend the model by adding the variability of *effective* exchange rates in equation (1). Since the effective exchange rate of a particular currency measures how that currency moves against the currencies of all its trading partners, it provides us with a proxy of systemwide exchange rate variations. Adding this variable then tests the proposition that systemwide uncertainty about exchange rates has negatively affected international trade flows. This yields the following equation:

$$X_{ijt} = a_t + b_t T_{ijt} + c_t Y_{jt} + e_t S_{ijt} + m_t E_{it} + u_{ijt},$$ (2)

with $i, j = 1, \ldots, n,$ $t = 1, 2,$

where E_{it} is the variability of the effective exchange rate of country i. The other variables were defined earlier. We use the same measures of variability as in the previous section. The results of estimating equation (2) are presented in table 8.6. It can be seen that the variability of the effective exchange rate has no significant additional influence on the trade flows of the fixed rate period (see row E-60). However, this variable appears to have a significant additional negative effect on the long-run growth rate of the trade flows during the flexible exchange rate period. This is especially the case when we use measures of *real* exchange rate variability. It should also be noted that in these cases the coefficients of the bilateral exchange rate variability are reduced. Thus we can conclude that the increase of the systemwide real exchange rate variability since 1973 has negatively affected the growth rate of trade. This is also the case for the trade flows between those countries (like the EMS-countries) which have maintained relatively stable bilateral exchange rates.

Using the results of table 8.6 and the procedure of table 8.4, we can compute the contribution of trade integration, income, and exchange rate variables to the decline of growth of international trade since 1973. The results are given in table 8.7. (We have done the computations with the results of the *real* exchange rate variability only.) The decline of the growth of GDP remains the most important variable. However, we now find that the exchange rate variability is more important than the trade integration variables in explaining the deceleration in international trade since 1973. This contrasts with the results of the previous section, where only the bilateral exchange rate variability was taken into account. The real exchange rate uncertainty now accounts for approximately one-third of the total drop in the growth rate of international trade. This result suggests that the systemwide uncertainty produced by the volatility of real exchange rates (as measured by the effective exchange rates) is an important additional explanation of the slowdown in the growth of international trade.

Table 8.6
Estimation results, equation (2): 1960–69 and 1973–84

Explanatory variables	Coefficients			
	Nominal variability		Real variability	
	Standard deviation	Mean absolute change	Standard deviation	Mean absolute change
Constant-60	2.53	3.03	4.68	4.39
	(2.4)	(2.8)	(3.1)	(2.8)
Constant-70	5.05	2.63	5.13	4.84
	(3.1)	(1.8)	(3.6)	(3.3)
Trade integration				
EEC-60	6.18	6.10	5.97	5.92
	(9.3)	(9.0)	(9.1)	(8.8)
EEC-70	−1.64	−0.85	−1.75	−1.63
	(−1.8)	(−1.0)	(−2.0)	(−1.9)
EEC-new	5.22	4.66	6.25	5.84
	(5.5)	(4.8)	(6.5)	(6.2)
JAP-60	12.35	12.25	12.29	12.22
	(12.4)	(11.7)	(13.4)	(13.2)
JAP-70	6.47	3.89	6.17	5.82
	(4.2)	(3.4)	(4.9)	(4.6)
Income growth				
Y-60	1.03	0.99	0.95	0.98
	(6.8)	(6.3)	(6.6)	(6.8)
Y-70	1.16	1.00	1.13	1.06
	(3.2)	(2.8)	(3.3)	(3.1)
Exchange rate				
S-60	0.01	−0.34	−1.02	−0.98
	(0.1)	(−0.7)	(−2.5)	(−1.9)
S-70	−0.21	−0.15	−0.27	−0.28
	(−1.9)	(−1.3)	(−2.1)	(−1.9)
E-60	−0.10	−0.04	0.54	0.34
	(−0.4)	(−0.1)	(1.0)	(0.4)
E-70	−0.33	0.00	−0.35	−0.40
	(−2.0)	(0.1)	(−2.4)	(−2.2)
Coefficient of determination (R^2)	0.76	0.76	0.78	0.77

Note: The numbers in parenthesis are t-statistics.

Table 8.7
Explanation of the decline in the growth rate of international trade from 1960–69 to 1973–84 (using the results of table 8.6)

Observed decline: 6.4 percent

Measure of exchange rate variability	Contribution of		
	Trade integration	Income growth	Exchange rates
Real			
Standard deviation	1.2	2.6	2.7
Absolute change	1.2	2.9	2.3

8.3   Conclusion

Since the start of the flexible exchange rate system in 1973, the industrialized countries have experienced a substantial decline in the growth rates of their bilateral trade flows. In this chapter we have attempted to explain this phenomenon. By using cross-sectional evidence pooled with observations of two periods (1960–69 and 1973–84), we were able to show that the long-run variability of the real exchange rates contributed in a significant way toward this phenomenon. In fact we found that close to 20 to 30 percent of the observed decline of the growth rate of international trade among the industrialized countries can be associated with the substantial increase of the long-run variability of real exchange rates. The other important factors that were isolated in this study are the decline in the growth rate of output (which accounts for approximately 50 percent of the decline in the growth rate of trade) and the slowdown of the trade integration process in the industrialized world since the early 1970s (which is responsible for 20 to 30 percent of this decline).

Most empirical studies have been unable to find negative effects of exchange rate variability. The reason we find such effects here are twofold. First, by using cross-sectional approaches, we were able to isolate the effects of trade integration among groups of countries. This is quite important as the evidence concerning trade among the EEC countries testifies. Since the early 1970s the trade integration process among the old EEC countries slowed down substantially. As a result these countries experienced a much larger deceleration of their bilateral trade than the rest of the industrialized world despite lower exchange rate variability. Thus studies that do not take these effects into account are likely to lead to biased results of the effects of exchange rate variability. Second, in contrast with most existing empirical studies, we have concentrated on long-run (yearly) exchange rate movements, which tend to lead to more pronounced uncertainty than short-term variations (weekly or monthly) against which insurance can be taken relatively cheaply.

8.4 Appendix A

Table 8.A1
Estimation results, equation (1): 1960–69 and 1973–84 (quarterly observations)

| | Coefficients | | | |
| | Nominal variability | | Real variability | |
Explanatory variables	Standard deviation	Mean absolute change	Standard deviation	Mean absolute change
Constant	0.68	0.76	0.48	0.63
	(2.5)	(2.8)	(1.2)	(1.5)
Trade integration				
EEC-60	1.53	1.52	1.54	1.54
	(9.0)	(9.0)	(9.1)	(9.1)
EEC-70	−0.17	−0.23	−0.23	−0.33
	(−0.6)	(−0.9)	(−0.9)	(−1.3)
EEC-new	1.23	1.21	1.22	1.28
	(5.3)	(4.8)	(5.3)	(5.5)
JAP-60	3.10	3.07	3.15	3.12
	(12.8)	(12.7)	(13.0)	(13.0)
JAP-70	0.89	0.92	0.89	0.93
	(3.7)	(3.8)	(3.7)	(3.9)
Income growth				
Y-60	1.01	0.99	1.05	1.03
	(6.5)	(6.5)	(6.8)	(6.8)
Y-70	0.89	0.94	0.87	0.94
	(2.6)	(2.7)	(2.5)	(2.7)
Exchange rate[a]				
S-60	−0.14	−0.36	−0.09	−0.04
	(−0.5)	(−1.0)	(0.3)	(−0.1)
S-70	−0.08	−0.10	−0.14	−0.19
	(−0.6)	(−1.0)	(−1.1)	(−1.6)
Coefficient of determination (R^2)	0.76	0.76	0.76	0.76

a. To obtain short-term measures of variability of the exchange rates (S-60 and S-70), we computed the standard deviations of the quarterly growth rates around the yearly averages; these numbers were then averaged for the two subperiods. The second measure is the mean absolute quarterly change in percent.

8.5   Appendix B: Data Sources and Definitions

The *bilateral exports* were obtained from the OECD, *Statistics of Foreign Trade, Overall Trade by Countries,* Series A. These are dollar figures. In order to compute the *real* growth rate of the export from country i to country j, the export figures were first converted into domestic currency using the dollar exchange rate from IMF, *International Financial Statistics* (IFS). This figure was then deflated using the export price index (or export unit value) from IFS. Ideally one should deflate the export figures using bilateral export price indexes. Since these are generally unavailable, we were forced to deflate the bilateral exports of each country by the aggregate export price index of that country. This is a potential source of errors.

The *real bilateral exchange rates* (R_{ijt}) were computed as follows:

$$R_{ijt} = \frac{E_{ijt} P_{jt}}{P_{it}},$$

where E_{ijt} is the index of the market exchange rate of currency j in units of currency i obtained from IFS (using the dollar rates of currency i and j); P_{jt} and P_{it} are the wholesale price indices of country j and i, respectively (source: IFS, line 63).

The *effective exchange rate* of country i is a weighted average of the indexes of the bilateral exchange rates of currency i with the nine other currencies in the sample. The weights are given by the export shares (source: OECD, *Statistics of Foreign Trade, Overall Trade by Countries,* Series A). The *real effective exchange rate* is defined in a similar way using the real bilateral exchange rates.

Notes

1. Representative studies are Hooper and Kohlhagen (1978) and Cushman (1983). The former find significant effects for some trade flows, however. For a survey of the literature see International Monetary Fund (1984). More recent studies have uncovered significant effects of exchange rate variability on trade. An example is the study by Akhtar and Hilton (1984). This study was recently criticized by Gotur (1985). Other recent studies finding significant effects are Coes (1981), Kenen and Rodrik (1985), and Thursby and Thursby (1986).

2. See Meltzer (1985) for a recent attempt to implement empirically this distinction between risk and uncertainty.

3. See note 1 for references.

4. In the long run when all adjustments have taken place, there is no reason why the growth rates of trade between countries forming a customs union should exceed the growth rate of their trade with other countries.

5. For a theoretical analysis of the effects of exchange rate uncertainty on international trade, see Hooper and Kohlhagen (1978).

6. This does not mean that these shocks may not have affected the trade flows of the ten industrialized countries in the sample with the rest of the world. To analyze this issue, one would have to increase the sample of countries.

7. We have experimented with regressions where the income elasticity is different between EEC countries and the other countries in the sample. In general, we do not find significant differences.

8. Technically, the trade integration and income variables are typically correlated. Omitting the former biases the coefficient of the income variable upward.

9. During the 1960–69 period, the average yearly growth rate of GDP in the ten countries in the sample was 5.3 percent; during 1973–83 this growth rate declined to 2.2 percent.

10. For example, the standard deviation of the yearly growth rates of the real exchange rates increased from 2.9 to 9.1 percent.

11. With intra-EEC we mean intra-original-EEC.

References

Akhtar, M. A., and R. Spence Hilton. 1984. Exchange Rate Uncertainty and International Trade: Some Conceptual Issues and New Estimates for Germany and the United States. Research paper no. 8403. Federal Reserve Bank of New York, May.

Coes, Donald. 1981. The Crawling Peg and Exchange Rate Uncertainty. In John Williamson (eds.), *Exchange Rate Rules: The Theory, Performance, and Prospects of the Crawling Peg*. New York: St Martin's, pp. 113–136.

Cushman, David, O. 1983. The Effects of Real Exchange Rate Risk on International Trade, *Journal of International Economics* 15 (August): 44–23.

Frenkel, Jacob. 1981. Flexible Exchange Rates and the Role of "News": Lessons from the 1970s. *Journal of Political Economy* 89 (August): 665–705.

Gotur, Padma. 1985. Effects of Exchange Rate Volatility on Trade: Some Further Evidence. *Staff Papers*, International Monetary Fund, 32 (September): 475–512.

Hooper, Peter, and Steven W. Kohlhagen. 1978. The Effect of Exchange Rate Uncertainty on the Prices and Volume of International Trade. *Journal of International Economics* 8 (November): 483–511.

International Monetary Fund. 1984. *Exchange Rate Volatility and International Trade.* Occasional paper no. 28. Washington, D.C., July.

Kenen, Peter, and Dani Rodrik. 1986. Measuring and Analyzing the Effects of Short-term Volatility in Real Exchange Rates. *Review of Economics and Statistics.* 68 (May):311–315.

Meltzer, Allan H. 1985. Variability of Prices, Output and Money under Fixed and Fluctuating Exchange Rates: An Empirical Study of Monetary Regimes in Japan and the United States. Unpublished manuscript.

Mussa, Michael. 1978. Empirical Regularities in the Behavior of Exchange Rates and Theories of the Foreign Exchange Market. In K. Brunner and A. H. Meltzer, (eds.), *Policies for Employment and Exchange Rates.* Vol. 11. Carnegie Rochester Conference Series.

Thursby, Marie C. 1981. The Resource Reallocation Costs of Fixed and Flexible Exchange Rates: A Multi-Country Extension, *Journal of International Economics* 11 (November):487–493.

Thursby, J. G., and Marie Thursby. 1986. Bilateral Trade Flows, the Linder Hypothesis, and Exchange Risk. Unpublished manuscript.

Williamson, John. 1983. *The Exchange Rate System.* Washington, D.C.: Institute of International Economics.

Index